The 30~Minute
Good Energy
Cookbook

Quick Recipes for Limitless Energy

250+ Metabolism~Boosting Meals,
120~Day Meal Plan,
and All~Inclusive Food List
to Bring Dr. Casey Means' Teachings to Your Table

Linda Holmes

First Printing Edition, 2024

Printed in the United States of America
Available from Amazon.com and other retail outlets

TABLE OF CONTENTS

INTRODUCTION

"We are eating ourselves to death."

Dr. Casey Means' words are drastic, but undeniably true.

Today, **nine of the ten leading causes of death for Americans**—including heart disease, diabetes, and cancer—are directly linked to our dietary and lifestyle choices, with many of these conditions rooted in **mismanaged blood sugar.** The good news? **We are in control of our health.** By making intentional changes to how we nourish our bodies, we can **reverse disease**, boost energy, and reclaim our vitality.

The idea that **nutrition can reverse heart disease and diabetes** may seem revolutionary, but it's backed by science. Research has shown time and again that the human body has an incredible capacity to heal when given the right fuel. By making the right dietary changes, we can lower blood sugar levels, reduce inflammation, and allow the body to repair itself at a cellular level.

Take heart disease, for instance: it's the leading cause of death in the U.S., but it's largely preventable—and even reversible—through dietary intervention. By reducing intake of ultra-processed foods and refined sugars, and increasing consumption of **whole, plant-based foods rich in fiber, healthy fats, and antioxidants**, we can **clear arterial blockages, improve circulation, and restore heart function.** Studies have shown that diets rich in fruits, vegetables, nuts, and healthy fats can lower cholesterol, reduce blood pressure, and dramatically lower the risk of heart attacks.

Diabetes, a condition once thought to be a lifelong burden, is now being reversed in people who adopt **low-glycemic, whole-food diets** that stabilize blood sugar and reduce insulin resistance. By eliminating sugar-laden, processed foods and focusing on **complex carbohydrates, lean proteins, and healthy fats**, individuals can regain control of their blood sugar and even, in many cases, achieve complete remission of Type 2 diabetes.

This isn't just about managing symptoms—it's about **taking full control of your health** and eradicating the root causes of chronic illness. Every meal is an opportunity to **heal, nourish, and strengthen your body.** With each bite of real, whole food, you are investing in your longevity, vitality, and well-being.

This knowledge should be empowering: **you have the power to change your health trajectory.** Through mindful nutrition and lifestyle choices, you can lower your risk of chronic disease, reverse existing conditions, and reclaim your energy, your life, and your future. It's not about restriction—it's about **choosing to nourish yourself** in a way that supports your body's natural ability to thrive.

This cookbook is your guide to doing exactly that. Inspired by the teachings of Dr. Casey Means, it offers you **nutritionally balanced, metabolism-boosting meals** that are both delicious and designed to optimize your metabolic health.

Every recipe is crafted to provide the ideal combination of **high fiber, high protein, and probiotics**, delivering all the essential nutrients your body needs to thrive. These meals are packed with the building blocks for robust metabolic function, helping you regulate blood sugar, reduce inflammation, and promote cellular energy production—all while fully embracing the rich, satisfying flavors of real, natural food.

Yet, this isn't just about improving your health—**it's about rediscovering the true joy and flavor of real food.** Processed foods have dulled our taste buds, making us believe that healthy eating is bland and boring. But nothing could be further from the truth. When you embrace whole, natural ingredients, you unlock a world of rich, vibrant flavors that enhance every meal. From **savory proteins and fresh, crunchy vegetables to tangy fermented foods packed with probiotics,** this cookbook brings out the **essence of real food.** These recipes aren't just a prescription for health—they are an invitation to celebrate food in its purest, most delicious form.

By following the recipes in this cookbook, you'll be fully **embracing a lifestyle of wellness and flavor.** Each meal is crafted to make healthy eating **both satisfying and joyful,** ensuring that you never feel deprived or restricted. Instead, you'll find yourself energized, nourished, and excited to eat in a way that supports both your metabolism and your taste buds. It's time to take control of your health—**one delicious, healing bite at a time.**

A Personal Note

If the absence of color pictures and the overall **minimal photographic content** in my cookbook caught your eye, **here's why that is:**

I've made a thoughtful choice to opt out of color printing **to reduce our ecological footprint,** which is also why this book is printed on recycled paper.

Moreover, I've put a lot of effort into making the instructions **super easy to follow and accessible to everyone,** regardless of your cooking experience.

I aimed to write them in a way that feels like I'm right there in the kitchen with you, guiding you through each step.

I know that pictures can be helpful, but I believe these **straightforward directions** will help you nail those recipes much better than a photo could.

I appreciate your understanding and support as I make choices that benefit our planet.

Thank you for allowing me to be part of your journey.

Please don't forget to redeem your 2 BONUSES!

The food list and the printable meal plan, designed to help you through your first 120 days, will ensure that you implement all of Dr. Casey's recommendations seamlessly.

Go to page 120 to download these amazing resources, which make every trip to the grocery store easy and every meal prep carefree!

GOOD ENERGY BUILDING HABITS

If you have read Casey Means' *Good Energy*, you are probably familiar with the habits you will have to develop to heal your body through food, but as a quick reminder in this chapter we will take a look at the rules and recommendations that Dr Means prescribes in her book.

FOOD

Takeaway:

Focus

on

The biggest problem plaguing American health and nutrition today is the dominance of **ultra-processed foods** in our diets, and the consequences are catastrophic. Over **60% of the calories** consumed by Americans come from these nutrient-poor, inflammatory, and highly addictive foods. These are not just minor health nuisances—**they are fueling a crisis of metabolic dysfunction**, leading to rampant obesity, Type 2 diabetes, heart disease, and even cognitive decline. And the worst part? This isn't inevitable. We have the power to break free from this cycle of disease, but it starts with a radical shift in how we nourish ourselves!

Whole foods are the answer—the key to reclaiming your health, boosting your energy, and reversing years of metabolic damage. When you choose whole, unprocessed foods like vibrant vegetables, fruits, lean proteins, and healthy fats, you are flooding your body with the essential nutrients it desperately needs to function optimally. These foods are naturally designed to **stabilize blood sugar, reduce inflammation, and fuel cellular energy production**, supporting everything from your brain to your immune system. You are literally feeding your body the tools it needs to fight off disease and thrive!

Let me be clear: **this is urgent.** By continuing to consume ultra-processed junk, you're not just inviting fatigue and weight gain—you're inviting a future filled with chronic diseases, endless medications, and preventable suffering. But it doesn't have to be this way! By taking control of your nutrition now, you can **transform your health, prevent life-threatening diseases, and experience a new level of vitality**. Every bite of whole food is a vote for your health, your energy, and your future.

SIX PRINCIPLES OF GOOD ENERGY EATING

Dr. Casey Means' **Six Principles of Good Energy Eating** offer a foundational guide for achieving optimal metabolic and overall health through the power of nutrition. These principles focus on unprocessed, nutrient-dense foods that support cellular function, gut health, and long-term vitality. Here's a breakdown of her six key rules:

1. Food Determines the Structure of Our Cells and Microbiome
The foods we eat provide the building blocks for every cell in our body. Whole, unprocessed foods rich in fiber, healthy fats, and proteins determine the structure and function of our cells, influencing everything from energy production to inflammation. The state of our gut microbiome, which plays a significant role in immunity and mental health, is also shaped by our diet.
Takeaway: Choose nutrient-dense, fiber-rich whole foods to build a strong, resilient cellular structure and a healthy gut microbiome.

2. Eating Is the Process of Matching Cellular Needs with Oral Inputs
Every bite you take communicates directly with your body at the cellular level. The nutrients (or lack thereof) in your food inform your body on how to function. If you're consuming processed, nutrient-poor foods, your cells receive confusing signals, leading to dysfunction, inflammation, and disease.
Conversely, whole, nourishing foods provide clear signals that support energy production and overall health.

foods that match your cellular needs—whole, unprocessed, and full of vital nutrients.

3. Food Is How You Communicate with Your Cells
Food is more than just fuel; it's a form of communication. When you eat nutrient-rich foods, your cells respond with efficient energy production, proper repair, and reduced inflammation. On the other hand, processed foods send signals of dysfunction, leading to metabolic issues like insulin resistance and chronic inflammation.
Takeaway: View food as a powerful tool for communication with your body, choosing options that support cellular health.

4. Extreme Food Cravings Are Feedback from Your Cells That You're Giving Mixed Messages
Cravings for sugar, processed foods, or excessive carbohydrates are signals that your cells are receiving confusing or inadequate information. These cravings often stem from a diet that causes blood sugar spikes and crashes or disrupts gut health. By stabilizing blood sugar and supporting your microbiome with balanced, whole foods, you can eliminate these cravings.
Takeaway: Recognize that extreme cravings are a sign of dietary imbalance, and address them by focusing on nutrient-dense, whole foods.

5. Ignore Diet Philosophies and Focus on Unprocessed Food
Dr. Means encourages breaking free from the confusion of competing diet trends—whether low-carb, paleo, vegan, or otherwise. Instead, the focus should be on eating **unprocessed, whole foods**. The closer the food is to its natural state, the better it is for your metabolic and overall health.
Takeaway: Prioritize unprocessed, whole foods like vegetables, fruits, healthy fats, and pasture-raised proteins over any specific diet trend.

6. Find Awe in Food
Dr. Means believes that finding awe in food and understanding its profound impact on our bodies can lead to more intentional and mindful eating. By appreciating the miracle of food's ability to nourish and heal, we can make better choices that support long-term health and well-being.
Takeaway: Approach food with awe and gratitude, recognizing its essential role in maintaining and optimizing your health.

FOOD TO AVOID

We need to stop eating ultra-processed food. **We are the food we eat**, and when we fill our bodies with chemically-laden, nutrient-devoid substances, we can expect nothing less than poor health in return. Ultra-processed foods are designed for convenience, not nourishment. They are loaded with **refined sugars, unhealthy fats, preservatives, and artificial additives** that disrupt our metabolism, trigger inflammation, and deplete our bodies of the vital nutrients we need to thrive.

By consuming these foods, we are essentially fueling our bodies with **empty calories**, leading to weight gain, fatigue, and a cascade of chronic diseases. It's no coincidence that as ultra-processed foods have taken over our plates, **rates of obesity, diabetes, heart disease, and even mental health disorders** have soared. The evidence is overwhelming: what we eat directly impacts our energy levels, immune function, mental clarity, and long-term health outcomes.

If we want to **live vibrant, healthy lives**, we must prioritize real, whole foods—foods that are alive with nutrients and free from harmful chemicals. Vegetables, fruits, whole grains, nuts, seeds, lean proteins, and healthy fats are the building blocks of a strong, resilient body. These foods provide the vitamins, minerals, and antioxidants our cells need to function properly, repair themselves, and protect us from disease. When we nourish our bodies with whole, unprocessed foods, we are giving ourselves the best possible chance to **prevent illness, feel energized, and live life to its fullest**.

It's time to reclaim our health by reclaiming our food choices. We are not powerless in the face of chronic disease—**we have the ability to transform our health** by choosing foods that heal rather than harm. Let your food be your medicine, and watch as your body responds with vitality, strength, and energy.

1. REFINED GRAINS
Refined grains are highly processed, stripped of their fiber and essential nutrients. They rapidly spike blood sugar and insulin levels, leading to inflammation and metabolic dysfunction. Even though whole grains retain more nutrients, they still pose a risk for insulin spikes and can contribute to gut issues. Dr. Means recommends avoiding both refined and whole grains for optimal metabolic function.
Avoid:
- White bread
- White pasta
- White rice and brown rice
- White flour-based products (e.g., cakes, cookies, pastries, croissants)
- Instant rice and couscous
- Regular and low-fiber cereals (e.g., corn flakes, sugary cereals)
- Tortillas (especially flour-based)
- Bagels
- Crackers
- Pretzels
- Pizza dough made from refined flour

2. REFINED SUGARS
Refined sugars are devoid of nutrients and contribute to rapid glucose spikes, leading to insulin resistance, oxidative stress, and mitochondrial dysfunction. Liquid forms of sugar, like those in sweetened beverages, are particularly harmful due to their fast absorption and immediate glucose spikes.
Avoid:
- Table sugar
- High-fructose corn syrup (HFCS)
- Brown sugar
- Agave syrup
- Maple syrup
- Honey (in large quantities)
- Sweetened beverages (e.g., soda, iced tea, lemonade, energy drinks)
- Fruit juices (e.g., orange juice, apple juice, grape juice)
- Sweetened coffee drinks (e.g., flavored lattes, frappuccinos)
- Sweetened milk and flavored yogurt
- Sports drinks (e.g., Gatorade, Powerade)
- Processed desserts (e.g., candy, cakes, cookies, ice cream)
- Jams, jellies, and fruit preserves
- Condiments high in sugar (e.g., ketchup, barbecue sauce, teriyaki sauce)

3. INDUSTRIAL SEED OILS
These oils are high in omega-6 fatty acids, which disrupt the body's balance of omega-6 to omega-3 and promote chronic inflammation. Industrial seed oils are extracted using harsh chemical processes and are found in most processed foods.
Avoid:
- Soybean oil
- Corn oil
- Canola oil
- Sunflower oil
- Safflower oil
- Peanut oil
- Grapeseed oil
- Margarine and vegetable shortening
- Foods fried in these oils (e.g., french fries, fried chicken, tempura)
- Pre-packaged snack foods containing these oils (e.g., chips, crackers, microwave popcorn)
- Salad dressings and mayonnaise made with these oils
- Frozen or processed meals (e.g., frozen pizza, ready-to-eat meals)

4. ULTRA-PROCESSED FOODS
Ultra-processed foods are manufactured through industrial processes and often combine refined sugars, refined grains, and seed oils. These foods are linked to metabolic disorders, increased inflammation, and a higher risk of chronic diseases like obesity and diabetes.
Avoid:
- Pre-packaged snacks (e.g., chips, cookies, crackers, granola bars)
- Fast food items (e.g., burgers, fried chicken, french fries, pizza)
- Instant noodles (e.g., ramen, cup noodles)
- Frozen dinners (e.g., frozen pizzas, microwaveable meals, TV dinners)
- Processed meats (e.g., hot dogs, sausages, bacon, salami, ham, bologna)
- Sweetened and flavored yogurts
- Sugary cereals and cereal bars
- Candy and chocolate bars
- Pre-packaged baked goods (e.g., muffins, doughnuts, cupcakes)
- Artificially flavored snacks (e.g., flavored crackers, snack cakes, potato chips)
- Meal replacement shakes and snack bars with processed ingredients

5. ARTIFICIAL SWEETENERS
Though marketed as healthier alternatives to sugar, artificial sweeteners can disrupt gut microbiota and cause glucose intolerance. They also maintain cravings for sweet flavors, leading to overconsumption.
Avoid:
- Aspartame (Equal, NutraSweet)
- Sucralose (Splenda)
- Saccharin (Sweet'N Low)
- Acesulfame potassium (Ace-K)
- Neotame
- Stevia in excess (though natural, overuse can still affect sweet cravings)
- Diet sodas and other sugar-free drinks
- Sugar-free gum and candies
- "Light" or "low-calorie" desserts and ice creams
- Protein shakes and bars sweetened with artificial sweeteners
- Pre-packaged sugar-free snacks or desserts (e.g., sugar-free cookies, cakes)

WHOLE, UNPROCESSED, ORGANIC FOOD

"We need to stop eating ultra-processed food. We are the food we eat."

Whole foods—those that are as close to their natural state as possible—are the foundation of a nutrient-rich, anti-inflammatory diet. Unlike processed foods, which are stripped of vital nutrients and packed with harmful additives, whole foods provide **the vitamins, minerals, fiber, and antioxidants** your body needs to function at its best. Eating whole foods helps stabilize blood sugar, promotes cellular repair, and supports metabolic health, all while reducing inflammation, which is at the core of most chronic diseases. They nourish your cells, help you feel energized, and can prevent or reverse conditions like diabetes, obesity, and cardiovascular disease.

ORGANIC
Organic foods are grown without the use of synthetic pesticides, herbicides, or genetically modified organisms (GMOs), all of which can harm your body over time. Organic produce has been shown to contain **higher levels of antioxidants** and other nutrients, while being free from the harmful chemicals found in conventionally grown foods. Studies show that long-term exposure to pesticides is linked to cancer, hormone disruption, and neurological issues. When you choose organic, you're not only protecting your own health, but also reducing the burden of toxic chemicals on the environment and farmworkers.

REGENERATIVE AGRICULTURE
Regenerative agriculture goes beyond organic by focusing on **building healthy soil, enhancing biodiversity, and sequestering carbon**, which helps combat climate change. Foods grown through regenerative farming methods are nutrient-dense because they are grown in **rich, living soil** that supports healthy plants and animals. This approach reduces erosion, restores natural ecosystems, and boosts the resilience of crops and livestock. By supporting regenerative agriculture, you are contributing to a healthier planet and a more sustainable future for food production.

GRASS-FED AND PASTURE-RAISED
Choosing **grass-fed and pasture-raised meats and dairy** ensures that the animals were raised on their natural diet of grass rather than grain. Grass-fed animals produce meat and dairy that is significantly higher in **omega-3 fatty acids**, which are anti-inflammatory and support brain, heart, and metabolic health. Grass-fed beef, for example, contains **two to five times more omega-3s** than grain-fed beef, along with higher levels of vitamins like **vitamin E** and **conjugated linoleic acid (CLA)**, a fat that has been shown to reduce the risk of heart disease and cancer.

Pasture-raised animals also live in more humane conditions, allowed to roam freely and engage in natural behaviors, which leads to better animal welfare and higher quality products. Industrially farmed animals, by contrast, are often confined, fed unnatural diets, and pumped with antibiotics, which not only affects the quality of the food but also contributes to antibiotic resistance.

WILD-CAUGHT
Wild-caught fish, as opposed to farm-raised, are harvested from their natural habitats, where they feed on a diet appropriate to their species. Wild-caught seafood contains **higher levels of omega-3s**, essential fats that reduce inflammation, improve heart health, and support brain function. They are also free from the **toxins and antibiotics** commonly found in farm-raised fish. Choosing wild-caught fish ensures you are consuming a cleaner, healthier protein source while supporting sustainable fishing practices that help preserve marine ecosystems.

WHY THESE CHOICES MATTER:
1. **Nutrient Density:** Foods grown in nutrient-rich soil or raised on natural diets contain significantly more vitamins, minerals, and healthy fats, which are essential for maintaining optimal metabolic health and reducing inflammation.
2. **Reducing Toxins:** Organic and grass-fed products are free from harmful pesticides, herbicides, antibiotics, and synthetic chemicals that disrupt hormonal balance, damage the gut, and contribute to chronic diseases.
3. **Environmental Impact:** Regenerative agriculture and sustainable fishing practices protect ecosystems, restore soil health, and help combat climate change by capturing carbon and reducing pollution.
4. **Animal Welfare:** Grass-fed, pasture-raised, and wild-caught animals are treated humanely, which translates to higher-quality food that's not tainted by stress hormones or antibiotics.
5. **Sustainability:** Choosing these food sources supports sustainable farming and fishing practices, which are crucial for the long-term health of the planet and food security.

These choices empower you to **nourish your body with clean, nutrient-dense food** while contributing to a food system that respects the earth and promotes longevity for future generations.

PRACTICAL ADVICE FOR INCORPORATING WHOLE, NUTRIENT-DENSE FOODS

To maintain high energy levels, support metabolic health, and foster long-term vitality, focusing on **whole, nutrient-dense foods** is critical. These foods offer the full range of vitamins, minerals, fiber, and antioxidants your body needs to function at its best, making them the foundation of any sustainable, health-promoting diet. Whole foods are naturally aligned with the body's biochemical needs, helping to **stabilize blood sugar**, support efficient mitochondrial function (energy production), and reduce inflammation—the root cause of many chronic diseases.

1. ELIMINATE ALL GRAINS
Dr. Means strongly advises against both refined and whole grains, arguing that they are unnecessary and can compromise metabolic health, especially when compared to other nutrient-dense alternatives. She emphasizes that the fiber, protein, and micronutrient content found in grains can be easily surpassed by more metabolically supportive foods like seeds, nuts, and legumes.

Grain Alternatives:
- **Cauliflower rice:** An easy and nutrient-dense replacement for white or brown rice. It is high in fiber and low in carbohydrates, offering a healthier option for those looking to stabilize blood sugar.
- **Nut-based flours:** Instead of bread and tortillas made from grains, opt for almond flour or coconut flour, which provide more fiber and healthy fats.
- **Vegetable noodles:** Replace pasta with zucchini, sweet potato, or beet noodles. These alternatives are packed with fiber, vitamins, and minerals.

2. PRIORITIZE HIGH-FIBER FOODS
Dr. Means stresses the importance of getting **50 grams or more of fiber per day** to improve gut health, support insulin sensitivity, and stabilize blood sugar levels. Fiber-rich foods are essential for maintaining a healthy gut microbiome and preventing chronic diseases like diabetes and heart disease.

High-Fiber Foods to Include:
- **Seeds:** Chia seeds (8g per 2 tbsp), flaxseeds, and basil seeds are fiber powerhouses, and they are excellent in smoothies, oatmeal replacements, or as toppings.
- **Legumes:** Lentils (15g per cup), split peas, and black beans are incredibly rich in fiber and also provide plant-based protein.
- **Vegetables:** Artichokes, Brussels sprouts, and broccoli are excellent sources of fiber while also delivering high doses of antioxidants and vitamins.

- **Nuts:** Almonds, hazelnuts, and pistachios not only provide fiber but also healthy fats, making them a filling and nutritious snack.

3. INCORPORATE PROBIOTIC FOODS FOR GUT HEALTH

Fermented, probiotic-rich foods are essential for maintaining a healthy gut, which is central to **optimal metabolic function and immune health.** Dr. Means recommends at least three servings of probiotic foods per day to boost the diversity of your gut microbiome and reduce inflammation.

Best Probiotic Foods to Include:
- **Sauerkraut and Kimchi:** These fermented vegetables are rich in beneficial bacteria that can improve gut health and digestion.
- **Unsweetened Yogurt and Kefir:** Choose dairy or non-dairy varieties that contain live active cultures, ensuring no added sugars.
- **Tempeh and Miso:** Fermented soy products like tempeh are rich in probiotics and provide a complete source of plant-based protein.

4. BALANCE OMEGA-3 AND OMEGA-6 INTAKE

Dr. Means emphasizes balancing **omega-3 fatty acids** with omega-6, as omega-6-heavy diets are linked to inflammation. To promote anti-inflammatory processes, it's crucial to increase your intake of omega-3s from whole food sources.

Omega-3 Rich Foods:
- **Wild-caught fish:** Salmon, mackerel, and sardines are among the best sources of omega-3 fatty acids, which support heart and brain health.
- **Seeds:** Chia, flaxseeds, and hemp seeds are excellent plant-based omega-3 sources and can be added to smoothies, salads, or baked goods.

5. EMPHASIZE PLANT DIVERSITY

Diversity in plant foods is crucial for gut health. Research shows that people who consume a wide variety of plant foods each week have healthier microbiomes. Dr. Means encourages consuming at least 30 different plant foods per week .

Key Tips:
- **Mix up your vegetables:** Rotate between leafy greens, cruciferous vegetables, and root vegetables.
- **Experiment with herbs and spices:** Use fresh herbs like parsley, cilantro, and basil to increase plant diversity while adding flavor.
- **Add more legumes and seeds:** Incorporate beans, lentils, and a variety of seeds (chia, flax, hemp) into your meals.

6. AVOID SUGARY FOODS AND BEVERAGES

Sugars, especially in liquid form, spike blood sugar and insulin levels, leading to metabolic dysfunction. Dr. Means emphasizes eliminating all added sugars, especially in sodas, juices, and sweetened coffee drinks.

Alternatives:
- **Natural sweeteners:** Use small amounts of stevia or monk fruit if needed, but aim to reduce the reliance on sweet tastes altogether.
- **Infused water:** Replace sugary beverages with water infused with fresh fruits or herbs for flavor without added sugar.

7. MINDFUL EATING AND PORTION CONTROL

Dr. Means highlights the importance of mindful eating to avoid overeating and better manage portion sizes. By slowing down and focusing on the food, you allow your body time to recognize fullness cues, which can help with portion control and prevent unnecessary blood sugar spikes.

Tips for Mindful Eating:
- **Eat without distractions:** Focus on your meal rather than multitasking with screens.
- **Chew thoroughly:** Taking time to chew aids digestion and helps you appreciate the flavors of whole, unprocessed foods.
- **Stop when satisfied:** Avoid the tendency to overeat by recognizing when you're comfortably full.

EXERCISES

Exercise must be a natural part of our daily lives, not just something we check off with a gym session. While gym memberships in the U.S. have **doubled since 2000,** so have obesity rates. This shows a clear disconnect between what we think is healthy and what truly benefits our bodies. While going to the gym and doing structured workouts is certainly good for us, it's not enough on its own. Dr. Casey Means emphasizes that true health requires **constant, low-level movement throughout the day.** This includes standing, walking, stretching, and taking breaks from sitting. You can incorporate this by using a standing desk, taking a few minutes to walk every half hour, or simply finding opportunities to move more regularly in your routine.

Dr. Means advocates for a **balanced approach to fitness,** built around consistency and variety, rather than extreme exercise routines. Here's a closer look at her practical recommendations for integrating movement into your life in ways that promote metabolic health and prevent chronic disease.

1. RESISTANCE TRAINING: BUILDING MUSCLE FOR METABOLIC HEALTH

Dr. Means strongly advocates for **resistance training** as a cornerstone of metabolic health. Muscle is more than just a means to strength—it's a **metabolic shield.** By building muscle, you increase your body's ability to clear glucose from the blood, which in turn improves **insulin sensitivity** and helps prevent conditions like Type 2 diabetes.

Key Benefits:
- Resistance training helps reduce abdominal fat, enhances glucose tolerance, and lowers blood pressure.
- Muscle mass correlates with better insulin sensitivity, which is vital for controlling blood sugar levels.

Practical Tips:
- Engage in resistance training at least **three times per week,** targeting all major muscle groups. You can use weights, resistance bands, or even bodyweight exercises like squats, push-ups, and pull-ups.
- As Dr. Means highlights, resistance training is particularly important for women entering middle age. The natural decline in estrogen makes it harder to maintain muscle mass, which can lead to metabolic slowdowns.

2. AEROBIC EXERCISE: FOCUS ON ZONE 2 TRAINING

Dr. Means recommends **Zone 2 aerobic training,** which involves maintaining a heart rate at 60-70% of your maximum. This type of moderate-intensity exercise is easy to maintain for long periods and confers numerous metabolic benefits without overstressing the body.

Key Benefits:
- Zone 2 exercise increases **mitochondrial efficiency,** helping your cells produce energy more effectively.
- It improves glucose uptake, which helps maintain stable blood sugar levels and supports long-term metabolic health.

Practical Tips:
- Aim for at least **150 minutes per week** of moderate aerobic exercise, such as brisk walking or light jogging. This can be divided into **30-minute sessions, five days a week.**
- You can easily monitor your heart rate during exercise using fitness trackers or by doing the "talk test"—if you can maintain a conversation but feel slightly breathless, you're likely in Zone 2.

3. HIGH-INTENSITY INTERVAL TRAINING (HIIT)

For those seeking a powerful metabolic boost, Dr. Means also recommends incorporating HIIT (High-Intensity Interval Training) into your routine. HIIT involves short bursts of intense exercise followed by periods of lower-intensity recovery.

Key Benefits:

- HIIT can significantly increase **mitochondrial biogenesis**, the process by which new mitochondria are formed, boosting energy production and enhancing metabolic flexibility.
- It's an effective way to improve cardiovascular health and insulin sensitivity in shorter timeframes.

Practical Tips:

- Incorporate HIIT once or twice a week. Sessions can be as short as 10-20 minutes but should include bursts of intense activity (e.g., sprinting, cycling, or jump squats) for 20-60 seconds, followed by recovery periods.

4. WALK REGULARLY: NON-EXERCISE ACTIVITY THERMOGENESIS (NEAT)

Dr. Means stresses that movement throughout the day is **just as important** as structured workouts. The modern sedentary lifestyle—marked by long periods of sitting—undermines metabolic health, even for those who exercise. She highlights the importance of **Non-Exercise Activity Thermogenesis (NEAT)**, which refers to all the low-intensity physical activities we do daily.

Key Benefits:

- Regular low-level activity helps regulate blood sugar, reduces inflammation, and improves mitochondrial function.
- Walking after meals, for example, can lower blood sugar spikes by up to **30%**.

Practical Tips:

- **Walk at least 7,000 steps a day**, gradually increasing to 10,000 steps per day. This simple habit can lower your risk of chronic diseases like heart disease, dementia, and Type 2 diabetes by **30-50%**.
- Take short walks throughout the day, particularly after meals, to keep glucose levels stable. Even standing up and moving for a few minutes every half hour can significantly improve metabolic markers.

5. INTEGRATE MOVEMENT INTO YOUR DAILY ROUTINE

Beyond formal exercise, Dr. Means encourages integrating movement into daily tasks to combat the negative effects of prolonged sitting. Regular muscle contractions, even at low intensity, are crucial for metabolic health.

Key Benefits:

- Frequent movement promotes **fat burning** and improves the efficiency of **glucose disposal**, reducing insulin resistance.

Practical Tips:

- Use a standing desk, take the stairs instead of the elevator, and incorporate short bursts of activity like air squats or stretches during work breaks.
- Treadmill desks, for instance, can help improve muscle mass and reduce fat mass when used consistently.

6. STRENGTHEN MITOCHONDRIA WITH EXERCISE

Exercise improves mitochondrial function, the cellular structures responsible for producing energy. **Regular physical activity** increases both the quantity and quality of mitochondria, enhancing your body's ability to use glucose and fats for energy.

Key Benefits:

- Exercise-induced mitochondrial biogenesis leads to better metabolic flexibility, allowing your body to switch more easily between burning carbohydrates and fats.

- More mitochondria also mean better resilience against oxidative stress and inflammation, both of which contribute to chronic disease.

SLEEP

Dr. Casey Means emphasizes that **sleep** is a foundational pillar for metabolic health, and its role in overall well-being cannot be overstated. Lack of sleep profoundly affects the body at the cellular and hormonal levels, impairing the body's ability to manage energy, regulate blood sugar, and reduce inflammation.

1. QUANTITY: PRIORITIZE 7-8 HOURS OF SLEEP

Dr. Means stresses that **7-8 hours of sleep** is essential to protect your body from metabolic dysfunction and what she refers to as "Bad Energy physiology." Research consistently shows that people who get less than 6.5 hours of sleep per night experience increased insulin resistance, which sets the stage for prediabetes, Type 2 diabetes, and other chronic diseases.

- A study highlighted by Dr. Means found that after just six nights of restricted sleep (four hours per night), participants exhibited a **40% reduction** in their body's ability to remove sugar from the bloodstream, mimicking glucose responses seen in prediabetes.
- Make sleep a non-negotiable priority. Create a bedtime routine that allows you to wind down without screens or bright lights, and aim to get 7-8 hours of uninterrupted sleep each night.

2. IMPACT ON INSULIN SENSITIVITY

Sleep deprivation wreaks havoc on insulin sensitivity, which is central to metabolic health. Dr. Means points to multiple studies showing that even short periods of sleep deprivation significantly impair the body's ability to regulate blood sugar. Sleep-deprived individuals may need to produce **50% more insulin** to achieve the same blood sugar control as those who are well-rested.

- When the body doesn't get enough rest, cortisol levels rise, further impairing insulin sensitivity and causing an elevated blood glucose response. This leads to an increased risk of **insulin resistance** and subsequent weight gain.
- Avoid late-night eating, which disrupts insulin sensitivity. Ensure your eating window ends several hours before bedtime to give your body time to digest and regulate blood sugar levels properly before sleep.

3. SLEEP QUALITY: MINIMALLY INTERRUPTED SLEEP

In addition to quantity, **sleep quality** plays a major role in metabolic health. Dr. Means notes that fragmented sleep is linked to an increased risk of metabolic disorders such as Type 2 diabetes, heart disease, and obesity. Poor sleep quality also affects the body's ability to efficiently manage blood sugar the following day, creating a vicious cycle.

- Inadequate deep and REM sleep reduces the body's ability to regulate glucose and increases inflammation. For optimal metabolic function, ensure a high proportion of your sleep is spent in deep sleep and REM stages, which are most restorative.
- Optimize your sleep environment. Keep the room cool, dark, and quiet. Consider blackout curtains, sound machines, or earplugs to minimize disturbances that could fragment sleep.

4. CONSISTENCY: KEEP REGULAR SLEEP-WAKE CYCLES

Consistency is key for aligning the body's **circadian rhythm**, which regulates metabolic processes. Dr. Means emphasizes that irregular sleep patterns, such as staying up late on weekends or working night shifts, can cause **social jet lag**, which increases the risk of metabolic diseases.

- A regular sleep schedule aligns the body's internal clock, promoting better insulin sensitivity and metabolic health. Disruptions to this cycle, even by just a few hours, can elevate the risk of conditions like prediabetes.
- Stick to a consistent sleep and wake time, even on weekends. Aim for a sleep window that varies by no more than one hour across the week.

5. SLEEP AND HUNGER HORMONES

Sleep deprivation has a profound effect on hunger hormones. Dr. Means references studies showing that lack of sleep increases **ghrelin** (the hunger hormone) and decreases **leptin** (the satiety hormone), leading to increased hunger and cravings for high-calorie, carbohydrate-rich foods. This hormonal imbalance drives overeating and weight gain, further exacerbating metabolic issues.

- Short-term sleep deprivation (even just a few nights) can lead to **increased calorie intake**, particularly from foods that spike blood sugar, worsening insulin resistance.
- To prevent overeating and support metabolic health, ensure you are well-rested. A good night's sleep will help regulate hunger hormones and reduce cravings for unhealthy foods the next day.

By optimizing both the **quantity and quality** of your sleep and maintaining consistent sleep habits, you can significantly improve your metabolic health. Poor sleep is not just about feeling tired—it disrupts nearly every system in your body, from your ability to regulate blood sugar to your hormone balance and energy production. Prioritizing sleep is one of the most powerful and actionable steps you can take to protect your health.

MENTAL HEALTH

Dr. Means emphasizes the strong connection between **metabolic health** and **mental well-being**, highlighting that both are deeply intertwined. Poor metabolic health—driven by inflammation, insulin resistance, and blood sugar dysregulation—can significantly impact brain function, mood, and overall mental health. Chronic conditions like anxiety, depression, and brain fog are often tied to underlying metabolic dysfunction. Here's a breakdown of her insights and recommendations on how to optimize mental health through lifestyle changes.

1. BLOOD SUGAR BALANCE FOR BRAIN HEALTH

Fluctuating blood sugar levels have a direct impact on brain function. Spikes in blood glucose can lead to rapid crashes, which result in feelings of irritability, anxiety, and fatigue. Over time, poor blood sugar control can contribute to cognitive decline, depression, and impaired focus.

- Stable blood sugar is crucial for keeping neurotransmitters in balance and maintaining steady energy levels in the brain. Blood sugar crashes can trigger the release of stress hormones like cortisol, leading to feelings of anxiety and difficulty concentrating.
- To maintain stable blood sugar levels, Dr. Means recommends **avoiding refined sugars and processed carbohydrates** and opting for whole foods with plenty of fiber, healthy fats, and protein to promote sustained energy release.

2. REDUCING INFLAMMATION TO PROTECT MENTAL HEALTH

Chronic, low-grade inflammation is a key driver of both metabolic and mental health issues. The brain is particularly vulnerable to inflammation, which can disrupt neurotransmitter function and lead to conditions such as depression, anxiety, and cognitive decline.

- **Neuroinflammation** has been directly linked to mood disorders like depression. By reducing systemic inflammation, we can support better mental clarity, emotional resilience, and cognitive function.
- Dr. Means advocates for an **anti-inflammatory diet** rich in omega-3 fatty acids (found in wild-caught fish, flaxseeds, and walnuts), and antioxidants from colorful fruits and vegetables. Avoiding inflammatory foods like processed oils and refined sugars is also key.

3. GUT HEALTH AND THE GUT-BRAIN CONNECTION

The **gut-brain axis** is a critical communication pathway between the digestive system and the brain. A healthy gut supports mental clarity and emotional well-being, while gut imbalances, such as dysbiosis (an imbalance in gut bacteria), are linked to mental health conditions like depression and anxiety.

- **70% of serotonin**, a neurotransmitter that regulates mood, is produced in the gut. An unhealthy gut can disrupt this process, affecting mood regulation and cognitive function.
- Dr. Means recommends incorporating **probiotic-rich foods** like sauerkraut, kimchi, and kefir, as well as **prebiotic fibers** from foods like garlic, onions, and asparagus to support a diverse and healthy gut microbiome.

4. PHYSICAL ACTIVITY AND ITS MENTAL HEALTH BENEFITS

Exercise is not just important for physical health—it has profound effects on mental health. Regular movement improves blood flow to the brain, reduces inflammation, and releases endorphins, which enhance mood and combat stress.

- **Aerobic exercise** and **resistance training** can improve symptoms of depression and anxiety by promoting neuroplasticity and boosting the production of feel-good chemicals like endorphins and serotonin.
- Dr. Means recommends incorporating **daily movement, even in small bursts,** such as walking, stretching, or practicing yoga, to enhance both mental and physical well-being.

5. SLEEP FOR MENTAL RESILIENCE

Quality sleep is essential for both mental and metabolic health. Sleep deprivation impairs cognitive function, emotional regulation, and increases the risk of developing anxiety and depression. It also worsens insulin resistance, creating a vicious cycle of poor health.

- **Lack of sleep** not only disrupts blood sugar regulation but also diminishes the brain's ability to repair itself and manage stress. This can lead to heightened anxiety, mood swings, and impaired decision-making.
- Dr. Means stresses the importance of prioritizing **7-8 hours of quality sleep** each night, maintaining a consistent sleep schedule, and creating a calming bedtime routine that limits screen time and promotes relaxation.

6. MANAGING STRESS TO SUPPORT MENTAL AND METABOLIC HEALTH

Chronic stress can disrupt both mental and metabolic health, leading to elevated cortisol levels, insulin resistance, and increased inflammation. Prolonged stress is a major contributor to anxiety, depression, and poor cognitive function.

- High cortisol levels, driven by stress, impair both mental clarity and metabolic regulation, creating a cycle of mental and physical exhaustion.
- Dr. Means encourages adopting stress-management practices such as **mindfulness, meditation, deep breathing exercises,** and spending time in nature to support mental well-being and reduce the physiological effects of stress on the body.

BREAKFAST RECIPES

Dr. Means recommends eating the bulk of your caloric needs in the morning, ideally with a savory breakfast, to give you a leveled energy boost that will last the whole day. The following recipes are specifically designed to keep you energized and full. They are also quick to make and easy to meal prep.

PANCAKES AND WAFFLES

PANCAKE/WAFFLE BATTER BASE

Prep Time: 10 minutes
Cook Time: 15 minutes
Serves: 6 pancakes

Ingredients:
- Base Flours: (Choose one or combine for a blend)
  - **Almond Flour** (1 cup): (Calories: 640, Protein: 24g, Fat: 56g, Carbs: 24g, Fiber: 12g)
  - **Coconut Flour** (1/2 cup): (Calories: 280, Protein: 10g, Fat: 18g, Carbs: 18g, Fiber: 10g)
  - **Cassava Flour** (1 cup): (Calories: 450, Protein: 3g, Fat: 0g, Carbs: 108g, Fiber: 3g)
- Binding Agents:
  - **Eggs** (3 large): (Calories: 210, Protein: 18g, Fat: 15g, Carbs: 1.2g)
  - **Mashed ripe banana** (1 medium): (Calories: 105, Protein: 1g, Fat: 0.4g, Carbs: 27g, Fiber: 3g) OR Unsweetened applesauce (1/2 cup): (Calories: 51, Protein: 0.2g, Fat: 0.1g, Carbs: 13.7g, Fiber: 2.1g)
  - **Flax eggs** (2 tablespoons ground flaxseed + 5 tablespoons water, let sit for 5 minutes): (Calories: 75, Protein: 3g, Fat: 6g, Carbs: 4g, Fiber: 3g) - Vegan Option
- Leavening Agents:
  - **Baking Powder** (1 teaspoon): (Negligible calories and macros)
  - **Baking Soda** (1/2 teaspoon): (Negligible calories and macros)
- Liquid:
  - **Unsweetened Milk** (1 cup): (Choose almond, coconut, or cashew milk for lower carbs)
  - Water (1 cup)
- Flavor Enhancers (Optional):
  - **Vanilla Extract** (1 teaspoon): (Calories: 12, Protein: 0g, Fat: 0g, Carbs: 0g, Fiber: 0g) - Adds warmth and subtle sweetness.
  - **Cinnamon** (1/2 teaspoon): (Calories: 6, Protein: 0g, Fat: 0g, Carbs: 2g, Fiber: 1g) - Provides blood sugar support and antioxidant benefits
  - **Nutmeg or Cardamom (pinch):** (Calories: ~1, negligible macros) - Adds warmth and complexity.
- Optional Add-Ins:
  - **Protein Powder** (1 scoop): (Calories and macros will vary based on the specific protein powder) - Boosts protein content for satiety and muscle support
  - **Chopped nuts or seeds** (1/4 cup): Adds healthy fats, protein, and texture.
  - (1/4 cup): Provides healthy fats and fiber.

Instructions:
1. Combine Dry ingredients in a large bowl, whisk together the chosen flour(s), baking powder, and baking soda.
2. Mix Wet ingredients in a separate bowl, whisk together the eggs (or flax eggs), mashed banana/applesauce, milk (or water), and any flavor enhancers.
3. Combine: Pour the wet ingredients into the dry ingredients and whisk until just combined. Don't overmix; a few lumps are okay
4. Rest (Optional): Let the batter rest for 5-10 minutes to allow the flours to absorb the liquid and thicken slightly
5. Cook: Heat a non-stick skillet or waffle iron over medium heat. Grease lightly with coconut oil or ghee.
6. Pour & Cook:
   - Pancakes: Pour 1/4 cup batter onto the hot skillet for each pancake. Cook for 2-3 minutes per side, or until golden brown and cooked through.
   - Waffles: Pour batter into the preheated waffle iron according to manufacturer's instructions. Cook until golden brown and crispy.

Technical Tips & Metabolic Health Considerations:
- Flour Power: Each flour has unique properties. Almond flour is naturally moist, coconut flour is highly absorbent, and cassava flour mimics wheat flour most closely. Experiment with different combinations to find your ideal texture and flavor
- Batter Consistency: The batter should be thick but pourable. If it's too thick, add a bit more milk or water; if it's too thin, add a tablespoon more flour
- Cooking Temperature: Adjust the heat as needed to ensure even cooking. If pancakes or waffles are browning too quickly, reduce the heat slightly
- Natural Sweetness: Rely on ripe bananas or applesauce for natural sweetness. If desired, add a touch of stevia or monk fruit extract, but remember, moderation is key even with natural sweeteners
- Protein & Fat Balance: Incorporate protein powder or Greek yogurt for a boost of protein, contributing to satiety and muscle support. Include healthy fats from nuts, seeds, or coconut milk for sustained energy and nutrient absorption
- Blood Sugar Stability: The combination of protein, fiber, and healthy fats in these pancakes/waffles helps to slow down the absorption of sugars, promoting stable blood sugar levels and preventing energy crashes
- Gut-Friendly Additions: Top your pancakes/waffles with berries for antioxidants and fiber, or add a dollop of unsweetened yogurt for probiotics to support a healthy gut microbiome

- Creative Toppings: Explore a variety of toppings like nut butter, chopped nuts, seeds, unsweetened coconut flakes, or a drizzle of honey or maple syrup (use sparingly)
- Why Ghee and not Butter? Ghee has several advantages over butter that make it a great choice. First, it's lactose- and casein-free, which means it's easier on the stomach for those sensitive to dairy. It also has a higher smoke point, so it's perfect for cooking at high heat without burning. Beyond that, ghee is packed with vitamins A, D, E, and K, along with conjugated linoleic acid (CLA) and butyrate, which are great for gut health and reducing inflammation. Its rich, nutty flavor makes it a versatile and delicious option for any dish!

Remember: This base recipe is your canvas. Feel free to adjust it to suit your preferences and dietary needs. Have fun experimenting with different flours, flavors, and toppings to create delicious and nourishing pancakes or waffles that fuel your body and mind!

Nutritional Information (per serving):
- Calories: 203
- Protein: 7g
- Fat: 14g
- Carbohydrates: 11g
- Fiber: 3g

FLAXSEED PANCAKES WITH WILD-CAUGHT SMOKED SALMON AND PROBIOTIC CREAM CHEESE

Prep Time: 20 minutes
Cook Time: 10 minutes
Serves: 4

Ingredients:
- 1 cup organic ground flaxseed
- 2 large organic, pasture-raised eggs
- 1/2 cup organic almond milk (or dairy-free alternative)
- 1 tbsp organic coconut oil or ghee
- 1 tsp organic vanilla extract
- 1/4 tsp organic baking soda
- Sea salt to taste
- 1/2 cup organic probiotic cream cheese (or dairy-free alternative)
- 4 slices wild-caught smoked salmon
- 1/4 cup organic fresh dill, chopped

Instructions:
1. In a bowl, mix ground flaxseed with eggs, almond milk, coconut oil or ghee, vanilla extract, baking soda, and salt.
2. Let the mixture rest for 10 minutes to thicken.
3. Cook on a non-stick skillet or griddle like regular pancakes.
4. Serve pancakes with probiotic cream cheese, smoked salmon, and chopped fresh dill.

Tip: For a lighter texture, allow the batter to rest for 10-15 minutes to allow the flaxseed to gel properly.

Nutritional Information (per serving):
- Calories: 347
- Protein: 18g
- Fat: 28g
- Carbohydrates: 7g
- Fiber: 6g

COCONUT FLOUR PANCAKES WITH BERRY COMPOTE

Prep Time: 15 minutes
Cook Time: 15 minutes
Serves: 4

Ingredients:
- 1/2 cup organic coconut flour
- 6 organic eggs
- 1/4 cup organic coconut milk
- 1 tsp organic vanilla extract
- 1/4 tsp sea salt

- 2 tbsp organic coconut oil for cooking

For the Berry Compote:
- 2 cups mixed organic berries
- 1 tbsp organic lemon juice

Instructions:
1. Whisk together coconut flour, eggs, coconut milk, vanilla, and salt until smooth.
2. Heat coconut oil in a skillet over medium heat.
3. Pour 1/4 cup batter for each pancake and cook until bubbles form, then flip.
4. For the compote, simmer berries and lemon juice in a small saucepan until softened.
5. Serve pancakes topped with berry compote.

Tip: Let the batter rest for 5 minutes before cooking to allow the coconut flour to absorb the liquid.

Nutritional Information (per serving):
- Calories: 280
- Protein: 12g
- Fat: 20g
- Carbohydrates: 18g
- Fiber: 10g

SAVORY SPINACH AND FETA WAFFLES WITH SMOKED SALMON

Prep Time: 15 minutes
Cook Time: 10 minutes
Serves: 4

Ingredients:
- For the Waffles:
  - 1 cup organic cassava flour
  - 2 organic eggs
  - 1/2 cup organic coconut milk (unsweetened)
  - 1/2 cup organic fresh spinach, finely chopped
  - 1/4 cup organic feta cheese, crumbled
  - 1 tsp organic garlic powder
  - 1/2 tsp organic baking powder
  - 2 tbsp organic avocado oil (for greasing waffle iron)
  - Sea salt & pepper to taste
- For the Toppings:
  - 100g wild-caught smoked salmon, sliced
  - 1 tbsp organic capers
  - 1 tbsp organic fresh dill, chopped
  - 1 tbsp organic lemon juice

Instructions:
1. In a bowl, whisk together cassava flour, eggs, coconut milk, chopped spinach, feta cheese, garlic powder, baking powder, salt, and pepper.
2. Preheat a waffle iron and grease with avocado oil. Pour the batter into the waffle iron and cook according to the manufacturer's instructions until crispy and golden.
3. Top each waffle with slices of smoked salmon, capers, fresh dill, and a drizzle of lemon juice.
4. Serve immediately, garnished with extra herbs and a squeeze of lemon if desired.

Tip: The saltiness of the smoked salmon pairs perfectly with the earthy spinach and tangy feta in the waffle, creating a balanced savory dish. For crispy waffles, be sure to preheat the waffle iron thoroughly and avoid opening it too early during cooking.

Nutritional Information (per serving):
- Calories: 353
- Protein: 14g
- Fat: 21g
- Carbohydrates: 27g
- Fiber: 3g

SAVORY CAULIFLOWER WAFFLES WITH POACHED EGGS AND AVOCADO SALSA

Prep Time: 20 minutes
Cook Time: 15 minutes
Serves: 4

Ingredients:
- For the Waffles:
  - 2 cups organic cauliflower, riced (about 1 small head)
  - 2 organic eggs
  - 1/4 cup organic almond flour
  - 1/4 cup organic Parmesan cheese, grated
  - 1/2 tsp organic garlic powder
  - 1/2 tsp organic baking powder
  - Sea salt & pepper to taste
  - 2 tbsp organic avocado oil (for greasing waffle iron)
- For the Toppings:
  - 4 organic poached eggs
  - 1 organic avocado, diced
  - 1/4 cup organic cherry tomatoes, diced
  - 1 tbsp organic cilantro, chopped
  - 1 tbsp organic lime juice

Instructions:
1. Prepare the Cauliflower Waffle Batter: In a bowl, combine riced cauliflower, eggs, almond flour, Parmesan, garlic powder, baking powder, salt, and pepper. Mix until a thick batter forms.
2. Cook the Waffles: Preheat a waffle iron and grease with avocado oil. Spoon the cauliflower batter into the waffle iron and cook until crispy and golden.
3. Make the Avocado Salsa: In a bowl, combine diced avocado, cherry tomatoes, cilantro, and lime juice. Season with salt and pepper to taste.
4. Poach the Eggs: Poach the eggs in simmering water with a splash of vinegar for 3-4 minutes until the whites are set and the yolks are still runny.
5. Serve: Top each cauliflower waffle with a poached egg and a generous spoonful of avocado salsa. Serve immediately.

Tip: To ensure crispy cauliflower waffles, squeeze out any excess moisture from the cauliflower before mixing it into the batter. The richness of the poached egg yolk complements the savory cauliflower waffles, while the avocado salsa adds a refreshing, tangy contrast.

Nutritional Information (per serving):
- Calories: 289
- Protein: 13g
- Fat: 22g
- Carbohydrates: 10g
- Fiber: 4g

BREAKFAST BOWLS

NATTO AND AVOCADO BREAKFAST BOWL

Prep Time: 10 minutes
Cook Time: 0 minutes
Serves: 2

Ingredients:
- 1 package organic natto
- 1 large organic avocado, diced
- 2 organic eggs, soft-boiled
- 1 tbsp organic coconut aminos
- 1 tsp organic sesame oil
- 1 tbsp organic fresh chives, chopped
- Sea salt and black pepper to taste

Instructions:
1. In a bowl, combine the natto, avocado, and soft-boiled eggs.
2. Drizzle with coconut aminos and sesame oil.
3. Sprinkle with chopped chives, salt, and pepper.
4. Serve immediately.

Tip: For a creamier texture, mash the avocado before mixing with the natto.

Nutritional Information (per serving):
- Calories: 320
- Protein: 18g
- Fat: 24g
- Carbohydrates: 8g
- Fiber: 6g

TURKEY SAUSAGE & ZUCCHINI BREAKFAST BOWL

Prep Time: 10 minutes
Cook Time: 15 minutes
Serves: 2

Ingredients:
- 6 oz pasture-raised ground turkey sausage
- 1 medium organic zucchini, spiralized
- 1/2 cup organic mushrooms, sliced
- 1 tbsp coconut oil
- 2 tbsp fermented kimchi (probiotic-rich)
- 1 tbsp tahini (sesame paste)
- 1 tsp sesame oil
- 1/2 tsp ground turmeric
- Sea salt and black pepper to taste

Instructions:
1. Cook the Turkey Sausage: Heat coconut oil in a skillet over medium heat. Add turkey sausage and break it up with a spatula. Cook for 5-7 minutes until browned and fully cooked.
2. Add the Veggies: Add the spiralized zucchini, sliced mushrooms, turmeric, and sesame oil to the skillet. Cook for another 3-4 minutes until the vegetables are tender.
3. Assemble the Bowl: Place the sausage and vegetable mix into bowls and top with a drizzle of tahini and a spoonful of fermented kimchi.

Tip: The combination of turmeric and sesame oil adds an earthy, aromatic element, while the kimchi brings a tangy heat that balances the richness of the turkey sausage.

Nutritional Information (per serving):
- Calories: 376
- Protein: 21g
- Fat: 30g
- Carbohydrates: 7g
- Fiber: 2g

SMOKED SALMON & AVOCADO BREAKFAST BOWL

Prep Time: 10 minutes
Cook Time: 5 minutes
Serves: 1

Ingredients:
- 3 oz wild-caught smoked salmon
- 1/2 organic avocado, sliced
- 1 cup organic baby spinach
- 2 tbsp fermented sauerkraut (preferably homemade, see recipe)
- 1 tbsp avocado oil
- 1 organic egg
- 1 tsp fresh lemon juice
- Sea salt and black pepper to taste
- Optional: Fresh dill for garnish

Instructions:

1. Wilt the Spinach: Heat avocado oil in a pan over medium heat. Add the spinach and sauté for 1-2 minutes until wilted. Season with sea salt and black pepper.
2. Cook the Egg: In the same pan, cook the egg sunny side up or to your preference.
3. Assemble the Bowl: In a bowl, arrange the smoked salmon, avocado slices, wilted spinach, sauerkraut, and cooked egg.
4. Finish with Lemon & Dill: Drizzle fresh lemon juice over the avocado and top the bowl with fresh dill.

Tip: To balance the flavors, use lemon juice to cut through the richness of the avocado and salmon, while the fermented sauerkraut adds a tangy, probiotic boost.

Nutritional Information (per serving):
- Calories: 460
- Protein: 23g
- Fat: 38g
- Carbohydrates: 9g
- Fiber: 5g

GRASS-FED BEEF & SWEET POTATO HASH BOWL

Prep Time: 10 minutes
Cook Time: 20 minutes
Serves: 2

Ingredients:
- 6 oz grass-fed ground beef
- 1 medium organic sweet potato, diced
- 1/2 cup organic red bell pepper, diced
- 1/2 cup organic onion, diced
- 1 tbsp ghee or coconut oil
- 1/4 tsp smoked paprika
- 1/4 tsp ground cumin
- 2 tbsp fermented salsa (preferably homemade, see recipe)
- Sea salt and black pepper to taste
- Optional: Fresh cilantro for garnish

Instructions:
1. Cook the Sweet Potatoes: Heat ghee in a skillet over medium heat. Add the diced sweet potatoes and cook for 10-12 minutes, stirring occasionally, until they are golden and tender.
2. Add Peppers and Onions: Add diced red bell pepper and onion to the skillet and cook for an additional 5-6 minutes until softened.
3. Brown the Beef: Push the veggies to the side of the pan and add ground beef. Cook for 4-5 minutes until browned and fully cooked, seasoning with smoked paprika, cumin, salt, and pepper.
4. Assemble the Bowl: In a bowl, layer the sweet potato hash and beef. Top with fermented salsa and fresh cilantro.

Tip: Cooking the sweet potatoes in ghee enhances their natural sweetness, while the smoked paprika and cumin give the dish a subtle, warming spice.

Nutritional Information (per serving):
- Calories: 460 kcal
- Protein: 23g
- Fat: 38g
- Carbohydrates: 9g
- Fiber: 5g

EGG AND MUSHROOM BREAKFAST BOWLS WITH SAUERKRAUT

Prep Time: 15 minutes
Cook Time: 20 minutes
Serves: 4

Ingredients:
- 4 large organic pasture-raised eggs
- 2 cups organic mushrooms, sliced
- 1 large organic zucchini, spiralized into noodles
- 1 organic onion, diced
- 2 organic garlic cloves, minced
- 2 tbsp organic extra-virgin olive oil
- 1 cup organic sauerkraut
- Sea salt and black pepper to taste
- 1/4 cup organic fresh dill, chopped

Instructions:
1. Heat oil in a large skillet over medium heat. Sauté onion and garlic until softened, about 5 minutes.
2. Add mushrooms and cook until browned and tender, about 5-7 minutes.
3. Stir in zucchini noodles and cook for another 2-3 minutes until tender. Season with salt and pepper.
4. In a separate skillet, fry the eggs to your desired doneness.
5. Divide the mushroom and zucchini mixture among four bowls. Top each with a fried egg and a spoonful of sauerkraut.
6. Garnish with fresh dill before serving.

Tip: For crispy edges on the fried eggs, cook them in a hot skillet with a generous amount of avocado oil.

Nutritional Information (per serving):
- Calories: 290 Kcal
- Protein: 14g
- Fat: 22g
- Carbohydrates: 10g
- Fiber: 4g

GINGER-TURMERIC PROBIOTIC SMOOTHIE BOWL

Prep Time: 10 minutes
Cook Time: 0 minutes
Serves: 2

Ingredients:
- 1 cup organic coconut yogurt (unsweetened, probiotic)
- 1/2 cup organic coconut milk (full-fat, no additives)
- 1 tsp organic fresh ginger, grated
- 1/2 tsp organic turmeric powder
- 1/2 tsp organic cinnamon (optional, for sweetness)
- 1 tbsp organic chia seeds
- 1/4 cup organic fresh pineapple (for tropical flavor and digestive enzymes)
- 1/2 cup organic spinach (optional for extra nutrients)
- 1 tbsp organic hemp seeds (for protein)
- Organic fresh berries and coconut flakes for topping

Instructions:
1. Blend the Smoothie Base: In a blender, combine the coconut yogurt, coconut milk, grated ginger, turmeric, cinnamon, chia seeds, fresh pineapple, and spinach (if using). Blend until smooth and creamy.
2. Pour into Bowls: Divide the smoothie mixture into two bowls. It should be thick enough to eat with a spoon.
3. Add Toppings: Top with fresh berries, hemp seeds, and coconut flakes for added crunch and flavor.
4. Serve Immediately: Enjoy this gut-boosting, nutrient-packed smoothie bowl for breakfast or a mid-day snack!

Nutritional Information (per serving):
- Calories: 266 kcal
- Protein: 7g
- Fat: 19g
- Carbohydrates: 18g
- Fiber: 5g

SAVORY BREAKFASTS

GOOD ENERGY ENGLISH BREAKFAST

Prep Time: 15 minutes
Cook Time: 25 minutes
Serves: 4

Ingredients:
- For the Sausages:
  - 4 organic, grass-fed pork sausages (choose brands without additives or preservatives like US Wellness Meats)
- For the Bacon:
  - 8 slices organic Irish-style bacon (rashers) from ButcherBox or Pederson's Farms
- For the White Pudding:
  - 4 slices organic, grain-free white pudding (such as the recipe below or specialty shops that offer it with no grains)
- For the Eggs:
  - 8 organic, pasture-raised eggs
  - 2 tbsp organic avocado oil (for frying)
  - Sea salt & pepper to taste
- For the Mushrooms:
  - 1 cup organic portobello mushrooms, sliced
  - 2 tbsp organic ghee (for cooking)
- For the Tomatoes:
  - 2 organic heirloom tomatoes, halved
  - 1 tbsp organic olive oil
- For the Sautéed Cabbage:
  - 2 cups organic green cabbage, sliced
  - 1 clove organic garlic, minced
  - 1 tbsp organic grass-fed butter
  - Sea salt & pepper to taste

Instructions:
1. Cook the Sausages and Bacon: In a large skillet over medium heat, cook the sausages for about 10-12 minutes until browned and cooked through. In a separate pan, cook the Irish bacon until crispy, about 4-5 minutes per side.
2. Prepare the White Pudding: If you're making your own grain-free white pudding, mix grass-fed ground pork, pasture-raised pork fat, onion, garlic, and herbs into a patty and cook in a pan until golden brown and crispy on both sides (about 4-5 minutes per side). If using pre-made white pudding, cook in the skillet until browned and crispy.
3. Sauté the Mushrooms and Tomatoes: In a skillet, heat ghee over medium heat. Add sliced mushrooms and sauté for 5-6 minutes until browned. Set aside. Add the tomatoes to the same pan and sear for 3 minutes until softened and slightly charred.
   Be sure not to overcrowd the mushrooms in the pan to allow them to caramelize properly.
4. Fry the Eggs: Heat avocado oil in a nonstick pan over medium heat. Fry the eggs to your preferred doneness (traditionally sunny-side-up or over easy). Season with sea salt and pepper.
5. Sauté the Cabbage: In a skillet, melt the grass-fed butter and add minced garlic. Sauté for 1 minute, then add the sliced cabbage. Cook for 5-7 minutes until tender but still slightly crisp. Season with salt and pepper.
6. Assemble and Serve: Arrange the sausages, bacon, white pudding, mushrooms, tomatoes, eggs, and sautéed cabbage on a plate.

Tip: Use a spoon to carefully baste the eggs with the oil in the pan for perfectly cooked whites and runny yolks. For extra probiotics and tang, serve with a side of fermented kimchi or sauerkraut.

Nutritional Information (per serving):
- Calories: 740
- Protein: 37g
- Fat: 61g
- Carbohydrates: 10g
- Fiber: 2g

GRAIN-FREE WHITE PUDDING

Prep Time: 10 minutes
Cook Time: 15 minutes
Serves: 4

Ingredients:
- 1/2 lb organic ground pork
- 1/4 lb pasture-raised pork fat (finely minced)
- 1/4 cup organic almond flour (for binding)
- 1/2 organic onion, finely minced
- 1 clove organic garlic, minced
- 1 tsp organic dried thyme
- 1/2 tsp organic ground sage
- Sea salt & pepper to taste

Instructions:
1. Mix the **Ingredients:**
   In a large bowl, combine ground pork, pork fat, almond flour, onion, garlic, thyme, sage, salt, and pepper.
2. Form the Patties:
   Shape the mixture into small, thick patties.
3. Cook the White Pudding:
   Heat a skillet over medium heat. Add the patties and cook for 4-5 minutes per side until golden brown and crispy.

Tip: To enhance flavor, sear the patties until a deep brown crust forms, locking in moisture.

Nutritional Information (per serving):
- Calories: 317
- Protein: 14g
- Fat: 28g
- Carbohydrates: 2g
- Fiber: 1g

BRUSSELS SPROUTS AND BACON HASH WITH FRIED EGGS

Prep Time: 15 minutes
Cook Time: 25 minutes
Serves: 4

Ingredients:
- 1 lb organic Brussels sprouts, trimmed and shredded
- 4 slices organic, pasture-raised bacon, chopped
- 1 organic onion, diced
- 2 tbsp organic coconut oil
- 4 organic, pasture-raised eggs
- Sea salt and black pepper to taste

Instructions:
1. Heat coconut oil in a large skillet over medium heat.
2. Add bacon and cook until crisp. Remove bacon and set aside.
3. Add onion to the skillet and cook until softened, about 5 minutes.
4. Add shredded Brussels sprouts and cook for 10-12 minutes, or until tender and slightly browned.
5. Stir in the cooked bacon.
6. Make four wells in the hash and crack an egg into each well.
7. Cover and cook for 3-4 minutes, or until the eggs are cooked to your liking.
8. Season with salt and pepper to taste.

Tip: Shredding the Brussels sprouts helps them cook more quickly and evenly.

Nutritional Information (per serving):
- Calories: 320
- Protein: 22g
- Fat: 26g

- Carbohydrates: 8g
- Fiber: 4g

SARDINE AND SWEET POTATO HASH

Prep Time: 15 minutes
Cook Time: 20 minutes
Serves: 4

Ingredients:

- 2 cans (4 oz each) wild-caught sardines in olive oil, drained
- 2 large organic sweet potatoes, peeled and diced
- 1 organic red bell pepper, diced
- 1 organic onion, diced
- 2 organic garlic cloves, minced
- 2 tbsp organic avocado oil
- 1 tsp organic smoked paprika
- 1/4 cup organic fresh parsley, chopped
- Sea salt and black pepper to taste

Instructions:

1. Heat avocado oil in a large skillet over medium heat.
2. Add sweet potatoes and cook for 10 minutes until tender.
3. Add bell pepper, onion, and garlic. Cook for another 5 minutes until vegetables are softened.
4. Stir in smoked paprika, salt, and pepper.
5. Gently fold in the sardines and cook for 2 minutes to warm through.
6. Garnish with fresh parsley and serve hot.

Tip: To ensure even cooking, cut the sweet potatoes into small, uniform pieces.

Nutritional Information (per serving):

- Calories: 400
- Protein: 20g
- Fat: 24g
- Carbohydrates: 28g
- Fiber: 6g

POACHED EGGS WITH SAUTÉED ASPARAGUS AND ANCHOVY SAUCE

Prep Time: 15 minutes
Cook Time: 15 minutes
Serves: 4

Ingredients:

- 4 large organic pasture-raised eggs
- 1 lb organic asparagus, trimmed
- 4 anchovy fillets, minced
- 2 organic garlic cloves, minced
- 1/4 cup organic extra-virgin olive oil
- 2 tbsp organic lemon juice
- Sea salt and black pepper to taste
- 1/4 cup organic fresh parsley, chopped

Instructions:

1. Bring a pot of water to a gentle simmer. Add a splash of vinegar (optional) to help the eggs set.
2. Crack each egg into a small bowl and gently slide it into the simmering water. Poach for 3-4 minutes until the whites are set but the yolks are still runny.
3. Remove the eggs with a slotted spoon and set aside.
4. In a large skillet, heat olive oil over medium heat. Sauté asparagus until tender, about 5-7 minutes.
5. Add minced garlic and anchovies, cooking for another 1-2 minutes until fragrant. Stir in lemon juice, salt, and pepper.
6. Serve the poached eggs over the sautéed asparagus, drizzling with the anchovy sauce.
7. Garnish with fresh parsley before serving.

Tip: Use fresh eggs for poaching, as they hold their shape better than older eggs.

Nutritional Information (per serving):

- Calories: 280
- Protein: 14g
- Fat: 24g
- Carbohydrates: 6g
- Fiber: 3g

CLOUD EGGS WITH PROSCIUTTO AND ASPARAGUS

Prep Time: 15 minutes
Cook Time: 10 minutes
Serves: 4

Ingredients:

- 4 organic, pasture-raised eggs, separated
- 4 slices organic prosciutto, chopped
- 1 bunch organic asparagus, trimmed
- 1/4 cup organic Parmesan cheese, grated
- 2 tbsp organic chives, finely chopped
- 2 tbsp organic ghee
- Sea salt and black pepper to taste

Instructions:

1. Preheat oven to 450°F (230°C).
2. Whip egg whites until stiff peaks form.
3. Gently fold in chopped prosciutto and Parmesan cheese.
4. Spoon mixture into 4 mounds on a parchment-lined baking sheet, creating a well in the center of each.
5. Bake for 3 minutes.
6. Carefully add an egg yolk to the center of each mound.
7. Bake for another 3-4 minutes until yolks are set but still runny.
8. Meanwhile, sauté asparagus in ghee until tender-crisp.
9. Serve cloud eggs over sautéed asparagus, garnished with chives.

Tip: Ensure your bowl and beaters are completely clean and dry before whipping egg whites for maximum volume.

Nutritional Information (per serving):

- Calories: 280
- Protein: 20g
- Fat: 22g
- Carbohydrates: 4g
- Fiber: 2g

BREAKFAST SALAD

Prep Time: 15 minutes
Cook Time: 10 minutes
Serves: 2

Ingredients:

- 4 cups organic mixed salad greens (e.g., spinach, arugula, kale)
- 2 organic pasture-raised eggs
- 4 slices organic, sugar-free bacon
- 1 small organic avocado, sliced
- 1/2 cup organic cherry tomatoes, halved
- 1/4 cup organic red onion, thinly sliced
- 1/4 cup organic walnuts, roughly chopped
- 2 tbsp organic pumpkin seeds

For the Dressing:

- 2 tbsp organic extra-virgin olive oil
- 1 tbsp organic apple cider vinegar
- 1 tsp organic Dijon mustard
- Sea salt and freshly ground black pepper to taste

Instructions:

1. **Cook the Bacon and Eggs:** In a skillet over medium heat, cook the bacon until crispy. Remove and set aside on a paper towel to drain. In the same skillet, fry the eggs to your desired doneness (sunny-side up or over-easy recommended).
2. **Prepare the Salad Base:** In a large bowl, combine the mixed salad greens, cherry tomatoes, and red onion.

3. **Make the Dressing:** In a small bowl, whisk together olive oil, apple cider vinegar, Dijon mustard, salt, and pepper.
4. **Assemble the Salad:** Divide the salad base between two plates and top each salad with a fried egg, sliced avocado, and crumbled bacon. Sprinkle walnuts and pumpkin seeds over the salads.

Tip: For an extra nutrient boost, add a handful of microgreens or sprouts to the salad base as well as a side of fermented vegetables.

Nutritional Information (per serving):
- Calories: 520
- Protein: 22g
- Fat: 44g
- Carbohydrates: 15g
- Fiber: 9g

30-MINUTE SHAKSHUKA

Prep Time: 10 minutes
Cook Time: 20 minutes
Serves: 4

Ingredients:
- 1 tbsp organic avocado oil
- 1 organic onion, diced
- 2 organic bell peppers (any color), diced
- 3 organic garlic cloves, minced
- 1 tsp organic ground cumin
- 1 tsp organic paprika
- 1/2 tsp organic chili powder (or cayenne, to taste)
- 1 can (14 oz) organic diced tomatoes
- 1/2 cup organic tomato sauce (no added sugars)
- 4 organic, pasture-raised eggs
- 1/4 cup organic feta cheese, crumbled (or dairy-free feta alternative)
- 2 tbsp organic fresh parsley, chopped
- Sea salt and freshly ground black pepper to taste

Instructions:
1. **Sauté the Vegetables:**
   1. In a large skillet or cast-iron pan, heat the avocado oil over medium heat.
   2. Add the diced onion and bell peppers. Sauté for 5-7 minutes until the vegetables are softened.
   3. Add the minced garlic, cumin, paprika, and chili powder (or cayenne). Cook for 1 minute, stirring constantly, until fragrant.
2. **Simmer the Sauce:**
   1. Pour in the diced tomatoes and tomato sauce. Stir to combine.
   2. Bring the mixture to a simmer and let it cook for 5-7 minutes, allowing the flavors to meld.
3. **Cook the Eggs:**
   1. Using the back of a spoon, create 4 wells or indentations in the tomato mixture.
   2. Crack the eggs directly into the wells.
   3. Cover the skillet and cook for 5-7 minutes, or until the egg whites are set and the yolks are cooked to your desired doneness.
4. **Finish and Serve:**
   1. Remove the skillet from heat.
   2. Sprinkle the crumbled feta cheese and chopped parsley over the top.
   3. Season with sea salt and freshly ground black pepper to taste.
   4. Serve the Shakshuka immediately, while the eggs are still hot.

Tip: For a richer flavor, sauté the onions and peppers in 1 tbsp of organic ghee instead of avocado oil.

Nutritional Information (per serving):
- Calories: 240
- Protein: 12g
- Fat: 14g

- Carbohydrates: 16g
- Fiber: 4g

BROCCOLI AND SALMON FRITTATA

Prep Time: 15 minutes
Cook Time: 20 minutes
Serves: 4

Ingredients:
- 8 organic, pasture-raised eggs
- 1 cup organic broccoli florets, chopped
- 8 oz wild-caught salmon, cooked and flaked
- 1/4 cup organic red onion, diced
- 2 tbsp organic fresh dill, chopped
- 2 tbsp organic ghee
- Sea salt and black pepper to taste

Instructions:
1. Preheat oven to 375°F (190°C).
2. In an oven-safe skillet, sauté broccoli and onion in ghee until tender.
3. Whisk eggs with dill, salt, and pepper.
4. Add flaked salmon to the skillet and pour egg mixture over.
5. Cook on stovetop for 5 minutes, then transfer to oven.
6. Bake for 15 minutes or until set and lightly golden.

Tip: For a fluffier frittata, separate the eggs and whip the whites before folding them into the yolks.

Nutritional Information (per serving):
- Calories: 320
- Protein: 26g
- Fat: 22g
- Carbohydrates: 6g
- Fiber: 2g

FLAXSEED AND EGG MUFFINS WITH SPINACH, MUSHROOMS, AND PROBIOTIC CHEESE

Prep Time: 15 minutes **Cook Time:** 15 minutes **Serves:** 4
Ingredients:
- 4 large organic, pasture-raised eggs
- 2 tbsp organic ground flaxseed
- 1/4 cup organic grated probiotic cheese (or dairy-free alternative)
- 1/4 cup organic fresh spinach, chopped
- 1/4 cup organic mushrooms, sliced
- 1 tsp organic dried thyme
- 2 tbsp organic ghee or coconut oil
- Sea salt and black pepper to taste

Instructions:
1. Preheat oven to 375°F (190°C). Grease a muffin tin with ghee or coconut oil.
2. Whisk eggs, ground flaxseed, and thyme in a bowl.
3. Stir in grated cheese, spinach, and mushrooms.
4. Pour the mixture into the muffin tin.
5. Bake for 12-15 minutes until eggs are set.
6. Serve warm.

Tip: Let the egg mixture rest for 5 minutes to allow the flaxseed to absorb excess moisture.

Nutritional Information (per serving):
- Calories: 176
- Protein: 9g
- Fat: 14g
- Carbohydrates: 2g
- Fiber: 1g

POWER WRAPS

These are perfect for a breakfast on the go or a easy lunch. Take a look at the no-grain wraps in the no-grain bread section.

POWER WRAPS WITH KIMCHI

Prep Time: 15 minutes
Cook Time: 15 minutes
Serves: 4

Ingredients:
- 1 lb organic, grass-fed ground beef
- 1 lb organic green beans, trimmed and cut into 1-inch pieces
- 2 organic garlic cloves, minced
- 1 organic red bell pepper, diced
- 2 tbsp organic tamari or coconut aminos
- 1 tbsp organic sesame oil
- 2 tbsp organic avocado oil
- Sea salt and black pepper to taste
- 8 large organic lettuce leaves (butter lettuce or romaine)
- 1/2 cup organic kimchi, chopped
- 2 tbsp organic green onions, sliced

Instructions:
1. In a large skillet, heat 1 tbsp avocado oil over medium-high heat. Add ground beef and cook until browned. Remove and set aside.
2. In the same skillet, heat the remaining 1 tbsp avocado oil. Add green beans and red bell pepper, and cook for 5-7 minutes until tender.
3. Add garlic and cook for another 1-2 minutes until fragrant.
4. Return the cooked beef to the skillet. Stir in tamari (or coconut aminos) and sesame oil. Cook for another 2-3 minutes until well combined.
5. Fill each lettuce leaf with the beef and green bean mixture. Top with chopped kimchi and green onions.
6. Serve immediately.

Tip: For added crunch, sprinkle chopped nuts like almonds or cashews over the lettuce wraps before serving.

Nutritional Information (per serving):
- Calories: 360
- Protein: 26g
- Fat: 24g
- Carbohydrates: 12g
- Fiber: 4g

LETTUCE-WRAPPED GRILLED CHICKEN WITH AVOCADO, CUCUMBER, AND SAUERKRAUT

Prep Time: 15 minutes
Cook Time: 15 minutes
Serves: 4 wraps

Ingredients:
- For the Chicken:
  - 2 organic, pasture-raised chicken breasts
  - 2 tbsp organic olive oil
  - 1 tsp organic garlic powder
  - 1 tsp organic smoked paprika
  - Sea salt & pepper to taste
- For the Wrap:
  - 8 large organic Romaine lettuce leaves (for wrapping)
  - 1 organic cucumber, thinly sliced
  - 1 organic avocado, sliced
  - 1/4 cup organic sauerkraut (probiotic-rich, unpasteurized)
  - 2 tbsp organic lemon juice

Instructions:
1. Prepare the Chicken: Preheat a grill or grill pan over medium heat. Rub the chicken breasts with olive oil, garlic powder, smoked paprika, salt, and pepper. Grill the chicken for 5-7 minutes per side, or until fully cooked (internal temperature of 165°F). Let rest for 5 minutes, then slice thinly. Resting the chicken after grilling helps retain moisture, ensuring the chicken stays juicy in the wrap.
2. Assemble the Wrap: Lay two Romaine leaves flat to form each wrap base. Layer with grilled chicken slices, cucumber, avocado, and sauerkraut. Drizzle with lemon juice and season with a pinch of sea salt.
3. Wrap and Serve: Fold the lettuce leaves around the filling like a burrito, tucking in the sides as you roll. Secure with a toothpick if necessary. These wraps are perfect for meal prepping and can be stored in an airtight container for up to 2 days.

Tip: Using crispy Romaine lettuce as a wrap keeps the texture light and refreshing while adding a satisfying crunch.

Nutritional Information (per wrap):
- Calories: 295
- Protein: 21g
- Fat: 21g
- Carbohydrates: 8g
- Fiber: 4g

COLLARD GREEN WRAP WITH GRASS-FED BEEF, BELL PEPPERS, AND TAHINI SAUCE

Prep Time: 20 minutes
Cook Time: 10 minutes
Serves: 4 wraps

Ingredients:
- For the Beef Filling:
  - 1 lb organic grass-fed ground beef
  - 1 tbsp organic avocado oil
  - 1 organic red bell pepper, thinly sliced
  - 1/2 organic red onion, thinly sliced
  - 1 clove organic garlic, minced
  - 1 tsp organic ground cumin
  - 1/2 tsp organic chili powder
  - Sea salt & pepper to taste
- For the Wrap:
  - 4 large organic collard green leaves
  - 1/2 organic carrot, julienned
  - 1/4 cup organic sauerkraut
- For the Tahini Sauce:
  - 2 tbsp organic tahini
  - 1 tbsp organic lemon juice
  - 1 tbsp filtered water (as needed to thin)
  - Sea salt & pepper to taste

Instructions:
1. Prepare the Beef Filling: In a skillet, heat avocado oil over medium heat. Add ground beef and cook for 5-7 minutes, breaking it up as it browns. Add garlic, red bell pepper, red onion, cumin, chili powder, salt, and pepper. Cook until the vegetables are softened and the beef is fully cooked, about 3-4 minutes.
2. Prepare the Collard Greens: To make the collard greens more pliable, blanch them in boiling water for 30 seconds, then transfer them to an ice bath to cool. Pat dry.
3. Make the Tahini Sauce: In a small bowl, whisk together tahini, lemon juice, and water until smooth. Season with salt and pepper. If too thick, add more water to reach the desired consistency.
4. Assemble the Wraps: Lay a collard leaf flat, place the beef mixture in the center, then top with julienned carrot and a spoonful of sauerkraut. Drizzle with tahini sauce.

5. Wrap and Serve: Fold the sides of the collard green over the filling, then roll tightly like a burrito. These wraps can be prepped ahead of time and stored in the fridge for up to 3 days.

Tip: Blanching the collard greens makes them tender and easier to wrap while retaining their vibrant color and nutrients. Collard greens are sturdy and hold up well in meal prep, keeping the wraps fresh and intact for several days.

Nutritional Information (per wrap):
- Calories: 380
- Protein: 22g
- Fat: 29g
- Carbohydrates: 9g
- Fiber: 3g

SWISS CHARD WRAPS WITH PASTURE-RAISED TURKEY, ROASTED VEGGIES, AND GARLIC-HERB DRESSING

Prep Time: 20 minutes
Cook Time: 15 minutes
Serves: 4 wraps

Ingredients:
- For the Roasted Vegetables:
  - 1 organic zucchini, sliced
  - 1 organic red bell pepper, sliced
  - 1 tbsp organic olive oil
  - 1/2 tsp organic dried oregano
  - Sea salt & pepper to taste
- For the Turkey:
  - 8 slices organic pasture-raised turkey breast (pre-cooked, nitrate-free, such as Applegate brand)
- For the Wrap:
  - 4 large organic Swiss chard leaves, stems removed
  - 1/2 organic avocado, sliced
  - 1/4 cup organic carrot, shredded
- For the Garlic-Herb Dressing:
  - 2 tbsp organic olive oil
  - 1 tbsp organic lemon juice
  - 1 tsp organic Dijon mustard (no added sugars)
  - 1 clove organic garlic, minced
  - 1 tbsp organic fresh parsley, chopped
  - Sea salt & pepper to taste

Instructions:
1. Roast the Vegetables: Preheat your oven to 400°F (200°C). Toss zucchini and red bell pepper slices with olive oil, oregano, salt, and pepper. Spread on a baking sheet and roast for 15 minutes, until tender and slightly caramelized.
2. Prepare the Swiss Chard Leaves: To soften the Swiss chard leaves, blanch them in boiling water for 30 seconds, then transfer to an ice bath. Pat dry with a clean towel.
3. Make the Garlic-Herb Dressing: In a small bowl, whisk together olive oil, lemon juice, Dijon mustard, garlic, parsley, salt, and pepper.
4. Assemble the Wraps: Lay a Swiss chard leaf flat. Layer 2 slices of turkey, roasted vegetables, avocado slices, and

shredded carrot in the center. Drizzle with garlic-herb dressing.
5. Wrap and Serve: Fold in the sides of the Swiss chard and roll tightly. These wraps can be stored in the fridge for up to 3 days and make an excellent meal-prep option.

Tip: Roasting the vegetables enhances their natural sweetness, while the garlic-herb dressing adds a fresh, zesty finish that complements the earthy flavor of the Swiss chard.

Nutritional Information (per wrap):
- Calories: 225
- Protein: 14g
- Fat: 16g
- Carbohydrates: 8g
- Fiber: 3g

MACKEREL LETTUCE WRAPS WITH SPICY CASHEW SAUCE

Prep Time: 15 minutes
Cook Time: 10 minutes
Serves: 4

Ingredients:
- For the Mackerel:
  - 4 fresh mackerel fillets
  - 1 tbsp organic avocado oil
  - Sea salt & pepper to taste
- For the Lettuce Wraps:
  - 8 large organic Romaine or Bibb lettuce leaves
  - 1 small organic cucumber, julienned
  - 1 organic carrot, julienned
  - 1/4 cup organic fresh cilantro, chopped
- For the Spicy Cashew Sauce:
  - 1/4 cup organic cashew butter (unsweetened)
  - 1 tbsp organic coconut aminos (grain-free soy sauce alternative)
  - 1 tbsp organic apple cider vinegar (unpasteurized)
  - 1 tsp organic chili flakes (optional for heat)
  - 2 tbsp water (to thin the sauce)

Instructions:
1. Cook the Mackerel: Heat avocado oil in a skillet over medium heat. Season the mackerel fillets with salt and pepper. Cook for about 4-5 minutes per side until cooked through and crispy on the outside.
2. Prepare the Spicy Cashew Sauce: In a small bowl, whisk together the cashew butter, coconut aminos, apple cider vinegar, chili flakes (if using), and water. Adjust the consistency by adding more water if needed.
3. Assemble the Lettuce Wraps: Place the cooked mackerel fillets on the lettuce leaves. Add the julienned cucumber, carrot, and cilantro on top of each fillet.
4. Serve: Drizzle the spicy cashew sauce over the wraps and serve immediately for a fresh, crunchy, and flavorful meal packed with protein and healthy fats.

Nutritional Information (per serving):
- Calories: 380
- Protein: 22g
- Fat: 30g
- Carbohydrates: 8g
- Fiber: 2g

VEGAN

NAVY BEAN AND AVOCADO BREAKFAST HASH

Prep Time: 15 minutes
Cook Time: 20 minutes
Serves: 4

Ingredients:
- 2 cups cooked organic navy beans
- 1 large organic sweet potato, diced

- 1 organic red bell pepper, diced
- 1 organic onion, diced
- 2 organic garlic cloves, minced
- 1 organic avocado, diced
- 2 tbsp organic coconut oil
- 1 tsp organic smoked paprika
- Sea salt and black pepper to taste

- 1/4 cup organic fresh cilantro, chopped

Instructions:
1. In a large skillet, heat coconut oil over medium heat. Sauté sweet potato, onion, and garlic until sweet potato is tender and slightly crispy, about 10 minutes.
2. Add red bell pepper and cook for another 5 minutes until softened.
3. Stir in navy beans, smoked paprika, salt, and pepper. Cook until heated through.
4. Remove from heat and gently fold in diced avocado.
5. Garnish with fresh cilantro before serving.

Tip: For even cooking, cut the sweet potato into small, evenly-sized cubes.

Nutritional Information (per serving):
- Calories: 307
- Protein: 7g
- Fat: 16g
- Carbohydrates: 37g
- Fiber: 10g

SCRAMBLED TOFU WITH SPINACH AND FERMENTED KIMCHI

Prep Time: 10 minutes
Cook Time: 10 minutes
Serves: 2

Ingredients:
- 8 oz firm tofu, crumbled
- 2 tbsp avocado oil
- 1/2 tsp turmeric
- 1 cup organic spinach, chopped
- 1/2 cup fermented kimchi
- 1 clove garlic, minced
- 1 tsp ground cumin
- Sea salt and black pepper to taste

Instructions:
1. Sauté the Tofu: Heat avocado oil in a large skillet over medium heat. Add crumbled tofu and turmeric, stirring well to coat the tofu in the yellow color.
2. Add Spinach and Garlic: Add garlic, cumin, and chopped spinach to the skillet. Cook for 2-3 minutes until the spinach wilts.
3. Add Kimchi: Stir in the fermented kimchi and cook for an additional 1-2 minutes to warm it through.
4. Serve: Season with salt and pepper, then serve the scrambled tofu immediately.

Tip: The turmeric gives the tofu a scrambled egg-like appearance while adding anti-inflammatory properties. Kimchi adds a spicy, tangy contrast that enhances the overall flavor.

Nutritional Information (per serving):
- Calories: 252
- Protein: 11g
- Fat: 21g
- Carbohydrates: 8g
- Fiber: 3g

PECAN "OATMEAL" WITH CARAMELIZED BANANAS AND COCONUT YOGURT

Prep Time: 10 minutes
Cook Time: 15 minutes
Serves: 2

Ingredients:
- 1 cup organic pecans, soaked overnight and drained
- 1/4 cup organic coconut flour
- 1 cup organic coconut milk
- 1 tsp organic vanilla extract
- 1/4 tsp sea salt

- 2 organic bananas, sliced
- 2 tbsp organic coconut oil
- 1/2 cup organic coconut yogurt
- 1 tsp organic cinnamon

Instructions:
1. In a food processor, pulse soaked pecans until finely chopped but not completely smooth.
2. Transfer to a saucepan and add coconut flour, coconut milk, vanilla, and salt. Cook over medium heat, stirring frequently, for 5-7 minutes until thickened.
3. In a separate skillet, melt coconut oil over medium heat. Add banana slices and cook for 2-3 minutes per side until caramelized.
4. Divide the pecan "oatmeal" between two bowls. Top with caramelized bananas, a dollop of coconut yogurt, and a sprinkle of cinnamon.

Tip: For a smoother texture, blend half of the pecan mixture until creamy before combining with the chopped pecans.

Nutritional Information (per serving):
- Calories: 689
- Protein: 7g
- Fat: 61g
- Carbohydrates: 34g
- Fiber: 9g

PECAN AND COCONUT "GRANOLA" WITH BERRY COMPOTE

Prep Time: 15 minutes
Cook Time: 20 minutes
Serves: 6

Ingredients:
- 2 cups organic pecans, roughly chopped
- 1 cup organic unsweetened coconut flakes
- 1/4 cup organic coconut oil, melted
- 1 tsp organic vanilla extract
- 1 tsp organic cinnamon
- 1/4 tsp sea salt
- 2 cups mixed organic berries (strawberries, blueberries, raspberries)
- 1/4 cup water
- 1 cup organic coconut yogurt

Instructions:
1. Preheat oven to 300°F (150°C).
2. In a large bowl, mix pecans, coconut flakes, melted coconut oil, vanilla, cinnamon, and salt.
3. Spread mixture on a baking sheet and bake for 15-20 minutes, stirring occasionally, until golden brown.
4. Meanwhile, in a saucepan, combine berries and water. Simmer over medium heat for 10 minutes until berries break down and sauce thickens.
5. Let the "granola" cool completely before serving.
6. Serve the pecan and coconut "granola" with berry compote and a dollop of coconut yogurt.

Tip: For clusters, press the granola mixture together on the baking sheet before baking and avoid stirring during cooking.

Nutritional Information (per serving):
- Calories: 420
- Protein: 6g
- Fat: 38g
- Carbohydrates: 16g
- Fiber: 8g

MEAT RECIPES

POULTRY

CAULIFLOWER AND CHICKEN NUGGETS

Prep Time: 20 minutes
Cook Time: 25 minutes
Serves: 4

Ingredients:
- 1 lb organic, pasture-raised chicken breast, cut into nugget-sized pieces
- 1 large head organic cauliflower, steamed and finely chopped
- 1 cup organic coconut flour
- 1/2 cup organic grated Parmesan cheese (optional)
- 1 organic egg, beaten
- 2 tbsp organic coconut oil
- Sea salt and black pepper to taste

Instructions:
1. Preheat oven to 400°F (200°C) and line a baking sheet with parchment paper.
2. In a large bowl, mix together chopped cauliflower, coconut flour, Parmesan cheese (if using), salt, and pepper.
3. Dip each chicken nugget piece into the beaten egg, then coat with the cauliflower mixture, pressing to adhere.
4. Place the coated chicken nuggets on the prepared baking sheet and brush with oil.
5. Bake for 20-25 minutes, turning halfway through, until golden and cooked through.
6. Serve with your favorite dipping sauce.

Tip: For extra flavor, add a teaspoon of smoked paprika or garlic powder to the cauliflower coating mixture.

Nutritional Information (per serving):
- Calories: 320
- Protein: 28g
- Fat: 20g
- Carbohydrates: 12g
- Fiber: 5g

COQ AU VIN WITH CAULIFLOWER PURÉE

Prep Time: 30 minutes
Cook Time: 1 hour 30 minutes
Serves: 6

Ingredients:
- 6 organic, pasture-raised chicken thighs
- 8 oz organic bacon, diced
- 1 large organic onion, diced
- 2 organic carrots, sliced
- 8 oz organic cremini mushrooms, quartered
- 3 organic garlic cloves, minced
- 2 cups organic red wine (preferably Burgundy)
- 1 cup organic bone broth
- 1 bouquet garni (thyme, parsley, bay leaf)
- 1/4 cup organic ghee
- 1 large organic cauliflower, cut into florets
- 1/4 cup organic coconut cream

- 2 tbsp organic avocado oil
- Sea salt and freshly ground black pepper to taste

Instructions:
1. In a large Dutch oven, cook diced bacon over medium heat until crispy. Remove and set aside, leaving the fat in the pot.
2. Season chicken thighs with salt and pepper. Brown them in the bacon fat, then set aside.
3. In the same pot, sauté onions, carrots, and mushrooms until softened (about 10 minutes).
4. Add garlic and cook for another minute.
5. Return chicken to the pot. Add wine, bone broth, and bouquet garni. Bring to a simmer, then cover and cook on low for about 1 hour.
6. Meanwhile, steam cauliflower until very tender.
7. In a food processor, blend steamed cauliflower with ghee and coconut cream until smooth.
8. When the chicken is tender, remove it from the pot. Increase heat and reduce the sauce until it thickens slightly.
9. Return chicken and bacon to the pot, warming through.
10. Serve the coq au vin over the cauliflower purée.

Tip: For maximum flavor, marinate the chicken in the red wine overnight before cooking. This will infuse the meat with a deeper, richer flavor and help tenderize it further.

Nutritional Information (per serving):
- Calories: 592
- Protein: 33g
- Fat: 42g
- Carbohydrates: 12g
- Fiber: 4g

NAVY BEAN AND CHICKEN STEW WITH PROBIOTIC RICH FERMENTED CARROTS

Prep Time: 20 minutes
Cook Time: 1 hour
Serves: 4

Ingredients:
- 1 lb organic, pasture-raised chicken thighs, diced
- 2 cups cooked organic navy beans
- 1 organic onion, diced
- 3 organic garlic cloves, minced
- 3 organic carrots, chopped
- 2 organic celery stalks, chopped

- 4 cups organic chicken broth
- 1 tbsp organic ghee
- 1 tsp organic thyme
- 1 tsp organic rosemary
- 1 bay leaf
- Sea salt and black pepper to taste
- 1/2 cup organic fermented carrots, chopped

Instructions:
1. In a large pot, heat ghee over medium heat. Sauté onion, garlic, carrots, and celery until softened, about 5 minutes.
2. Add diced chicken and cook until browned.
3. Stir in navy beans, chicken broth, thyme, rosemary, and bay leaf. Bring to a boil, then reduce heat and simmer for 45 minutes.
4. Season with sea salt and black pepper to taste.
5. Remove bay leaf and stir in fermented carrots just before serving.

Tip: For added flavor, deglaze the pot with a splash of apple cider vinegar after browning the chicken.

Nutritional Information (per serving):
- Calories: 412
- Protein: 35g
- Fat: 16g
- Carbohydrates: 32g
- Fiber: 8g

CHIA AND HERB-CRUSTED CHICKEN TENDERS WITH FERMENTED CARROT SLAW

Prep Time: 20 minutes
Cook Time: 20 minutes
Serves: 4

Ingredients:
- 1 lb organic, pasture-raised chicken tenders
- 1/2 cup organic chia seeds
- 1/2 cup organic almond flour
- 1 tbsp organic dried oregano
- 1 tbsp organic dried thyme
- 1 tbsp organic garlic powder
- 1/2 tsp sea salt
- 1/2 tsp black pepper
- 2 organic eggs, beaten
- 3 tbsp organic avocado oil
- 1 cup organic shredded fermented carrots (preferably homemade, see recipe)
- 2 cups organic green cabbage, finely shredded
- 1 organic apple, julienned
- 2 tbsp organic apple cider vinegar
- 2 tbsp organic extra-virgin olive oil

Instructions:
1. Preheat oven to 400°F (200°C) and line a baking sheet with parchment paper.
2. In a shallow dish, mix chia seeds, almond flour, oregano, thyme, garlic powder, salt, and pepper.
3. Dip chicken tenders in beaten eggs, then coat with the chia seed mixture.
4. In a skillet, heat avocado oil over medium heat. Sear chicken tenders for 2-3 minutes per side until golden brown.
5. Transfer chicken tenders to the prepared baking sheet and bake for 10-12 minutes until cooked through.
6. In a bowl, combine fermented carrots, cabbage, apple, apple cider vinegar, and olive oil. Toss to mix.
7. Serve chicken tenders alongside the fermented carrot slaw.

Tip: For a more cohesive crust, press the chia mixture firmly onto the chicken tenders before searing.

Nutritional Information (per serving):
- Calories: 498

- Protein: 31g
- Fat: 33g
- Carbohydrates: 19g
- Fiber: 10g

BROCCOLI AND CHEDDAR-STUFFED CHICKEN BREASTS

Prep Time: 20 minutes
Cook Time: 25 minutes
Serves: 4

Ingredients:
- 4 organic, pasture-raised chicken breasts
- 1 cup organic broccoli florets, finely chopped
- 1/2 cup organic full-fat grass-fed cheddar cheese, shredded
- 1/2 cup organic full-fat grass-fed Greek yogurt (optional for a creamier filling)
- 2 tbsp organic full-fat grass-fed ghee, melted
- Sea salt and black pepper to taste

Instructions:
1. Preheat oven to 375°F (190°C).
2. In a bowl, mix broccoli, cheddar cheese, and coconut yogurt.
3. Cut a pocket into each chicken breast and stuff with the broccoli mixture.
4. Secure with toothpicks if necessary.
5. Brush chicken breasts with melted ghee and season with salt and pepper.
6. Place in a baking dish and bake for 25 minutes, or until chicken is cooked through.
7. Let rest for 5 minutes before serving.

Tip: For even cooking, ensure the chicken breasts are of uniform thickness. Pound them if necessary. Serve with a side of Brussel sprouts (see side recipes) and sauerkraut for a complete meal.

Nutritional Information (per serving):
- Calories: 350
- Protein: 38g
- Fat: 20g
- Carbohydrates: 3g
- Fiber: 1g

AVOCADO AND CHICKEN ZOODLE ALFREDO

Prep Time: 20 minutes
Cook Time: 15 minutes
Serves: 4

Ingredients:
- 1 lb organic, pasture-raised chicken breast, sliced into strips
- 2 large organic zucchinis, spiralized into noodles
- 2 large organic avocados
- 1/4 cup organic nutritional yeast
- 2 organic garlic cloves, minced
- 1/4 cup organic coconut milk
- 2 tbsp organic lemon juice
- 2 tbsp organic avocado oil
- Sea salt and black pepper to taste
- 1/4 cup organic fresh basil, chopped

Instructions:
1. Heat avocado oil in a large skillet over medium heat. Cook chicken strips until browned and cooked through, about 5-7 minutes. Remove and set aside.
2. In a blender, blend avocados, nutritional yeast, garlic, coconut milk, lemon juice, salt, and pepper until smooth.
3. In the same skillet, cook zoodles for 2-3 minutes until just tender.
4. Add chicken back to the skillet and pour avocado sauce over. Toss to coat.
5. Serve hot, garnished with fresh basil.

Tip: To prevent the zoodles from becoming watery, sprinkle them with salt and let them sit in a colander for 10 minutes, then pat dry before cooking.

Nutritional Information (per serving):
- Calories: 420
- Protein: 30g
- Fat: 28g
- Carbohydrates: 12g
- Fiber: 8g

DUCK CONFIT WITH ROASTED ROOT VEGETABLES AND KIMCHI

Prep Time: 5 minutes + 24 hours (for curing)
Cook Time: 3 hours
Serves: 4

Ingredients:
- 4 organic, pasture-raised duck legs
- 1/4 cup sea salt
- 2 tbsp organic fresh thyme leaves
- 2 organic bay leaves, crumbled
- 2 cups organic duck fat or ghee
- 2 organic parsnips, peeled and cut into batons
- 2 organic carrots, peeled and cut into batons
- 1 organic rutabaga, peeled and cut into batons
- 2 tbsp organic avocado oil
- 1/2 cup organic kimchi

Instructions:
1. Mix salt, thyme, and bay leaves. Rub mixture all over duck legs. Refrigerate for 24 hours.
2. Preheat oven to 250°F (120°C).
3. Rinse salt mixture off duck legs and pat dry.
4. Place legs in a baking dish and cover with melted duck fat or ghee.
5. Cook for 2.5-3 hours until meat is very tender.
6. In the last 45 minutes, toss root vegetables with avocado oil, salt, and pepper. Roast in the oven until caramelized.
7. Serve duck legs with roasted vegetables and a side of kimchi.

Tip: Save the duck fat after cooking for future use. It's excellent for roasting potatoes or other vegetables.

Nutritional Information (per serving):
- Calories: 845
- Protein: 33g
- Fat: 72g
- Carbohydrates: 18g
- Fiber: 5g

BLACKBERRY-GLAZED DUCK BREAST WITH RASPBERRY CAULIFLOWER MASH

Prep Time: 20 minutes
Cook Time: 25 minutes
Serves: 4

Ingredients:
- 4 organic, pasture-raised duck breasts (6 oz each)
- 1 cup organic blackberries
- 1 tbsp organic balsamic vinegar
- 1 tbsp organic fresh thyme leaves
- 2 tbsp organic ghee
- 1 large organic cauliflower head, cut into florets
- 1 cup organic raspberries
- 2 tbsp organic extra-virgin olive oil
- 1/4 cup organic, full-fat, grass-fed cream
- Sea salt and black pepper to taste

Instructions:
1. Score the duck skin in a diamond pattern. Season with salt and pepper.
2. In a small saucepan, mash blackberries with balsamic vinegar and thyme. Simmer for 10 minutes until syrupy.
3. Place duck breasts skin-side down in a cold skillet. Turn heat to medium and cook for 8-10 minutes until skin is crispy.

4. Flip and cook for another 4-5 minutes for medium-rare. Rest for 5 minutes before slicing.
5. Steam cauliflower until tender. Blend with raspberries, coconut oil, and coconut cream until smooth.
6. Serve sliced duck over cauliflower mash, drizzled with blackberry glaze.

Tip: For extra crispy duck skin, pat the breasts dry before cooking and start in a cold pan to render fat slowly.

Nutritional Information (per serving):
- Calories: 512
- Protein: 28g
- Fat: 42g
- Carbohydrates: 14g
- Fiber: 6g

EGG-STUFFED BELL PEPPERS WITH TURKEY AND SPINACH

Prep Time: 15 minutes
Cook Time: 25 minutes
Serves: 4

Ingredients:
- 4 large organic bell peppers, tops cut off and seeds removed
- 4 large organic pasture-raised eggs
- 1/2 lb organic ground turkey
- 2 cups organic spinach, chopped
- 1 organic onion, diced
- 2 organic garlic cloves, minced
- 1 tsp organic ground cumin
- 1/2 tsp organic smoked paprika
- 2 tbsp organic extra-virgin olive oil
- Sea salt and black pepper to taste
- 1/4 cup organic fresh parsley, chopped

Instructions:
1. Preheat oven to 375°F (190°C).
2. Heat oil in a skillet over medium heat. Sauté onion and garlic until softened, about 5 minutes.
3. Add ground turkey, cumin, and smoked paprika. Cook until turkey is browned, about 5 minutes.
4. Stir in spinach and cook until wilted. Season with salt and pepper.
5. Stuff the bell peppers with the turkey-spinach mixture, creating a small well in each one.
6. Crack an egg into each bell pepper.
7. Place stuffed bell peppers in a baking dish and bake for 20-25 minutes, until the eggs are set.
8. Garnish with fresh parsley before serving.

Tip: To prevent the bell peppers from tipping over, trim a small slice off the bottom of each one to create a flat surface.

Nutritional Information (per serving):
- Calories: 310
- Protein: 22g
- Fat: 20g
- Carbohydrates: 12g
- Fiber: 4g

CELERIAC "PASTA" WITH TURKEY MEATBALLS AND SAUERKRAUT

Prep Time: 15 minutes
Cook Time: 30 minutes
Serves: 4

Ingredients:
- 2 medium organic celeriac (celery root), spiralized
- 1 lb organic ground turkey
- 1 egg organic pasture-raised egg
- 1 tsp organic dried oregano
- 1 tbsp organic coconut oil
- 1/2 cup organic sauerkraut

Instructions:

1. Make the Meatballs: Preheat the oven to 375°F (190°C). Mix ground turkey, egg, oregano, salt, and pepper. Form into meatballs and bake for 20 minutes, or until fully cooked.
2. Cook the Celeriac Noodles: Sauté celeriac noodles in coconut oil for 5-7 minutes until tender but slightly firm.
3. Serve: Plate the celeriac noodles with turkey meatballs and sauerkraut on the side for a probiotic boost.

Tip: Celeriac noodles have a mild, slightly nutty flavor and a firm texture, making them a great low-carb alternative. You can add some organic or homemade marinara sauce for a saucier pasta.

Nutritional Information (per serving):

- Calories: 274
- Protein: 22g
- Fat: 15g
- Carbohydrates: 14g
- Fiber: 4g

CHICKEN LIVER AND APPLE SKILLET WITH CARAMELIZED ONIONS

Prep Time: 10 minutes
Cook Time: 20 minutes
Serves: 4

Ingredients: 1 lb, pasture-raised chicken livers, sliced thinly

- 2 organic apples, cored and thinly sliced
- 2 organic onions, thinly sliced
- 2 tbsp organic ghee
- 1 tsp organic ground cinnamon
- 1/2 tsp organic ground nutmeg
- Sea salt and freshly ground black pepper to taste

Instructions:

1. In a large skillet, heat 1 tbsp of ghee over medium heat and add the onions and cook, stirring occasionally, for about 10-15 minutes until caramelized.
2. Push the caramelized onions to the side of the skillet and add the remaining ghee.
3. Add the apples and cook for about 3-4 minutes until slightly tender.
4. Add the sliced livers, cinnamon, and nutmeg. Cook for about 4-5 minutes until the livers are browned and cooked through.
5. Stir the livers, apples, and onions together and season with salt and pepper.

Tip: For extra sweetness and a touch of acidity, add a splash of apple cider vinegar to the skillet just before serving.

Nutritional Information (per serving):

- Calories: 260
- Protein: 20g
- Fat: 14g
- Carbohydrates: 16g
- Fiber: 4g

CHICKEN LIVER PÂTÉ WITH FERMENTED VEGGIE GARNISH

Prep Time: 20 minutes
Cook Time: 25 minutes
Serves: 6 (as an appetizer)

Ingredients:

- 1 lb organic, pasture-raised chicken livers cleaned and trimmed
- 1 large organic onion, finely chopped
- 3 organic cloves, minced
- 2 tbsp organic ghee -1/4 cup organic coconut cream
- 1 tbsp organic fresh thyme leaves
- Sea salt and freshly ground black pepper to taste
- 1/4 cup organic sauerkraut or fermented carrots (for garnish)
- Organic vegetable crudités (such as cucumber slices, carrot sticks, and bell pepper strips) for serving

Instructions:

1. Cook the Livers:
   1. In a large skillet, heat 2 tbsp of ghee over medium heat.
   2. Sauté the chopped onion for about 5 minutes until softened.
   3. Add the garlic and chicken livers. Cook for about 8-10 minutes until the livers are browned and cooked through.
2. Blend the Pâté:
   1. Transfer the liver mixture to a food processor. Add the coconut cream, thyme leaves, salt, and pepper.
   2. Blend until smooth and creamy. Taste and adjust seasoning as needed.
3. Serve:
   1. Spoon the pâté into a serving dish and garnish with sauerkraut or fermented carrots.
   2. Serve with vegetable crudités.

Tip: For a smoother pâté pass the blended mixture through a fine-mesh sieve.

Nutritional Information (per serving):

- Calories: 180
- Protein: 12g
- Fat: 14g
- Carbohydrates: 4g
- Fiber: 1g

ALMOND FLOUR POTSTICKERS WITH CHICKEN & ZUCCHINI FILLING

Prep Time: 30 minutes
Cook Time: 20 minutes
Serves: 4 (makes about 16 potstickers)

Ingredients:

For the Almond Flour Dough:

- 1 1/2 cups almond flour
- 1 tbsp coconut flour
- 1 large organic egg
- 2 tbsp coconut oil, melted
- Pinch of sea salt

For the Filling:

- 8 oz organic ground chicken
- 1/2 cup organic zucchini, finely shredded and squeezed to remove excess moisture
- 1 tbsp coconut aminos
- 1 clove garlic, minced
- 1 tsp fresh ginger, grated
- 1 tbsp green onions, finely chopped
- 1 tbsp avocado oil (for cooking)

For Dipping Sauce:

- 2 tbsp coconut aminos
- 1 tbsp rice vinegar
- 1/2 tsp sesame oil (optional)
- Optional: Sesame seeds for garnish

Instructions:

1. Make the Almond Flour Dough: In a bowl, mix almond flour, coconut flour, egg, melted coconut oil, and a pinch of salt. Stir until a dough forms. Wrap in plastic and let rest in the refrigerator for 15 minutes.
2. Prepare the Filling: In a bowl, mix ground chicken, zucchini, garlic, ginger, green onions, and coconut aminos. Set aside.
3. Assemble the Potstickers: Roll out the dough between two sheets of parchment paper to about 1/8-inch thickness. Cut out circles (about 3 inches wide) using a cookie cutter or glass. Place a spoonful of the filling in the center of each circle and fold the dough over, pressing the edges together to seal.
4. Cook the Potstickers: Heat avocado oil in a skillet over medium heat. Place the potstickers in the pan and cook for

2-3 minutes on each side until golden. Add a splash of water to the pan, cover, and steam for 5-7 minutes until the filling is cooked through.
5. Make the Dipping Sauce: Whisk together coconut aminos, rice vinegar, and sesame oil. Garnish with sesame seeds if desired.

Tip: When making the almond flour dough, chilling it helps firm it up for easier rolling and shaping. Also, squeezing out the moisture from the zucchini ensures that the filling isn't too watery, making the potstickers crispier.

Nutritional Information (per serving):
- Calories: 417
- Protein: 19g
- Fat: 33g
- Carbohydrates: 10g
- Fiber: 4g

DAIKON RADISH NOODLES WITH CRISPY DUCK AND GINGER SAUCE

Prep Time: 15 minutes
Cook Time: 25 minutes
Serves: 4

Ingredients:
- 1 large organic daikon radish, spiralized
- 2 organic duck breasts, skin-on
- 2 tbsp organic coconut aminos
- 1 tbsp organic fresh ginger, minced
- 1 tbsp organic sesame oil
- 1 tbsp organic fresh scallions, chopped

Instructions:
1. Cook the Duck: Score the duck skin and season with salt. Heat a pan over medium heat and cook the duck skin-side down for 6-7 minutes until crispy. Flip and cook for another 4-5 minutes. Let rest before slicing.
2. Prepare the Sauce: In a small pan, heat sesame oil, ginger, and coconut aminos. Simmer for 3-4 minutes.
3. Cook the Daikon Noodles: Lightly sauté daikon radish noodles in the duck fat for 3-4 minutes until tender.
4. Serve: Plate the daikon noodles, top with sliced duck breast, and drizzle with the ginger sauce. Garnish with scallions.

Tip: Sautéing the daikon noodles in duck fat enhances their flavor and adds richness to the dish.

Nutritional Information (per serving):
- Calories: 410
- Protein: 27g
- Fat: 30g
- Carbohydrates: 8g
- Fiber: 2g

BEEF

BEEF BOURGUIGNON WITH MASHED CELERY ROOT AND LACTO-FERMENTED CARROTS

Prep Time: 30 minutes
Cook Time: 3 hours
Serves: 6

Ingredients:
- 3 lbs grass-fed beef chuck, cut into 2-inch cubes
- 8 oz organic bacon, diced
- 2 organic carrots, sliced
- 1 organic onion, diced
- 8 oz organic cremini mushrooms, quartered
- 3 organic garlic cloves, minced
- 2 cups organic red wine (Burgundy)
- 2 cups organic beef bone broth
- 1 bouquet garni (thyme, parsley, bay leaf)
- 2 large organic celery roots, peeled and cubed
- 1/4 cup organic ghee
- 1/4 cup organic coconut cream
- 1/2 cup lacto-fermented carrots
- Sea salt and freshly ground black pepper to taste

Instructions:
1. In a large Dutch oven, cook bacon until crispy. Remove and set aside.
2. Brown beef cubes in bacon fat. Remove and set aside.
3. Sauté onions, carrots, and mushrooms until softened.
4. Return beef and bacon to the pot. Add wine, broth, and bouquet garni.
5. Simmer covered for 2.5-3 hours until beef is tender.

6. Meanwhile, boil celery root until tender. Mash with ghee and coconut cream.
7. Serve beef bourguignon over mashed celery root with a side of lacto-fermented carrots.

Tip: For deeper flavor, marinate the beef in red wine overnight before cooking.

Nutritional Information (per serving):
- Calories: 665
- Protein: 45g
- Fat: 45g
- Carbohydrates: 15g
- Fiber: 4g

POWER CHILI

Prep Time: 20 minutes
Cook Time: 40 minutes
Serves: 4

Ingredients:
- 2 cups cooked organic navy beans
- 1 lb organic, grass-fed ground beef
- 1 organic red bell pepper, diced
- 1 organic green bell pepper, diced
- 1 organic onion, diced
- 3 organic garlic cloves, minced
- 2 organic carrots, chopped
- 2 cups organic diced tomatoes (no added sugar)
- 2 cups organic vegetable broth
- 1 tbsp organic chili powder
- 1 tsp organic cumin
- 1 tsp organic paprika

- 1/4 tsp organic cayenne pepper (optional)
- Sea salt and black pepper to taste
- 1/4 cup organic fresh cilantro, chopped

Instructions:
1. In a large pot, cook ground beef over medium heat until browned. Remove from the pot and set aside.
2. In the same pot, add diced onion, garlic, bell peppers, and carrots. Sauté until vegetables are soft.
3. Add chili powder, cumin, paprika, cayenne pepper, salt, and black pepper. Stir to combine.
4. Add cooked navy beans, diced tomatoes, vegetable broth, and browned beef. Bring to a boil.
5. Reduce heat and let it simmer uncovered for 30 minutes until the chili thickens.
6. Serve hot, garnished with fresh cilantro.

Tip: For deeper flavor, let the chili simmer on low heat for an additional hour, stirring occasionally.

Nutritional Information (per serving):
- Calories: 430
- Protein: 31g
- Fat: 17g
- Carbohydrates: 38g
- Fiber: 10g

BLACK BEAN AND GRASS-FED BEEF CHILI WITH FERMENTED JALAPEÑOS

Prep Time: 15 minutes
Cook Time: 1 hour
Serves: 6

Ingredients:
- 1 lb grass-fed ground beef
- 2 cups cooked organic black beans
- 1 organic onion, diced
- 3 organic garlic cloves, minced
- 2 organic bell peppers, diced
- 1 can (14 oz) organic diced tomatoes
- 2 tbsp organic tomato paste
- 2 cups organic beef bone broth
- 2 tbsp organic chili powder
- 1 tsp organic ground cumin
- 1 tsp organic oregano
- 2 tbsp organic ghee
- Sea salt and black pepper to taste
- 1/4 cup fermented jalapeños, chopped

Instructions:
1. In a large pot, heat ghee over medium heat. Brown the beef.
2. Add onion, garlic, and bell peppers. Sauté until softened.
3. Stir in tomatoes, tomato paste, broth, and spices. Simmer for 30 minutes.
4. Add black beans and simmer for another 20 minutes.
5. Serve topped with fermented jalapeños.

Tip: For deeper flavor, use a combination of ancho and chipotle chili powders.

Nutritional Information (per serving):
- Calories: 400
- Protein: 27g
- Fat: 22g
- Carbohydrates: 26g
- Fiber: 8g

KALBI-INSPIRED GRILLED SHORT RIBS WITH RADISH SALAD AND FERMENTED GARLIC

Prep Time: 30 minutes (plus 4 hours marinating)
Cook Time: 10 minutes
Serves: 4

Ingredients:
- 2 lbs grass-fed beef short ribs, cut flanken style
- 1/4 cup coconut aminos
- 2 tbsp organic sesame oil
- 1 organic Asian pear, grated
- 3 organic garlic cloves, minced
- 1 tbsp organic ginger, grated
- 1/4 tsp organic black pepper
- 2 cups organic radishes, thinly sliced
- 1 organic cucumber, thinly sliced
- 2 tbsp organic apple cider vinegar
- 1 tbsp organic avocado oil
- 1/4 cup organic green onions, chopped
- 2 tbsp organic sesame seeds
- 1/4 cup fermented garlic cloves, minced

Instructions:
1. Mix coconut aminos, sesame oil, pear, garlic, ginger, and pepper. Marinate ribs for 4 hours.
2. Grill ribs for 3-4 minutes per side.
3. Toss radishes and cucumber with vinegar, avocado oil, and sesame seeds.
4. Serve ribs with radish salad, topped with green onions and fermented garlic.

Tip: Let the grilled ribs rest for 5 minutes before cutting to retain juices.

Nutritional Information (per serving):
- Calories: 635
- Protein: 33g
- Fat: 50g
- Carbohydrates: 13g
- Fiber: 3g

BIBIMBAP-INSPIRED CAULIFLOWER RICE BOWL

Prep Time: 25 minutes
Cook Time: 20 minutes
Serves: 4

Ingredients:
- 1 large organic cauliflower, riced
- 1 lb grass-fed ground beef
- 2 organic carrots, julienned
- 1 organic zucchini, julienned
- 2 cups organic spinach
- 1 cup organic shiitake mushrooms, sliced
- 4 organic eggs
- 2 tbsp organic coconut oil
- 2 tbsp organic sesame oil
- 2 tbsp coconut aminos
- 1 tbsp organic apple cider vinegar
- 1 tbsp organic ginger, grated
- 2 organic garlic cloves, minced
- 1/4 cup organic green onions, chopped

Instructions:
1. Sauté cauliflower rice in coconut oil until tender. Set aside.
2. In the same pan, cook ground beef with half the garlic and ginger.
3. Separately sauté carrots, zucchini, spinach, and mushrooms in sesame oil.
4. Mix coconut aminos, apple cider vinegar, and remaining garlic and ginger for sauce.
5. Fry eggs sunny-side up.

6. Assemble bowls: cauliflower rice, beef, vegetables, egg, sauce, and green onions.

Tip: For extra texture, crisp the bottom layer of cauliflower rice in the pan before assembling.

Nutritional Information (per serving): Balanced protein and vegetables, rich in vitamins and minerals.

Nutritional Information (per serving):
- Calories: 445
- Protein: 25g
- Fat: 32g
- Carbohydrates: 18g
- Fiber: 6g

BULGOGI WITH CAULIFLOWER RICE AND KIMCHI

Prep Time: 30 minutes (plus 2 hours marinating)
Cook Time: 15 minutes
Serves: 4

Ingredients:
- 1 lb grass-fed sirloin, thinly sliced
- 1 organic Asian pear, grated
- 3 organic garlic cloves, minced
- 1 tbsp organic ginger, grated
- 3 tbsp coconut aminos
- 1 tbsp organic sesame oil
- 1/4 tsp organic black pepper
- 1 large organic cauliflower, riced
- 2 tbsp organic ghee
- 4 organic green onions, sliced
- 1 tbsp organic sesame seeds
- 1/2 cup organic kimchi
- Cauliflower rice for serving (see recipe)

Marinade Instructions:
1. Mix Asian pear, garlic, ginger, coconut aminos, sesame oil, and black pepper.
2. Marinate beef for 2 hours in the refrigerator.

Cooking Instructions:
1. Heat a large skillet over medium-high heat.
2. Cook marinated beef in batches until browned.
3. In another pan, sauté cauliflower rice in ghee until tender.
4. Serve bulgogi over cauliflower rice, garnished with green onions and sesame seeds.
5. Accompany with kimchi for probiotic benefits.

Tip: Freeze the beef for 30 minutes before slicing to achieve paper-thin slices easily.

Nutritional Information (per serving):
- Calories: 400
- Protein: 26g
- Fat: 27g
- Carbohydrates: 15g
- Fiber: 4g

BLACK BEAN AND GRASS-FED LAMB MEATBALLS WITH MINT COCONUT YOGURT SAUCE

Prep Time: 25 minutes
Cook Time: 20 minutes
Serves: 4

Ingredients:
- 1 lb grass-fed ground lamb
- 1 cup cooked organic black beans, mashed
- 1 organic egg
- 2 organic garlic cloves, minced
- 1 tsp organic ground cumin
- 1 tsp organic dried oregano
- 2 tbsp organic avocado oil
- 1 cup organic coconut yogurt
- 1/4 cup organic fresh mint, chopped
- 1 organic lemon, juiced

- Sea salt and black pepper to taste

Instructions:
1. In a large bowl, mix lamb, mashed beans, egg, garlic, cumin, oregano, salt, and pepper.
2. Form into small meatballs.
3. Heat avocado oil in a skillet over medium heat. Cook meatballs for 8-10 minutes, turning occasionally.
4. For the sauce, mix coconut yogurt, mint, and lemon juice. Season with salt.
5. Serve meatballs with mint yogurt sauce.

Tip: Chill the meatball mixture for 30 minutes before forming for easier handling.

Nutritional Information (per serving):
- Calories: 450
- Protein: 24g
- Fat: 33g
- Carbohydrates: 14g
- Fiber: 5g

LENTIL AND GRASS-FED BEEF MEATBALLS WITH TOMATO-BASIL SAUCE

Prep Time: 25 minutes
Cook Time: 30 minutes
Serves: 4

Ingredients:
- 1 lb grass-fed ground beef
- 1 cup cooked organic lentils, mashed
- 1 organic egg, beaten
- 2 organic garlic cloves, minced
- 1/4 cup organic fresh parsley, chopped
- 1/4 cup organic coconut flour
- 2 tbsp organic avocado oil
- 1 can (14 oz) organic crushed tomatoes
- 1/2 cup organic fresh basil, chopped
- Sea salt and black pepper to taste

Instructions:
1. Preheat oven to 375°F (190°C).
2. In a large bowl, mix ground beef, mashed lentils, egg, garlic, parsley, coconut flour, salt, and pepper.
3. Form the mixture into meatballs.
4. Heat avocado oil in an oven-safe skillet over medium heat. Brown meatballs on all sides, about 5 minutes.
5. Add crushed tomatoes and basil to the skillet. Bring to a simmer.
6. Transfer the skillet to the oven and bake for 20 minutes.
7. Serve meatballs with tomato-basil sauce.

Tip: For even browning, avoid overcrowding the skillet when searing the meatballs.

Nutritional Information (per serving):
- Calories: 460
- Protein: 30g
- Fat: 26g
- Carbohydrates: 23g
- Fiber: 8g

BROCCOLI AND BEEF STIR-FRY WITH SESAME GINGER SAUCE

Prep Time: 15 minutes
Cook Time: 15 minutes
Serves: 4

Ingredients:
- 1 lb grass-fed beef sirloin, thinly sliced
- 2 cups organic broccoli florets
- 1 organic red bell pepper, thinly sliced
- 1 organic carrot, julienned
- 2 organic garlic cloves, minced
- 1 tbsp organic ginger, grated
- 2 tbsp organic coconut aminos
- 2 tbsp organic sesame oil

- 1 tbsp organic avocado oil
- 1 tbsp organic sesame seeds
- Sea salt and black pepper to taste

Instructions:
1. Heat avocado oil in a large skillet over medium-high heat. Add beef and cook until browned, about 3-4 minutes. Remove and set aside.
2. In the same skillet, add sesame oil. Sauté garlic and ginger until fragrant.
3. Add broccoli, bell pepper, and carrot. Cook for 5-7 minutes until vegetables are tender.
4. Stir in coconut aminos, sesame seeds, salt, and pepper.
5. Return beef to the skillet and toss to combine. Cook for another 2 minutes.
6. Serve hot.

Tip: To keep the beef tender, do not overcook it. Sear quickly over high heat and remove before adding vegetables.

Nutritional Information (per serving):
- Calories: 350
- Protein: 28g
- Fat: 20g
- Carbohydrates: 16g
- Fiber: 4g

BEEF AND BROCCOLI RABE STUFFED ACORN SQUASH

Prep Time: 20 minutes
Cook Time: 45 minutes
Serves: 4

Ingredients:
- 2 organic acorn squash, halved and seeded
- 1 lb organic, grass-fed ground beef
- 1 bunch organic broccoli rabe, chopped
- 1 organic onion, diced
- 2 organic garlic cloves, minced
- 1 tbsp organic coconut aminos
- 1 tsp organic ground cumin
- 2 tbsp organic extra-virgin olive oil
- Sea salt and black pepper to taste
- 1/4 cup organic toasted pumpkin seeds

Instructions:
1. Preheat oven to 400°F (200°C).
2. Place the acorn squash halves cut-side down on a baking sheet. Roast for 25-30 minutes until tender.
3. In a skillet, heat avocado oil over medium heat. Add the ground beef and cook, breaking it up as it cooks, until browned.

4. Add the onion and garlic, sautéing until softened.
5. Stir in the chopped broccoli rabe, coconut aminos, cumin, salt, and pepper. Cook for 5-7 minutes until the greens are wilted.
6. Flip the roasted acorn squash halves over and scoop the beef and broccoli rabe mixture into the cavities.
7. Bake for an additional 15-20 minutes.
8. Serve the stuffed acorn squash warm, topped with toasted pumpkin seeds.

Nutritional Information (per serving):
- Calories: 400
- Protein: 30g
- Fat: 22g
- Carbohydrates: 24g
- Fiber: 8g

EGGPLANT LASAGNA WITH GRASS-FED GROUND BEEF

Prep Time: 15 minutes
Cook Time: 35 minutes
Serves: 4

Ingredients:
- 2 large organic eggplants, sliced lengthwise
- 1 lb grass-fed ground beef
- 1 cup organic tomato sauce (no added sugar)
- 1/2 cup organic full-fat Greek yogurt (for probiotics)
- 2 cloves organic garlic, minced
- 1 tbsp organic olive oil

Instructions:
1. Preheat the Oven: Preheat to 375°F (190°C).
2. Cook the Beef: Heat olive oil in a pan, add garlic, and sauté. Add beef and cook until browned. Stir in tomato sauce and simmer for 10 minutes.
3. Assemble the Lasagna: Layer the eggplant slices in a baking dish, top with the beef mixture, and repeat. Spread yogurt over the top.
4. Bake: Bake for 25 minutes until the eggplant is tender.

Tip: Coconut yogurt adds creaminess and probiotics without the need for dairy.

Nutritional Information (per serving):
- Calories: 365
- Protein: 27g
- Fat: 23g
- Carbohydrates: 14g
- Fiber: 5g

PORK

WALNUT-CRUSTED PORK CHOPS WITH ROASTED BRUSSELS SPROUTS AND APPLE CIDER REDUCTION

Prep Time: 20 minutes
Cook Time: 30 minutes
Serves: 4

Ingredients:
- 4 organic, pasture-raised pork chops (6 oz each)
- 1/2 cup organic walnuts, finely chopped
- 2 tbsp organic fresh thyme, chopped
- 2 tbsp organic extra-virgin olive oil
- 1 lb organic Brussels sprouts, halved
- 1 cup organic apple cider
- 1 tbsp organic apple cider vinegar
- Sea salt and black pepper to taste

Instructions:
1. Preheat oven to 400°F (200°C).

2. In a shallow bowl, mix together chopped walnuts and thyme.
3. Brush the pork chops with 1 tbsp oil and season with salt and pepper. Press the walnut-thyme mixture onto the top of each pork chop.
4. Toss the Brussels sprouts with the remaining 1 tbsp oil, salt, and pepper. Spread on a baking sheet.
5. Place the pork chops and Brussels sprouts in the oven and bake for 20-25 minutes, until the pork is cooked through and the Brussels sprouts are tender.
6. In a small saucepan, bring the apple cider to a simmer. Cook for 10-15 minutes, until reduced by half and thickened slightly. Stir in the apple cider vinegar.
7. Serve the walnut-crusted pork chops with the roasted Brussels sprouts and drizzle with the apple cider reduction.

Tip: For extra flavor, sear the pork chops in a hot skillet for 2-3 minutes per side before baking. Serve with leafy greens and fermented vegetables for extra fiber and probiotics.

Nutritional Information (per serving):
- Calories: 430

- Protein: 32g
- Fat: 26g
- Carbohydrates: 16g
- Fiber: 6g

ROASTED FENNEL AND PORK SAUSAGE WITH APPLE CIDER GLAZE

Prep Time: 15 minutes
Cook Time: 30 minutes
Serves: 4

Ingredients:
- 2 organic fennel bulbs, sliced lengthwise
- 1 lb organic Italian sausage, casings removed
- 1 organic apple, diced
- 1/4 cup organic apple cider
- 2 tbsp organic ghee
- 1 tbsp organic fresh thyme leaves
- Sea salt and black pepper to taste

Instructions:
1. Preheat oven to 400°F (200°C).
2. In a large bowl, toss fennel slices with 1 tbsp melted ghee, salt, and pepper. Spread on a baking sheet.
3. In a separate bowl, combine sausage meat, diced apple, and thyme. Form into small patties.
4. Arrange sausage patties on the baking sheet with the fennel.
5. Roast for 25-30 minutes, until sausage is cooked through and fennel is tender.
6. While roasting, simmer apple cider in a saucepan until reduced by half and slightly thickened. Stir in remaining 1 tbsp ghee.
7. Drizzle the apple cider glaze over the roasted fennel and sausage before serving.

Tip: For a richer flavor, use bone-in pork sausage and remove the casings before cooking.

Nutritional Information (per serving):
- Calories: 410
- Protein: 26g
- Fat: 28g
- Carbohydrates: 16g
- Fiber: 5g

FENNEL AND SAUSAGE STUFFED PORK TENDERLOIN

Prep Time: 20 minutes
Cook Time: 30 minutes
Serves: 4

Ingredients:
- 1 lb organic, pasture-raised pork tenderloin
- 1 organic fennel bulb, finely diced
- 1/2 lb organic Italian sausage, casings removed
- 1/4 cup organic onion, finely chopped
- 2 organic garlic cloves, minced
- 1 tbsp organic fresh sage, chopped
- 2 tbsp organic ghee
- Sea salt and black pepper to taste

Instructions:
1. Preheat oven to 375°F (190°C).
2. Butterfly the pork tenderloin by cutting lengthwise almost all the way through, then opening it like a book.
3. In a skillet, melt 1 tbsp ghee over medium heat. Sauté onion and garlic until softened.
4. Add sausage meat and cook until browned, breaking it apart as it cooks. Stir in diced fennel and sage. Season with salt and pepper.
5. Spread the sausage mixture evenly over the opened pork tenderloin. Roll it up tightly and tie with kitchen twine.
6. Heat the remaining ghee in a skillet. Sear the pork tenderloin on all sides until browned.

7. Transfer the skillet to the oven and roast for 25-30 minutes, until the internal temperature of the pork reaches 145°F (63°C).
8. Let rest for 10 minutes before slicing and serving.

Tip: For a crispier crust, sear the pork tenderloin in a cast iron skillet before roasting. Serve with a fresh carrot salad and sauerkraut.

Nutritional Information (per serving):
- Calories: 450
- Protein: 42g
- Fat: 28g
- Carbohydrates: 8g
- Fiber: 2g

PECAN AND APPLE STUFFED PORK TENDERLOIN WITH SAUERKRAUT

Prep Time: 20 minutes
Cook Time: 40 minutes
Serves: 4

Ingredients:
- 1 lb organic, pasture-raised pork tenderloin
- 1 organic apple, finely chopped
- 1/2 cup organic pecans, finely chopped
- 2 organic garlic cloves, minced
- 1 tbsp organic fresh thyme leaves
- 2 tbsp organic ghee
- Sea salt and black pepper to taste
- 1/2 cup organic sauerkraut

Instructions:
1. Preheat oven to 375°F (190°C).
2. In a skillet, melt ghee over medium heat. Sauté apple, pecans, garlic, and thyme until the apple is tender. Season with salt and pepper.
3. Butterfly the pork tenderloin by slicing it lengthwise, being careful not to cut all the way through. Open it like a book.
4. Spread the apple-pecan mixture evenly over the pork. Roll up the pork and secure with kitchen twine.
5. Season the outside of the pork with salt and pepper.
6. Place the stuffed pork tenderloin in a baking dish and roast for 35-40 minutes, until the pork is cooked through.
7. Let rest for 5 minutes before slicing.
8. Serve the stuffed pork tenderloin with a side of sauerkraut.

Tip: For added flavor, brine the pork tenderloin in a mixture of water, salt, and apple cider vinegar for 2 hours before stuffing and roasting.

Nutritional Information (per serving):
- Calories: 420
- Protein: 32g
- Fat: 28g
- Carbohydrates: 10g
- Fiber: 4g

SHEET PAN PORK TENDERLOIN WITH GRAPES, WALNUTS, AND BLUE CHEESE

Prep Time: 15 minutes
Cook Time: 25 minutes
Serves: 4

Ingredients:
- 1.5 lbs organic, pasture-raised pork tenderloin
- 1 cup organic red grapes, halved
- 1 cup organic green grapes, halved
- 1/2 cup organic walnuts, roughly chopped
- 2 tbsp organic extra-virgin olive oil, divided
- 2 tbsp organic fresh rosemary, chopped
- 3 organic garlic cloves, minced
- Sea salt and freshly ground black pepper to taste
- 1/4 cup organic blue cheese, crumbled (or dairy-free blue cheese alternative)

- 1 tbsp organic balsamic vinegar (optional, for drizzling)

Instructions:
1. Preheat your oven to 400°F (200°C). Line a baking sheet with parchment paper.
2. Rub the pork tenderloin with 1 tbsp of olive oil, minced garlic, chopped rosemary, salt, and pepper and place the pork tenderloin in the center of the prepared baking sheet.
3. In a bowl, toss the halved grapes and chopped walnuts with the remaining 1 tbsp of olive oil, salt, and pepper.
4. Arrange the grape and walnut mixture around the pork tenderloin on the baking sheet.
5. Roast in the preheated oven for 20-25 minutes, or until the pork tenderloin reaches an internal temperature of 145°F (63°C) and the grapes are slightly caramelized. Stir the grapes and walnuts halfway through cooking.
6. Remove the pork tenderloin from the oven and let it rest for 5 minutes before slicing.
7. Slice the pork tenderloin into medallions and arrange them on a serving platter.
8. Top with the roasted grapes and walnuts and sprinkle crumbled blue cheese over the top. Drizzle with balsamic vinegar if desired.

Tip: To add an extra layer of flavor, marinate the pork tenderloin in a mixture of olive oil, garlic, rosemary, and a splash of balsamic vinegar for 30 minutes before cooking.

Nutritional Information (per serving):
- Calories: 420
- Protein: 30g
- Fat: 28g
- Carbohydrates: 12g
- Fiber: 2g

LEMON-ROSEMARY PORK CHOPS WITH ROASTED ASPARAGUS AND PICKLED ONIONS

Prep Time: 10 minutes
Cook Time: 20 minutes
Serves: 4

Ingredients:
- 4 organic bone-in pork chops
- 2 tbsp organic fresh rosemary, chopped
- 1 tbsp organic lemon zest
- 2 tbsp organic avocado oil
- 1 lb organic asparagus, trimmed
- 1/2 cup organic pickled onions

Instructions:
1. Preheat the Oven: Preheat the oven to 425°F (220°C).
2. Season the Pork Chops: Rub the pork chops with rosemary, lemon zest, and avocado oil. Let it sit for 10 minutes.
3. Prepare the Asparagus: Toss the asparagus with avocado oil, salt, and pepper, then spread it on a sheet pan.
4. Roast: Place the pork chops on the sheet pan with the asparagus. Roast for 15-20 minutes, until the pork is golden and the asparagus is tender.
5. Serve with Pickled Onions: Plate the pork chops and asparagus with a side of pickled onions for a tangy, probiotic-rich addition.

Tip: The bright lemon and rosemary flavor pairs beautifully with the rich pork, while the pickled onions add an extra layer of flavor.

Nutritional Information (per serving):
- Calories: 410
- Protein: 31g
- Fat: 28g
- Carbohydrates: 8g
- Fiber: 3g

LAMB

NAVY BEAN AND LAMB STEW WITH SPINACH AND HERBS

Prep Time: 20 minutes
Cook Time: 1 hour 30 minutes
Serves: 4

Ingredients:
- 1 lb grass-fed lamb stew meat, cubed
- 2 cups cooked organic navy beans
- 1 organic onion, diced
- 3 organic garlic cloves, minced
- 3 organic carrots, chopped
- 2 organic celery stalks, chopped
- 4 cups organic lamb or beef bone broth
- 1 tbsp organic ghee
- 1 tsp organic dried thyme
- 1 tsp organic dried rosemary
- 1 bay leaf
- Sea salt and black pepper to taste
- 2 cups organic spinach, chopped
- 1/4 cup organic fresh cilantro, chopped

Instructions:
1. In a large pot, heat ghee over medium heat. Sauté onion, garlic, carrots, and celery until softened, about 5 minutes.
2. Add lamb and cook until browned on all sides.
3. Stir in navy beans, broth, thyme, rosemary, bay leaf, salt, and pepper. Bring to a boil, then reduce heat and simmer for 1 hour 30 minutes.
4. Add spinach in the last 10 minutes of cooking and stir until wilted.
5. Remove bay leaf and garnish with fresh cilantro before serving.

Tip: For more tender lamb, cook the stew on low heat for an additional 30 minutes.

Nutritional Information (per serving):
- Calories: 460
- Protein: 35g
- Fat: 22g
- Carbohydrates: 29g
- Fiber: 8g

BRUSSELS SPROUTS AND GROUND LAMB MEATBALLS WITH TZATZIKI SAUCE

Prep Time: 20 minutes
Cook Time: 25 minutes
Serves: 4

Ingredients:
- 1 lb organic, grass-fed ground lamb
- 1 cup organic Brussels sprouts, finely chopped
- 1 organic onion, finely chopped
- 2 organic garlic cloves, minced
- 1 organic egg, beaten
- 1/4 cup organic coconut flour
- 1 tsp organic ground cumin
- 1 tsp organic dried oregano
- 2 tbsp organic extra-virgin olive oil
- Sea salt and black pepper to taste

For the Tzatziki Sauce:
- 1 cup organic full-fat grass-fed yogurt
- 1/2 organic cucumber, grated and squeezed dry
- 1 organic garlic clove, minced
- 1 tbsp organic fresh dill, chopped

- 1 tbsp organic lemon juice
- Sea salt and black pepper to taste

Instructions:

1. Preheat oven to 375°F (190°C).
2. In a large bowl, mix ground lamb, Brussels sprouts, onion, garlic, egg, coconut flour, cumin, oregano, salt, and pepper.
3. Form the mixture into meatballs.
4. Heat oil in an oven-safe skillet over medium heat. Brown meatballs on all sides, about 5 minutes.
5. Transfer the skillet to the oven and bake for 20 minutes.
6. For the sauce, mix yogurt with cucumber, garlic, dill, lemon juice, salt, and pepper.
7. Serve meatballs with tzatziki sauce.

Tip: For even browning, avoid overcrowding the skillet when searing the meatballs.

Nutritional Information (per serving):

- Calories: 460
- Protein: 28g
- Fat: 36g
- Carbohydrates: 11g
- Fiber: 4g

ZUCCHINI BOATS WITH SPICED LAMB AND ANCHOVY GREMOLATA

Prep Time: 20 minutes
Cook Time: 30 minutes
Serves: 4

Ingredients:

- 4 medium organic zucchini, halved lengthwise
- 1 lb organic, grass-fed ground lamb
- 1 organic onion, diced
- 2 organic garlic cloves, minced
- 1 tsp organic ground cumin
- 1 tsp organic paprika
- 1/4 cup organic fresh parsley, chopped

For the Gremolata:

- 1/4 cup organic fresh parsley, finely chopped
- 2 organic garlic cloves, minced
- 4 anchovy fillets, minced
- 1 tbsp organic lemon zest

Instructions:

1. Preheat oven to 375°F (190°C).
2. Scoop out the flesh from the zucchini halves, leaving about 1/4 inch of flesh attached to the skin. Chop the scooped zucchini flesh and set aside.
3. In a skillet, brown ground lamb with onion and garlic over medium heat. Drain excess fat.
4. Add cumin, paprika, chopped zucchini flesh, and parsley to the skillet. Cook for 5-7 minutes until zucchini is tender.
5. For the gremolata, combine parsley, garlic, anchovies, and lemon zest in a small bowl.
6. Fill zucchini boats with the lamb mixture and bake for 20-25 minutes until zucchini is tender.
7. Top with gremolata and serve hot.

Tip: For a more intense flavor, toast the cumin and paprika in a dry skillet for a minute before adding them to the lamb mixture.

Nutritional Information (per serving):

- Calories: 360
- Protein: 25g
- Fat: 24g
- Carbohydrates: 12g
- Fiber: 4g

WALNUT AND HERB-CRUSTED LAMB CHOPS

Prep Time: 20 minutes
Cook Time: 15 minutes
Serves: 4

Ingredients:

- 8 organic, grass-fed lamb chops
- 1 cup organic walnuts, finely chopped
- 1/4 cup organic fresh rosemary, chopped
- 1/4 cup organic fresh thyme, chopped
- 2 organic garlic cloves, minced
- 2 tbsp organic Dijon mustard
- 2 tbsp organic avocado oil
- Sea salt and black pepper to taste

Instructions:

1. Preheat oven to 400°F (200°C).
2. In a bowl, combine chopped walnuts, rosemary, thyme, garlic, salt, and pepper.
3. Brush lamb chops with Dijon mustard and press the walnut-herb mixture onto both sides to coat.
4. Heat avocado oil in an oven-safe skillet over medium-high heat. Sear lamb chops for 2-3 minutes per side until golden brown.
5. Transfer the skillet to the oven and bake for 8-10 minutes, until the lamb chops reach your desired doneness.
6. Let rest for 5 minutes before serving.

Tip: For a more intense flavor, toast the walnuts in a dry skillet for 2-3 minutes before chopping and using in the crust. Serve with a high-fiber side and sauerkraut for a probiotic add-on.

Nutritional Information (per serving):

- Calories: 480
- Protein: 28g
- Fat: 38g
- Carbohydrates: 6g
- Fiber: 2g

DUKKAH-SPICED LAMB CHOPS WITH CREAMY CAULIFLOWER MASH

Prep Time: 15 minutes (plus 30 minutes marinating)
Cook Time: 20 minutes
Serves: 4

Ingredients:

- 4 organic, grass-fed lamb chops
- 2 tbsp organic dukkah
- 1 tbsp organic avocado oil
- 1 large organic cauliflower, cut into florets
- 1/2 cup organic coconut cream
- 2 tbsp organic ghee
- Sea salt and black pepper to taste

Instructions:

1. Rub lamb chops with dukkah and let marinate for 30 minutes at room temperature.
2. Preheat oven to 400°F (200°C).
3. Steam cauliflower florets until tender.
4. Mash cooked cauliflower with coconut cream and ghee. Season with salt and pepper.
5. Heat avocado oil in an oven-safe skillet over medium-high heat. Sear lamb chops for 2-3 minutes per side.
6. Transfer skillet to the oven and roast for 10-12 minutes for medium-rare.
7. Serve lamb chops with creamy cauliflower mash.

Tip: For a richer flavor, deglaze the skillet with a splash of red wine after searing the lamb chops.

Nutritional Information (per serving):

- Calories: 480
- Protein: 38g
- Fat: 32g
- Carbohydrates: 12g
- Fiber: 4g

EGGPLANT AND LAMB KOFTA SKEWERS WITH CREAMY TAHINI SAUCE

Prep Time: 25 minutes
Cook Time: 15 minutes
Serves: 4

Ingredients:

- 1 lb organic, grass-fed ground lamb
- 1 medium organic eggplant, diced
- 1 organic onion, finely chopped
- 2 organic garlic cloves, minced
- 1/4 cup organic fresh parsley, chopped
- 1 tsp organic ground cumin
- 1 tsp organic ground coriander
- 1/2 tsp organic smoked paprika
- Sea salt and black pepper to taste
- 2 tbsp organic avocado oil
- 1 organic lemon, cut into wedges

For the Tahini Sauce:

- 1/2 cup organic tahini
- 1/4 cup organic water
- 2 tbsp organic lemon juice
- 1 organic garlic clove, minced
- Sea salt and black pepper to taste

Instructions:

1. Preheat grill to medium-high heat.
2. In a large bowl, combine ground lamb, diced eggplant, onion, garlic, parsley, cumin, coriander, paprika, salt, and pepper. Mix well.
3. Form the mixture into small kofta (meatballs) and thread them onto skewers.
4. Brush the kofta skewers with avocado oil.
5. Grill for 10-15 minutes, turning occasionally, until cooked through.
6. While the kofta are grilling, prepare the tahini sauce by whisking together tahini, water, lemon juice, garlic, salt, and pepper in a bowl until smooth.
7. Serve the grilled kofta skewers with the creamy tahini sauce and lemon wedges on the side.

Tip: Salting the diced eggplant and letting it sit for 15 minutes before adding it to the kofta mixture helps draw out excess moisture and prevents the kofta from becoming soggy. Serve with a high fiber side or salad and remember to add ½ cup of your favorite fermented vegetable.

Nutritional Information (per serving):

- Calories: 400
- Protein: 28g
- Fat: 28g
- Carbohydrates: 12g
- Fiber: 5g

OTHER MEAT RECIPES

ELK BURGERS WITH CARAMELIZED ONIONS AND AVOCADO

Prep Time: 20 minutes
Cook Time: 20 minutes
Serves: 4

Ingredients:

- 1 lb organic, grass-fed elk ground meat
- 1 organic avocado, sliced
- 1 organic onion, thinly sliced
- 2 tbsp organic ghee
- 1 tbsp organic apple cider vinegar
- 1 tsp organic dried thyme
- Sea salt and black pepper to taste
- 4 large organic lettuce leaves (for buns)

Instructions:

1. In a large skillet, melt 1 tbsp ghee over medium heat. Add the sliced onions and cook for 15-20 minutes, stirring occasionally, until caramelized and softened.
2. Deglaze the pan with apple cider vinegar and continue cooking for 2-3 minutes until the onions are deeply browned and jammy. Remove from heat and set aside.
3. In a bowl, mix the elk ground meat with dried thyme, salt, and pepper until well combined.
4. Form the mixture into four equal-sized patties.
5. In the same skillet, heat the remaining 1 tbsp ghee over medium-high heat.
6. Cook the elk burgers for 4-5 minutes per side, or until cooked to your desired doneness.
7. Serve the elk burgers on lettuce leaves, topped with the caramelized onions and sliced avocado.

Tip: For a juicier burger, handle the meat as little as possible when forming the patties. Serve with sauerkrauts and a high-fiber salad for a complete meal.

Nutritional Information (per serving):

- Calories: 380
- Protein: 30g
- Fat: 28g
- Carbohydrates: 8g
- Fiber: 4g

ELK TENDERLOIN WITH ROASTED BEETS AND HORSERADISH CREAM

Prep Time: 20 minutes
Cook Time: 25 minutes
Serves: 4

Ingredients:

- 1 lb organic, grass-fed elk tenderloin
- 3 organic beets, peeled and cut into wedges
- 2 tbsp organic organic extra-virgin olive oil
- 1 cup organic full-fat grass-fed Greek yogurt
- 2 tbsp organic prepared horseradish
- 1 tbsp organic lemon juice
- Sea salt and black pepper to taste
- 2 tbsp organic fresh parsley, chopped

Instructions:

1. Preheat oven to 400°F (200°C).
2. Toss the beet wedges with 1 tbsp oil, salt, and pepper. Spread on a baking sheet and roast for 20-25 minutes, until tender.
3. In a small bowl, mix the yogurt, horseradish, and lemon juice. Season with salt and pepper.
4. Heat the remaining 1 tbsp oil in a large skillet over medium-high heat.
5. Season the elk tenderloin with salt and pepper. Sear the tenderloin in the hot skillet for 3-4 minutes per side, until a nice crust forms.
6. Transfer the skillet to the oven and roast the tenderloin for an additional 10-12 minutes, or until it reaches your desired doneness.
7. Let the elk tenderloin rest for 5 minutes, then slice it into medallions.
8. Serve the elk tenderloin slices with the roasted beets and a dollop of the horseradish cream. Garnish with fresh parsley.

Tip: Use a meat thermometer to ensure the elk tenderloin is cooked to your preferred doneness, usually around 130°F (55°C) for medium-rare.

Nutritional Information (per serving):

- Calories: 380
- Protein: 36g
- Fat: 22g
- Carbohydrates: 12g
- Fiber: 4g

ELK MEATLOAF WITH CAULIFLOWER MASH AND SAUERKRAUT

Prep Time: 20 minutes
Cook Time: 1 hour
Serves: 4

Ingredients:

- 1 lb organic, grass-fed elk ground meat
- 1 organic egg, beaten
- 1/2 cup organic almond flour
- 1 organic onion, finely chopped
- 2 organic garlic cloves, minced
- 1 tbsp organic fresh thyme, chopped
- 1 tbsp organic Dijon mustard (without added sugar)
- Sea salt and black pepper to taste
- 1 large organic cauliflower, cut into florets
- 2 tbsp organic ghee
- 1/2 cup organic coconut milk
- Sea salt and black pepper to taste
- 1 cup organic sauerkraut

Instructions:

1. Preheat oven to 375°F (190°C).
2. In a large bowl, mix together elk ground meat, egg, almond flour, onion, garlic, thyme, Dijon mustard, salt, and pepper until well combined.
3. Shape the mixture into a loaf and place in a baking dish.
4. Bake for 45-50 minutes, or until the internal temperature reaches 160°F (70°C).
5. While the meatloaf is baking, steam the cauliflower florets until tender, about 10-12 minutes.
6. In a blender or food processor, blend the steamed cauliflower with ghee and coconut milk until smooth. Season with salt and pepper.
7. Serve slices of elk meatloaf with cauliflower mash and a side of sauerkraut.

Tip: For a deeper flavor, sauté the onion and garlic in a bit of ghee before adding them to the meatloaf mixture.

Nutritional Information (per serving):

- Calories: 450
- Protein: 30g
- Fat: 28g
- Carbohydrates: 18g
- Fiber: 6g

BISON AND SWEET POTATO SHEPHERD'S PIE

Prep Time: 20 minutes
Cook Time: 40 minutes
Serves: 4

Ingredients:

- 1 lb organic, grass-fed ground bison
- 2 medium organic sweet potatoes, peeled and cubed
- 1 cup organic carrots, diced
- 1 cup organic peas
- 1 organic onion, diced
- 2 organic garlic cloves, minced
- 1 cup organic beef bone broth
- 2 tbsp organic tomato paste
- 2 tbsp organic coconut oil
- 1 tsp organic dried thyme
- Sea salt and black pepper to taste
- 1/4 cup organic coconut milk

Instructions:

1. Preheat oven to 375°F (190°C).
2. In a large pot, cook sweet potatoes in boiling water until tender, about 15 minutes. Drain and mash with coconut milk, salt, and pepper.
3. In a large skillet, heat 1 tbsp coconut oil over medium heat. Add onion and garlic, and sauté until softened.
4. Add ground bison and cook until browned. Stir in carrots and peas, cooking for another 5 minutes.
5. Mix in bone broth, tomato paste, thyme, salt, and pepper. Simmer for 10 minutes until the mixture thickens.
6. Transfer the bison mixture to a baking dish and spread mashed sweet potatoes over the top.
7. Bake for 25 minutes, until the top is slightly golden.
8. Let rest for 5 minutes before serving.

Tip: For extra flavor, use roasted garlic in the mashed sweet potatoes.

Nutritional Information (per serving):

- Calories: 420
- Protein: 36g
- Fat: 20g
- Carbohydrates: 25g
- Fiber: 5g

BISON CHILI WITH SPAGHETTI SQUASH

Prep Time: 20 minutes
Cook Time: 40 minutes
Serves: 4

Ingredients:

- 1 lb organic, grass-fed ground bison
- 1 medium organic spaghetti squash
- 1 organic onion, diced
- 2 organic garlic cloves, minced
- 1 organic red bell pepper, diced
- 1 can (14 oz) organic diced tomatoes
- 1 cup organic beef broth
- 2 tbsp organic chili powder
- 1 tsp organic cumin
- 1 tsp organic smoked paprika
- 2 tbsp organic extra-virgin olive oil
- Sea salt and black pepper to taste
- 1/4 cup organic fresh cilantro, chopped

Instructions:

1. Preheat oven to 400°F (200°C).
2. Cut the spaghetti squash in half lengthwise and remove seeds. Brush with olive oil, season with salt and pepper, and place cut-side down on a baking sheet. Roast for 30-40 minutes, until tender.
3. In a large pot, heat 1 tbsp oil over medium heat. Sauté onion and garlic until softened.
4. Add ground bison and cook until browned.
5. Stir in bell pepper, diced tomatoes, beef broth, chili powder, cumin, smoked paprika, salt, and pepper. Simmer for 20 minutes.
6. Use a fork to scrape out the spaghetti squash strands and divide them among serving bowls.
7. Serve the bison chili over the spaghetti squash, garnished with fresh cilantro.

Tip: For deeper flavor, let the chili simmer for an extra 15-20 minutes. Serve with a high-fiber side and fermented jalapenos for a spicy probiotic kick.

Nutritional Information (per serving):

- Calories: 380
- Protein: 30g
- Fat: 22g
- Carbohydrates: 18g
- Fiber: 6g

BISON SHORT RIB RAGU WITH CREAMY CAULIFLOWER MASH

Prep Time: 20 minutes
Cook Time: 2 hours 30 minutes
Serves: 4

Ingredients:

- 2 lbs organic, grass-fed bison short ribs
- 1 organic onion, diced
- 2 organic carrots, diced
- 2 organic celery stalks, diced
- 3 organic garlic cloves, minced
- 1 can (28 oz) organic crushed tomatoes
- 1 cup organic beef bone broth
- 2 tbsp organic tomato paste
- 1 tbsp organic dried oregano
- 1 tbsp organic dried thyme
- 2 tbsp organic extra-virgin olive oil
- Sea salt and black pepper to taste

For the Cauliflower Mash:

- 1 large organic cauliflower, cut into florets
- 1/2 cup organic coconut cream
- 2 tbsp organic ghee
- Sea salt and black pepper to taste

Instructions:

1. Preheat oven to 325°F (160°C).
2. Season bison short ribs with salt and pepper.
3. Heat olive oil in a Dutch oven over medium-high heat. Sear short ribs on all sides until browned. Remove and set aside. Alternatively you can use a slow cooker.
4. Add onion, carrots, celery, and garlic to the pot. Sauté until softened.
5. Stir in crushed tomatoes, bone broth, tomato paste, oregano, and thyme. Bring to a simmer.
6. Return short ribs to the pot, cover, and transfer to the oven. Braise for 2-2.5 hours, until the meat is fork-tender.
7. While the ragu braises, steam cauliflower florets until tender.
8. Mash cooked cauliflower with coconut cream and ghee. Season with salt and pepper.
9. Remove short ribs from the pot and shred the meat.
10. Serve the bison ragu over creamy cauliflower mash.

Tip: For a richer ragu, deglaze the Dutch oven with a splash of red wine after browning the short ribs.

Nutritional Information (per serving):

- Calories: 520
- Protein: 42g
- Fat: 34g
- Carbohydrates: 20g
- Fiber: 6g

SLOW-COOKED VENISON STEW WITH ROOT VEGETABLES

Prep Time: 20 minutes
Cook Time: 3 hours
Serves: 4

Ingredients:

- 1.5 lbs wild venison, cubed
- 2 tbsp ghee
- 2 medium carrots, chopped
- 2 medium parsnips, chopped
- 1 large sweet potato, diced
- 1 medium onion, chopped
- 2 cloves garlic, minced
- 2 cups organic beef broth
- 1 tsp fresh thyme
- 1 bay leaf
- Sea salt and black pepper to taste

Instructions:

1. Brown the Venison: Heat ghee in a large pot. Brown the venison on all sides, about 8 minutes.
2. Sauté the Vegetables: Add carrots, parsnips, sweet potato, onion, and garlic to the pot. Sauté for 5-7 minutes.
3. Simmer the Stew: Add beef broth, thyme, and bay leaf. Simmer on low heat for 3 hours, until the venison is tender.
4. Season & Serve: Discard the bay leaf. Season with salt and pepper before serving.

Tip: Venison is naturally lean, so slow-cooking it with ghee and root vegetables ensures it stays tender and flavorful.

Nutritional Information (per serving):

- Calories: 435
- Protein: 39g
- Fat: 17g
- Carbohydrates: 30g
- Fiber: 6g

CAULIFLOWER GNOCCHI WITH SAGE BROWN BUTTER AND CRISPY PANCETTA

Prep Time: 20 minutes
Cook Time: 15 minutes
Serves: 4

Ingredients:

- 1 medium organic cauliflower, steamed and mashed
- 1 cup organic almond flour
- 1 organic pasture-raised egg yolk
- 1 tbsp organic ghee
- 2 tbsp organic fresh sage, chopped
- 4 slices organic pancetta, chopped

Instructions:

1. Make the Gnocchi: In a bowl, mix mashed cauliflower, almond flour, egg yolk, salt, and pepper until a dough forms. Roll into small gnocchi shapes.
2. Cook the Gnocchi: Boil water in a large pot and cook the gnocchi until they float, about 2-3 minutes.
3. Brown the Butter: In a pan, melt ghee and add sage. Cook until the butter turns golden brown. Add the pancetta and cook until crispy.
4. Serve: Toss the gnocchi in the sage brown butter and crispy pancetta mixture.

Tip: Browning the butter adds a nutty, rich flavor to the dish, while the crispy pancetta provides a salty crunch.

Nutritional Information (per serving):

- Calories: 320
- Protein: 11g
- Fat: 26g
- Carbohydrates: 10g
- Fiber: 3g

EGGPLANT CRUST PIZZA WITH GOAT CHEESE AND PROSCIUTTO

Prep Time: 15 minutes
Cook Time: 30 minutes
Serves: 4

Ingredients:

- For the crust:
  - 2 medium organic eggplants, peeled and sliced into thin rounds
  - 2 tbsp organic olive oil
  - Sea salt and black pepper to taste
- For the toppings:
  - 4 oz organic goat cheese
  - 2 oz organic prosciutto
  - 1 cup organic cherry tomatoes, halved
  - 1/2 cup organic arugula
  - 1 tbsp organic balsamic vinegar (optional, no added sugar)

Instructions:

1. Preheat your oven to 400°F (200°C). Arrange the sliced eggplant on a parchment-lined baking sheet. Drizzle with olive oil and season with salt and pepper. Roast for 20-25 minutes, flipping halfway through, until the slices are golden and slightly crisp. Roasting the eggplant in thin slices ensures it becomes crispy enough to serve as a stable pizza base.
2. Remove the roasted eggplant slices from the oven. Spread a layer of goat cheese over each slice. Top with halved cherry tomatoes and torn pieces of prosciutto.
3. Place the eggplant pizzas back in the oven and bake for an additional 5-7 minutes until the goat cheese is slightly melted and bubbly.
4. Remove from the oven and top each eggplant pizza with fresh arugula and a drizzle of balsamic vinegar, if using. Serve immediately.

Tip: The creamy goat cheese complements the smoky prosciutto, while the fresh arugula adds a peppery finish that balances the richness of the toppings.

Nutritional Information (per serving):

- Calories: 250
- Protein: 9g
- Fat: 20g
- Carbohydrates: 10g
- Fiber: 4g

FISH AND SEAFOOD RECIPES

SALMON

GRILLED SALMON WITH RASPBERRY-BLACKBERRY SALSA

Prep Time: 15 minutes
Cook Time: 10 minutes
Serves: 4

Ingredients:

- 4 wild-caught salmon fillets (6 oz each)
- 1 cup organic raspberries
- 1 cup organic blackberries
- 1/2 organic red onion, finely chopped
- 1/4 cup organic fresh cilantro, chopped
- 1 organic lime, juiced
- 2 tbsp organic extra-virgin olive oil
- Sea salt and black pepper to taste

Instructions:

1. Preheat grill to medium-high heat.
2. Season salmon fillets with salt and pepper. Grill for 4-5 minutes per side, or until fully cooked.
3. In a bowl, combine raspberries, blackberries, red onion, cilantro, lime juice, and olive oil. Gently mix to combine.
4. Serve grilled salmon topped with the berry salsa.

Tip: For a more intense flavor, let the salsa sit for 15 minutes before serving to allow the flavors to meld.

Nutritional Information (per serving):

- Calories: 420
- Protein: 34g
- Fat: 28g
- Carbohydrates: 14g
- Fiber: 6g

WALNUT-CRUSTED SALMON WITH ROASTED BEETS AND HORSERADISH CREAM

Prep Time: 20 minutes
Cook Time: 30 minutes
Serves: 4

Ingredients:

- 4 wild-caught salmon fillets (6 oz each)
- 1/2 cup organic walnuts, finely chopped
- 2 tbsp organic parsley, finely chopped

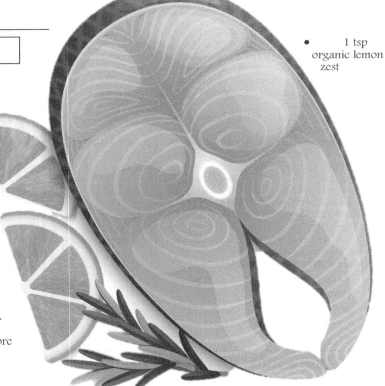

- 1 tsp organic lemon zest
- 2 tbsp organic avocado oil
- 3 organic beets, peeled and cut into wedges
- 1/2 cup organic coconut yogurt
- 1 tbsp organic prepared horseradish
- 1 tbsp organic lemon juice
- Sea salt and black pepper to taste

Instructions:

1. Preheat oven to 400°F (200°C).
2. In a shallow bowl, mix together chopped walnuts, parsley, and lemon zest.
3. Brush salmon fillets with 1 tbsp avocado oil and season with salt and pepper. Press the walnut mixture onto the top of each fillet.
4. Toss beet wedges with remaining 1 tbsp avocado oil, salt, and pepper. Spread on a baking sheet.

5. Roast the salmon and beets for 20-25 minutes, until the salmon is cooked through and the beets are tender.
6. In a small bowl, mix together coconut yogurt, horseradish, and lemon juice. Season with salt and pepper.
7. Serve the walnut-crusted salmon with the roasted beets and a dollop of horseradish cream.

Tip: For a more intense walnut flavor, toast the chopped walnuts in a dry skillet for 2-3 minutes before mixing with the parsley and lemon zest.

Nutritional Information (per serving):
- Calories: 420
- Protein: 34g
- Fat: 26g
- Carbohydrates: 12g
- Fiber: 4g

CHIA-CRUSTED WILD SALMON WITH ROASTED FENNEL AND LEMON-CAPER YOGURT

Prep Time: 20 minutes
Cook Time: 20 minutes
Serves: 4

Ingredients:
- 4 wild-caught salmon fillets (6 oz each)
- 1/4 cup organic chia seeds
- 1 tbsp organic lemon zest
- 2 organic fennel bulbs, sliced
- 2 tbsp organic avocado oil
- 1/2 cup organic full-fat Greek yogurt
- 2 tbsp organic capers, minced
- 1 organic lemon, juiced
- 2 tbsp organic fresh dill, chopped
- Sea salt and black pepper to taste

Instructions:
1. Preheat oven to 400°F (200°C).
2. Mix chia seeds with lemon zest, salt, and pepper.
3. Press the mixture onto the top of each salmon fillet.
4. Toss sliced fennel with 1 tbsp avocado oil, salt, and pepper. Spread on a baking sheet.
5. Place salmon on top of fennel and drizzle with remaining avocado oil.
6. Roast for 15-20 minutes until salmon is cooked through and fennel is caramelized.
7. Mix yogurt with capers, lemon juice, and dill.
8. Serve salmon and fennel with a dollop of the yogurt sauce.

Tip: Soak chia seeds in a little water for 5 minutes before mixing with lemon zest. This helps them adhere better to the salmon.

Nutritional Information (per serving):
- Calories: 480
- Protein: 37g
- Fat: 31g
- Carbohydrates: 9g
- Fiber: 5g

BLACK BEAN AND WILD-CAUGHT SALMON CAKES WITH MANGO SALSA

Prep Time: 25 minutes
Cook Time: 15 minutes
Serves: 4

Ingredients:
- 1 can (14 oz) wild-caught salmon, drained
- 1 cup cooked organic black beans, mashed
- 1 organic egg, beaten
- 1/4 cup organic red bell pepper, finely diced
- 2 tbsp organic coconut flour
- 1 tbsp organic lime juice

- 1 tsp organic cumin
- 1/4 cup organic cilantro, chopped
- 2 tbsp organic coconut oil for frying
- 1 organic mango, diced
- 1/4 organic red onion, finely diced
- 1 small organic jalapeño, seeded and minced
- 1 tbsp organic extra-virgin olive oil

Instructions:
1. Mix salmon, mashed beans, egg, bell pepper, coconut flour, half the lime juice, cumin, and half the cilantro.
2. Form into 8 patties.
3. Heat coconut oil in a skillet over medium heat. Cook patties for 3-4 minutes per side until golden.
4. For salsa, combine mango, red onion, jalapeño, remaining lime juice and cilantro, and olive oil.
5. Serve cakes topped with mango salsa.

Tip: Chill the patties for 30 minutes before cooking to help them hold together better.

Nutritional Information (per serving):
- Calories: 370
- Protein: 26g
- Fat: 19g
- Carbohydrates: 24g
- Fiber: 7g

GRILLED SALMON WITH HEMP SEED PESTO AND ROASTED BROCCOLI

Prep Time: 20 minutes
Cook Time: 20 minutes
Serves: 4

Ingredients:
- 4 wild-caught salmon fillets (6 oz each)
- 1 head organic broccoli, cut into florets
- 2 tbsp organic avocado oil, divided
- Sea salt and black pepper to taste

For the Hemp Seed Pesto:
- 1 cup organic fresh basil leaves
- 1/2 cup organic hemp seeds
- 1/4 cup organic extra-virgin olive oil
- 2 organic garlic cloves
- 1 tbsp organic lemon juice
- 1/4 tsp sea salt

Instructions:
1. Preheat grill to medium-high heat.
2. Toss broccoli florets with 1 tbsp avocado oil, salt, and pepper. Spread on a baking sheet.
3. Roast broccoli for 15-20 minutes, until tender and slightly charred.
4. In a food processor, blend basil, hemp seeds, olive oil, garlic, lemon juice, and salt to make the pesto.
5. Brush salmon fillets with remaining 1 tbsp avocado oil and season with salt and pepper.
6. Grill salmon for 5-7 minutes per side, until cooked through.
7. Serve grilled salmon topped with the hemp seed pesto, accompanied by the roasted broccoli.

Tip: For a deeper, richer pesto flavor, toast the hemp seeds in a dry skillet for 2-3 minutes before blending.

Nutritional Information (per serving):
- Calories: 420
- Protein: 34g
- Fat: 28g
- Carbohydrates: 8g
- Fiber: 4g

MACKEREL

KOREAN-STYLE GRILLED MACKEREL WITH SESAME BOK CHOY AND KOMBUCHA VINAIGRETTE

Prep Time: 20 minutes
Cook Time: 15 minutes
Serves: 4

Ingredients:
- 4 wild-caught mackerel fillets
- 2 tbsp organic sesame oil
- 1 tbsp organic ginger, grated
- 2 organic garlic cloves, minced
- 2 tbsp coconut aminos
- 4 heads organic baby bok choy, halved
- 1 tbsp organic avocado oil
- 2 tbsp organic sesame seeds
- 1/4 cup organic extra-virgin olive oil
- 2 tbsp unflavored kombucha
- 1 tsp organic mustard
- Sea salt and organic black pepper to taste

Instructions:
1. Marinate mackerel in sesame oil, ginger, garlic, and coconut aminos for 15 minutes.
2. Grill mackerel for 3-4 minutes per side.
3. Sauté bok choy in avocado oil until tender. Sprinkle with sesame seeds.
4. Whisk olive oil, kombucha, and mustard for the vinaigrette.
5. Serve grilled mackerel with bok choy and drizzle with vinaigrette.

Tip: Don't overcook the mackerel; it should be just opaque in the center.

Nutritional Information (per serving):
- Calories: 470
- Protein: 30g
- Fat: 36g
- Carbohydrates: 6g
- Fiber: 2g

ROASTED ASPARAGUS WITH MACKEREL AND AVOCADO CREAM

Prep Time: 15 minutes
Cook Time: 20 minutes
Serves: 4

Ingredients:
- For the Roasted Asparagus:
  - 1 bunch organic asparagus, trimmed
  - 2 tbsp organic avocado oil
  - 1 tsp organic garlic powder
  - Sea salt & pepper to taste
- For the Mackerel:
  - 4 fresh mackerel fillets, grilled or baked
  - 1 tbsp organic lemon juice
  - Sea salt & pepper to taste
- For the Avocado Cream:
  - 1 large organic avocado, mashed
  - 1 tbsp organic lemon juice
  - 1 tbsp organic coconut yogurt (unsweetened, probiotic-rich)
  - Sea salt & pepper to taste

Instructions:
1. Roast the Asparagus: Preheat the oven to 400°F (200°C). Toss the asparagus with avocado oil, garlic powder, salt, and pepper. Spread on a baking sheet and roast for 15-20 minutes until tender and slightly crispy.
2. Cook the Mackerel: Grill or bake the mackerel fillets seasoned with lemon juice, salt, and pepper. Cook for about 5-6 minutes per side until fully cooked.
3. Prepare the Avocado Cream: In a bowl, mash the avocado and mix with lemon juice, coconut yogurt, salt, and pepper until smooth.
4. Assemble the Dish: Plate the roasted asparagus with the grilled mackerel on top. Drizzle the avocado cream over the dish or serve it on the side for dipping.

Tip: If you are a fish in the morning kind of person, this is also a perfect breakfast or brunch.

Nutritional Information (per serving):
- Calories: 430
- Protein: 28g
- Fat: 33g
- Carbohydrates: 8g
- Fiber: 5g

MACKEREL PATTIES WITH CASHEW DIP

Prep Time: 15 minutes
Cook Time: 10 minutes
Serves: 4

Ingredients:
- For the Mackerel Patties:
  - 2 fresh mackerel fillets, cooked and flaked
  - 1 organic egg, beaten
  - 2 tbsp organic almond flour
  - 1 tbsp organic fresh parsley, chopped
  - 1 clove organic garlic, minced
  - 1 tsp organic Dijon mustard (no added sugar)
  - Sea salt & pepper to taste
  - 2 tbsp organic avocado oil (for frying)
- For the Cashew Dip:
  - 1/2 cup organic raw cashews, soaked for 2-4 hours
  - 1 tbsp organic lemon juice
  - 1 clove organic garlic
  - 1 tbsp organic olive oil
  - Sea salt to taste

Instructions:
1. Prepare the Mackerel Patties: In a bowl, mix the flaked mackerel, beaten egg, almond flour, parsley, garlic, Dijon mustard, salt, and pepper. Form the mixture into small patties.
2. Fry the Patties: Heat avocado oil in a skillet over medium heat. Fry the patties for 3-4 minutes per side, until golden brown and crispy. Set aside on a paper towel to drain excess oil.
3. Make the Cashew Dip: Drain the soaked cashews and blend with lemon juice, garlic, olive oil, and a pinch of salt until smooth and creamy.
4. Serve the crispy mackerel patties with the cashew dip for a savory, satisfying snack.

Nutritional Information (per serving):
- Calories: 380
- Protein: 20g
- Fat: 29g
- Carbohydrates: 10g
- Fiber: 2g

MACKEREL AND SWEET POTATO NOURISH BOWL WITH PROBIOTIC PICKLED RADISHES

Prep Time: 20 minutes
Cook Time: 30 minutes
Serves: 4

Ingredients:
- For the Mackerel:
  - 4 fresh mackerel fillets
  - 1 tbsp organic avocado oil
  - 1 tsp organic turmeric powder
  - Sea salt & pepper to taste
- For the Nourish Bowl:
  - 2 large organic sweet potatoes, cubed
  - 2 tbsp organic avocado oil
  - 4 cups organic mixed greens (arugula, spinach)
  - 1/4 cup organic pumpkin seeds, toasted
- For the Probiotic Pickled Radishes:
  - 1/2 cup organic radishes, thinly sliced
  - 1/4 cup organic apple cider vinegar (unpasteurized)
  - 1 tbsp organic fresh dill, chopped
  - Sea salt to taste

Instructions:
1. Pickle the Radishes: In a small bowl, combine the radish slices with apple cider vinegar, fresh dill, and a pinch of salt. Let sit for at least 15 minutes or refrigerate for up to 24 hours to allow the flavors to develop.
2. Roast the Sweet Potatoes: Preheat the oven to 400°F (200°C). Toss the sweet potato cubes with avocado oil, turmeric, salt, and pepper. Spread on a baking sheet and roast for 25-30 minutes until golden and tender.
3. Cook the Mackerel: Heat avocado oil in a skillet over medium heat. Season the mackerel fillets with salt, pepper, and turmeric powder. Cook for 4-5 minutes per side until crispy and cooked through.
4. Assemble the Nourish Bowl: In a large bowl, layer the mixed greens and roasted sweet potatoes. Add the cooked mackerel fillets and sprinkle with toasted pumpkin seeds.
5. Serve: Top with the probiotic pickled radishes for a zesty, gut-friendly touch and serve immediately for a hearty, nutrient-dense meal.

Nutritional Information (per serving):
- Calories: 490
- Protein: 28g
- Fat: 30g
- Carbohydrates: 27g
- Fiber: 6g

SARDINES

SARDINE AND VEGETABLE SKEWERS WITH LEMON-HERB MARINADE

Prep Time: 20 minutes
Cook Time: 10 minutes
Serves: 4

Ingredients:
- 2 cans (4 oz each) wild-caught sardines in olive oil, drained and cut into chunks
- 1 organic red bell pepper, cut into chunks
- 1 organic zucchini, sliced into rounds
- 1 organic red onion, cut into chunks
- 1 organic lemon, zested and juiced
- 2 tbsp organic extra-virgin olive oil
- 2 tbsp organic fresh oregano, chopped
- 2 tbsp organic fresh parsley, chopped
- Sea salt and black pepper to taste

Instructions:
1. Preheat grill to medium-high heat.
2. In a bowl, mix lemon zest, lemon juice, olive oil, oregano, parsley, salt, and pepper.
3. Thread sardine chunks, bell pepper, zucchini, and red onion onto skewers.
4. Brush the skewers with the lemon-herb marinade.
5. Grill the skewers for 2-3 minutes per side until vegetables are tender and sardines are heated.
6. Serve immediately.

Tip: Soak wooden skewers in water for 30 minutes before grilling to prevent burning.

Nutritional Information (per serving):
- Calories: 220
- Protein: 16g
- Fat: 16g
- Carbohydrates: 8g
- Fiber: 2g

SARDINE AND ZUCCHINI NOODLES WITH PESTO

Prep Time: 15 minutes
Cook Time: 10 minutes
Serves: 4

Ingredients:
- 2 cans (4 oz each) wild-caught sardines in olive oil, drained
- 4 medium organic zucchinis, spiralized into noodles
- 1 cup organic fresh basil leaves
- 1/4 cup organic pine nuts
- 1/4 cup organic extra-virgin olive oil
- 2 organic garlic cloves
- 1/4 cup organic Parmesan cheese (optional)
- Sea salt and black pepper to taste

Instructions:
1. In a food processor, combine basil, pine nuts, olive oil, garlic, and Parmesan cheese. Blend until smooth. Season with salt and pepper.
2. In a large skillet, heat a bit of the olive oil from the sardines over medium heat. Add zucchini noodles and sauté for 2-3 minutes until tender.
3. Stir in the pesto and cook for another 2 minutes until heated through.
4. Gently fold in the sardines and cook for 1 minute to warm.
5. Serve immediately.

Tip: Toast the pine nuts in a dry skillet for 2-3 minutes before adding to the food processor for a richer, nuttier flavor.

Nutritional Information (per serving):
- Calories: 380
- Protein: 20g
- Fat: 30g
- Carbohydrates: 10g
- Fiber: 4g

SPAGHETTI SQUASH WITH PUTTANESCA SAUCE AND SARDINES

Prep Time: 10 minutes
Cook Time: 40 minutes
Serves: 4

Ingredients:

- 1 large organic spaghetti squash
- 1 can wild-caught sardines, drained
- 1/2 cup organic olives, chopped
- 2 tbsp organic capers
- 1 cup organic tomato sauce (no added sugars)
- 1 tbsp organic olive oil
- 2 cloves organic garlic, minced

Instructions:

1. Roast the Squash: Preheat the oven to 400°F (200°C). Cut spaghetti squash in half, remove the seeds, and roast cut-side down for 35-40 minutes until tender.
2. Make the Puttanesca Sauce: Heat olive oil in a pan over medium heat. Add garlic and sauté until fragrant. Stir in tomato sauce, olives, capers, and sardines. Simmer for 10 minutes.
3. Scrape the Squash: Use a fork to scrape out the spaghetti squash strands.
4. Serve: Top the spaghetti squash with puttanesca sauce.

Tip: Sardines add a rich, briny flavor that complements the bold flavors of puttanesca sauce.

Nutritional Information (per serving):

- Calories: 300
- Protein: 15g
- Fat: 18g
- Carbohydrates: 20g
- Fiber: 5g

SHRIMP

CHIA AND CITRUS MARINATED SHRIMP SKEWERS WITH GARLIC KALE

Prep Time: 30 minutes (plus 1 hour marinating)
Cook Time: 15 minutes
Serves: 4

Ingredients:

- 1 lb wild-caught shrimp, peeled and deveined
- 2 tbsp organic chia seeds
- 1 organic orange, juiced
- 1 organic lemon, juiced
- 2 organic garlic cloves, minced
- 1/4 cup organic extra-virgin olive oil
- 1 tsp organic smoked paprika
- 1/4 tsp sea salt
- 1/4 tsp black pepper
- 4 cups organic kale, chopped
- 1 tbsp organic avocado oil

Instructions:

1. In a bowl, mix chia seeds, orange juice, lemon juice, 1 minced garlic clove, olive oil, smoked paprika, salt, and pepper. Add shrimp and marinate in the refrigerator for 1 hour.
2. Preheat grill or grill pan to medium-high heat.
3. Thread shrimp onto skewers and grill for 2-3 minutes per side until opaque and cooked through.
4. In a skillet, heat avocado oil over medium heat. Sauté kale with a pinch of salt and the remaining garlic until wilted, about 5 minutes.
5. Serve shrimp skewers over a bed of garlic kale.

Tip: Soak wooden skewers in water for 30 minutes before grilling to prevent burning.

Nutritional Information (per serving):

- Calories: 320
- Protein: 25g
- Fat: 22g
- Carbohydrates: 9g
- Fiber: 3g

AVOCADO AND CUCUMBER GAZPACHO WITH SHRIMP

Prep Time: 15 minutes
Cook Time: 5 minutes (for shrimp)
Serves: 4

Ingredients:

- 2 large organic avocados, peeled and pitted
- 1 organic cucumber, peeled and chopped
- 1 cup organic coconut water
- 1/4 cup organic fresh cilantro, chopped
- 1 organic lime, juiced
- 1 organic garlic clove, minced
- 1 tbsp organic apple cider vinegar
- 1/2 lb wild-caught shrimp, peeled and deveined
- 2 tbsp organic avocado oil
- Sea salt and black pepper to taste

Instructions:

1. In a blender, combine avocados, cucumber, coconut water, cilantro, lime juice, garlic, and apple cider vinegar. Blend until smooth.
2. Season with salt and pepper, and refrigerate for at least 30 minutes to chill.
3. Heat avocado oil in a skillet over medium heat. Sauté shrimp until pink and cooked through, about 3-4 minutes.
4. Serve gazpacho topped with sautéed shrimp.

Tip: Chill the serving bowls in the freezer for a few minutes before ladling in the gazpacho for an extra-refreshing experience.

Nutritional Information (per serving):

- Calories: 310
- Protein: 15g
- Fat: 25g
- Carbohydrates: 12g
- Fiber: 7g

CAULIFLOWER FRIED "RICE" WITH SHRIMP

Prep Time: 15 minutes
Cook Time: 20 minutes
Serves: 4

Ingredients:

- 1 head organic cauliflower, riced
- 1 lb organic, wild-caught shrimp, peeled and deveined
- 2 organic eggs, beaten
- 1 organic onion, diced
- 2 organic carrots, diced
- 2 organic garlic cloves, minced
- 2 tbsp organic coconut aminos
- 1 tbsp organic sesame oil
- 2 tbsp organic coconut oil
- Sea salt and black pepper to taste
- 2 tbsp organic green onions, sliced

Instructions:

1. In a large skillet or wok, heat 1 tbsp coconut oil over medium-high heat.

2. Add the beaten eggs and scramble them, breaking them into small pieces. Remove from the skillet and set aside.
3. Add the remaining 1 tbsp coconut oil to the skillet. Sauté the onion, carrots, and garlic until softened.
4. Add the riced cauliflower and shrimp. Cook for 5-7 minutes, stirring frequently, until the shrimp is cooked through and the cauliflower is tender.
5. Stir in the scrambled eggs, coconut aminos, and sesame oil. Season with salt and pepper.
6. Serve the cauliflower fried "rice" hot, garnished with sliced green onions.

Tip: For a more uniform texture, pulse the cauliflower florets in a food processor until they resemble rice grains.

Nutritional Information (per serving):
- Calories: 340
- Protein: 24g
- Fat: 20g
- Carbohydrates: 16g
- Fiber: 6g

JICAMA AND SHRIMP CEVICHE WITH COCONUT LIME DRESSING

Prep Time: 20 minutes
Cook Time: 0 minutes (plus 30 minutes marinating)
Serves: 4

Ingredients:
- 1 lb wild-caught shrimp, peeled, deveined, and chopped
- 2 cups organic jicama, peeled and diced
- 1 organic avocado, diced
- 1/4 cup organic red onion, finely chopped
- 1/4 cup organic fresh cilantro, chopped
- 2 organic limes, juiced
- 1/4 cup organic coconut milk
- 1 tbsp organic avocado oil
- Sea salt and black pepper to taste
- 1/4 cup organic coconut yogurt

Instructions:
1. In a large bowl, combine shrimp and lime juice. Let marinate for 30 minutes, stirring occasionally.
2. In a separate bowl, whisk together coconut milk, avocado oil, salt, and pepper to make the dressing.
3. Drain excess lime juice from the shrimp and add jicama, avocado, red onion, and cilantro.
4. Pour the coconut lime dressing over the mixture and toss gently to combine.
5. Serve chilled, topped with a dollop of coconut yogurt.

Tip: For a more "cooked" texture in the shrimp, marinate for up to 2 hours, stirring occasionally.

Nutritional Information (per serving):
- Calories: 320
- Protein: 24g
- Fat: 20g
- Carbohydrates: 14g
- Fiber: 7g

SHRIMP AND ZOODLES WITH GARLIC BUTTER SAUCE

Prep Time: 10 minutes
Cook Time: 15 minutes
Serves: 4

Ingredients:
- 1 lb organic, wild-caught shrimp, peeled and deveined
- 4 medium organic zucchini, spiralized into zoodles
- 4 tbsp organic organic extra-virgin olive oil
- 4 organic garlic cloves, minced
- 1/4 cup organic lemon juice
- 1/4 cup organic fresh parsley, chopped
- Sea salt and freshly ground black pepper to taste
- Optional: Red pepper flakes (for a touch of heat)

Instructions:
1. Prepare the Zoodles:
   1. Lightly salt the zucchini noodles and place them in a colander for 10 minutes to draw out excess moisture. Pat dry with paper towels.
2. Sauté the Shrimp:
   1. Heat 2 tbsp of the oil in a large skillet over medium-high heat.
   2. Add the shrimp and cook for 2-3 minutes per side, until pink and cooked through. Remove from the skillet and set aside.
3. Make the Garlic Butter Sauce:
   1. In the same skillet, melt the remaining 2 tbsp of oil over medium heat.
   2. Add the minced garlic and cook for 1 minute, stirring constantly, until fragrant.
   3. Stir in the lemon juice, chopped parsley, salt, pepper, and red pepper flakes (if using).
4. Combine and Serve:
   1. Add the zoodles to the skillet and toss to coat with the garlic butter sauce. Cook for 2-3 minutes, until the zoodles are slightly softened but still retain a bit of crunch.
   2. Return the cooked shrimp to the skillet and toss to combine.
   3. Serve the Shrimp and Zoodles immediately, while hot.

Tip: For a richer flavor, add a tablespoon of organic white wine to the garlic butter sauce after adding the garlic and cook for 1 minute before adding the lemon juice and parsley.

Nutritional Information (per serving):
- Calories: 280
- Protein: 24g
- Fat: 18g
- Carbohydrates: 8g
- Fiber: 3g

CHAWANMUSHI (SAVORY STEAMED CUSTARD) WITH WILD-CAUGHT SHRIMP AND SEAWEED

Prep Time: 15 minutes
Cook Time: 20 minutes
Serves: 4

Ingredients:
- 4 large organic eggs
- 2 cups organic chicken broth
- 1 tbsp organic coconut aminos
- 1 tbsp organic rice vinegar
- 8 pieces wild-caught shrimp, peeled and deveined
- 1 sheet organic nori (seaweed), torn into small pieces
- 1 tbsp organic fresh chives, chopped

Instructions:
1. Prepare the Custard Mixture:
   In a bowl, whisk the eggs, chicken broth, coconut aminos, and rice vinegar until well combined. Strain the mixture to remove any bubbles for a smooth texture.
2. Assemble the Chawanmushi:
   Divide the shrimp and nori evenly among four small bowls. Pour the egg mixture over the shrimp and seaweed. Cover each bowl with foil.
3. Steam the Custard:
   Set up a steamer or a large pot with a steamer insert. Steam the bowls for 15-20 minutes until the custard is just set and the shrimp are cooked through. Use gentle heat for steaming to ensure the custard remains silky and smooth.
4. Garnish with fresh chives and serve hot.
   Tip: Chawanmushi is best enjoyed warm, with the delicate custard melting in your mouth alongside the briny flavor of the shrimp and seaweed.

Nutritional Information (per serving):
- Calories: 160, Protein: 18g, Fat: 7g, Carbohydrates: 3g, Fiber: 0g

WHITE FISH

White fish is a versatile and popular category of fish that includes many different species: **Cod** has a mild, slightly sweet flavor and flaky, dense flesh that makes it perfect for dishes like fish and chips, while halibut is the oiliest of the white fish with a firm, meaty texture that holds up well to grilling, pan-frying, or baking. **Haddock** has a clean, white, soft flesh with a subtle sweet taste and is often used in fish and chips or smoked for a distinctive flavor. **Sole**, which includes varieties like Dover sole and lemon sole, has a delicate, mild flavor and firm flesh that is often pan-fried or served whole. Sea bass has a firm, meaty flesh that is excellent for grilling, frying, searing, or baking. Other popular types of white fish include pollock, grouper, red snapper, flounder, monkfish, tilapia, catfish, and branzino.

White fish are generally low in fat and calories, high in protein, easy to digest, and rich in B vitamins, selenium, phosphorus, and other minerals, making them a healthy choice for many diets. When selecting white fish, it's important to consider the thickness, flakiness, and fat content of the fish and match it to the appropriate cooking method. Thicker fillets are better for grilling or searing, while thinner fillets are best for poaching, steaming, or using in soups and stews. Flaky fish like cod break apart easily after cooking, while firmer fish like halibut and sea bass hold together better. Lean fish can dry out more easily, while fatty fish stay moist. With so many different types of white fish available, it's easy to find one that suits your taste preferences and cooking needs.

BLACK BEAN AND WILD-CAUGHT COD CEVICHE

Prep Time: 20 minutes
Marinating Time: 2 hours
Serves: 4

Ingredients:
- 1 lb wild-caught cod, diced
- 1 cup cooked organic black beans
- 1/2 cup organic lime juice (about 4-5 limes)
- 1 organic red onion, finely diced
- 1 organic bell pepper, finely diced
- 1 organic jalapeño, seeded and minced
- 1/4 cup organic cilantro, chopped
- 1 organic avocado, diced
- 2 tbsp organic extra-virgin olive oil
- Sea salt to taste

Instructions:
1. In a glass bowl, combine cod and lime juice. Marinate in the refrigerator for 2 hours.
2. Drain excess lime juice, leaving a small amount.
3. Add black beans, red onion, bell pepper, jalapeño, and cilantro to the fish.
4. Gently fold in avocado and olive oil. Season with salt.
5. Serve chilled.

Tip: For the best texture, use very fresh fish and cut it into uniform pieces.

Nutritional Information (per serving):
- Calories: 280
- Protein: 24g
- Fat: 13g
- Carbohydrates: 18g
- Fiber: 7g

FLAXSEED-CRUSTED WILD COD WITH ROASTED FENNEL AND LEMON-CAPER AIOLI

Prep Time: 20 minutes
Cook Time: 25 minutes
Serves: 4

Ingredients:
- 4 wild-caught cod fillets (6 oz each)
- 1/4 cup organic ground flaxseed
- 2 tbsp organic fresh thyme leaves
- 2 organic fennel bulbs, sliced
- 2 tbsp organic avocado oil
- 1/2 cup organic mayonnaise (preferably homemade with avocado oil, see recipe)
- 2 tbsp organic capers, minced
- 1 organic lemon, zested and juiced
- 1 organic garlic clove, minced
- Sea salt and black pepper to taste

Instructions:
1. Preheat oven to 400°F (200°C).
2. Mix ground flaxseed with thyme, salt, and pepper.
3. Press the mixture onto both sides of each cod fillet.
4. Toss sliced fennel with 1 tbsp avocado oil, salt, and pepper. Spread on a baking sheet.
5. Place cod on top of fennel and drizzle with remaining avocado oil.
6. Roast for 20-25 minutes until cod is cooked through and fennel is caramelized.
7. For the aioli, mix mayonnaise with capers, lemon zest, lemon juice, and garlic.
8. Serve cod and fennel with a dollop of lemon-caper aioli.

Tip: To prevent the flaxseed crust from becoming soggy, pat the cod fillets dry before coating and avoid overcrowding the baking sheet.

Nutritional Information (per serving):
- Calories: 420
- Protein: 34g
- Fat: 28g
- Carbohydrates: 10g
- Fiber: 5g

LEMON BAKED COD WITH PISTACHIO CRUST

Prep Time: 15 minutes
Cook Time: 20 minutes
Serves: 4

Ingredients:
- 4 wild-caught cod fillets (6 oz each)
- 1/2 cup organic pistachios, finely chopped
- 1/4 cup organic almond flour
- 1/4 cup organic fresh parsley, chopped
- 1 organic lemon, zested and juiced
- 2 organic garlic cloves, minced
- 2 tbsp organic extra-virgin olive oil
- Sea salt and freshly ground black pepper to taste
- Lemon wedges (for serving)

Instructions:
1. Preheat the Oven: Preheat your oven to 375°F (190°C). Line a baking sheet with parchment paper.
2. Prepare the Pistachio Crust:
   1. In a bowl, combine chopped pistachios, almond flour, chopped parsley, lemon zest, minced garlic, salt, and pepper. Mix well.
   2. Add 1 tbsp of olive oil and mix until the crust mixture is moistened and crumbly.
3. Prepare the Cod:
   1. Place the cod fillets on the prepared baking sheet. Drizzle with the remaining 1 tbsp of olive oil and the lemon juice. Season with salt and pepper.
   2. Press the pistachio mixture onto the top of each cod fillet, ensuring an even layer.
4. Bake the Cod: Bake the cod in the preheated oven for 15-20 minutes, or until the fish is opaque and flakes easily with a fork, and the crust is golden brown.
5. Serve: Serve the cod fillets hot, garnished with lemon wedges.

Tip: For an extra burst of flavor, you can marinate the cod fillets in a mixture of lemon juice, olive oil, and garlic for 30 minutes before adding the pistachio crust.

Nutritional Information (per serving):

- Calories: 350
- Protein: 32g
- Fat: 20g
- Carbohydrates: 8g
- Fiber: 3g

WALNUT-CRUSTED HALIBUT WITH ROASTED ASPARAGUS AND LEMON-DILL YOGURT SAUCE

Prep Time: 20 minutes
Cook Time: 25 minutes
Serves: 4

Ingredients:

- 4 wild-caught halibut fillets (6 oz each)
- 1/2 cup organic walnuts, finely chopped
- 2 tbsp organic fresh dill, chopped
- 1 tbsp organic lemon zest
- 2 tbsp organic avocado oil
- 1 lb organic asparagus, trimmed
- 1 cup organic coconut yogurt
- 1 tbsp organic lemon juice
- Sea salt and black pepper to taste

Instructions:

1. Preheat oven to 400°F (200°C).
2. In a shallow bowl, mix together chopped walnuts, dill, and lemon zest.
3. Brush the halibut fillets with 1 tbsp avocado oil and season with salt and pepper. Press the walnut mixture onto the top of each fillet.
4. Toss the asparagus with the remaining 1 tbsp avocado oil, salt, and pepper. Spread on a baking sheet.
5. Place the halibut and asparagus in the oven and bake for 20-25 minutes, until the fish is cooked through and the asparagus is tender.
6. In a small bowl, mix the coconut yogurt with lemon juice and season with salt and pepper.
7. Serve the walnut-crusted halibut with the roasted asparagus and a dollop of lemon-dill yogurt sauce.

Tip: For a more vibrant color, use a combination of green and purple asparagus.

Nutritional Information (per serving):

- Calories: 410
- Protein: 36g
- Fat: 24g
- Carbohydrates: 12g
- Fiber: 4g

MOROCCAN FISH TAGINE WITH SPICES & PRESERVED LEMON

Prep Time: 15 minutes
Cook Time: 30 minutes
Serves: 4

Ingredients:

- 1 lb wild-caught cod or sea bass, cut into chunks
- 2 tbsp ghee or coconut oil
- 1 medium onion, sliced
- 2 cloves garlic, minced
- 1 medium carrot, sliced
- 1 medium zucchini, sliced
- 1 tsp ground cumin
- 1 tsp ground coriander
- 1 tsp paprika
- 1/2 tsp ground cinnamon
- 1 cup organic diced tomatoes
- 1/2 cup organic vegetable broth
- 1 preserved lemon, chopped (preferably homemade, see recipe)
- 2 tbsp fresh cilantro, chopped (for garnish)
- Sea salt and black pepper to taste

Instructions:

1. Sauté the Vegetables: Heat ghee or coconut oil in a large pot over medium heat. Add onions, garlic, carrots, and zucchini. Sauté for 5-7 minutes until softened.
2. Add the Spices and Liquids: Stir in cumin, coriander, paprika, and cinnamon. Add diced tomatoes, broth, and preserved lemon. Simmer for 10 minutes.
3. Cook the Fish: Nestle the fish chunks into the vegetable mixture. Simmer for 8-10 minutes until the fish is cooked through and tender.
4. Garnish with Cilantro: Serve the stew in bowls, garnished with fresh cilantro.

Tip: Preserved lemon adds a unique tang and slight bitterness to the stew, balancing the warmth of the spices. Adjust the amount of preserved lemon based on your taste preference.

Nutritional Information (per serving):

- Calories: 270
- Protein: 26g
- Fat: 14g
- Carbohydrates: 13g
- Fiber: 4g

PARSNIP NOODLES WITH ALMOND PESTO AND WILD-CAUGHT COD

Prep Time: 10 minutes
Cook Time: 20 minutes
Serves: 4

Ingredients:

- 4 large organic parsnips, spiralized
- 4 fillets wild-caught cod
- 1/4 cup organic almonds, toasted
- 1/2 cup organic fresh basil
- 2 tbsp organic olive oil
- 1 tbsp organic lemon juice

Instructions:

1. Prepare the Cod: Preheat the oven to 375°F (190°C). Drizzle cod with olive oil, season with salt and pepper, and bake for 12-15 minutes until flaky.
2. Make the Pesto: In a food processor, blend almonds, basil, lemon juice, and olive oil until smooth.
3. Cook the Parsnip Noodles: Sauté parsnip noodles in olive oil for 5 minutes until tender.
4. Serve: Toss parsnip noodles with almond pesto and top with baked cod.

Tip: Toasted almonds in the pesto add a rich, nutty flavor that pairs beautifully with mild cod.

Nutritional Information (per serving):

- Calories: 390
- Protein: 31g
- Fat: 21g
- Carbohydrates: 22g
- Fiber: 7g

OTHER FISH AND SEAFOOD

AVOCADO AND CRAB STUFFED PORTOBELLO MUSHROOMS

Prep Time: 15 minutes
Cook Time: 20 minutes
Serves: 4

Ingredients:

- 4 large organic portobello mushrooms, stems removed
- 1 cup organic lump crab meat
- 1 large organic avocado, diced
- 1/4 cup organic red bell pepper, finely diced
- 1/4 cup organic red onion, finely diced
- 2 organic garlic cloves, minced
- 1 organic lemon, juiced
- 2 tbsp organic avocado oil
- Sea salt and black pepper to taste
- 1/4 cup organic fresh parsley, chopped

Instructions:

1. Preheat oven to 375°F (190°C).
2. Brush portobello mushrooms with 1 tbsp avocado oil and place on a baking sheet, gill side up.
3. In a bowl, mix crab meat, avocado, red bell pepper, red onion, garlic, lemon juice, salt, and pepper.
4. Stuff each mushroom cap with the crab and avocado mixture.
5. Drizzle with remaining avocado oil and bake for 20 minutes.
6. Garnish with fresh parsley before serving.

Tip: For extra flavor, lightly grill the mushrooms before stuffing them to add a smoky dimension.

Nutritional Information (per serving):

- Calories: 280
- Protein: 18g
- Fat: 20g
- Carbohydrates: 10g
- Fiber: 5g

RAINBOW TROUT WITH LEMON-HERB BUTTER AND ROASTED VEGETABLES

Prep Time: 15 minutes
Cook Time: 25 minutes
Serves: 4

Ingredients:

- 4 wild-caught rainbow trout fillets (6 oz each)
- 2 tbsp organic ghee, melted
- 1 organic lemon, thinly sliced
- 2 tbsp organic fresh dill, chopped
- 2 tbsp organic fresh parsley, chopped
- 2 cups organic baby carrots
- 2 cups organic Brussels sprouts, halved
- 2 tbsp organic extra-virgin olive oil
- Sea salt and black pepper to taste

Instructions:

1. Preheat oven to 400°F (200°C).
2. Toss baby carrots and Brussels sprouts with oil, salt, and pepper. Spread on a baking sheet and roast for 15 minutes.
3. Meanwhile, place trout fillets on a separate baking sheet lined with parchment paper.
4. Brush fillets with melted ghee and sprinkle with dill and parsley. Top with lemon slices.
5. After the vegetables have roasted for 15 minutes, place the trout in the oven and roast for an additional 10 minutes,

or until the fish is cooked through and flakes easily with a fork.
6. Serve the trout with roasted vegetables.

Tip: For extra flavor, drizzle the vegetables with a bit of the lemon-herb ghee before serving.

Nutritional Information (per serving):

- Calories: 450
- Protein: 36g
- Fat: 28g
- Carbohydrates: 14g
- Fiber: 6g

RAINBOW TROUT AND VEGETABLE PARCHMENT PACKETS WITH MISO BUTTER

Prep Time: 15 minutes
Cook Time: 15 minutes
Serves: 4

Ingredients:

- 4 wild-caught rainbow trout fillets (6 oz each)
- 2 cups organic mixed vegetables (zucchini, bell peppers, cherry tomatoes), sliced
- 4 tbsp organic ghee, softened
- 2 tbsp organic white miso paste
- 1 tbsp organic ginger, grated
- 2 organic garlic cloves, minced
- 1 organic lemon, sliced
- Sea salt and black pepper to taste

Instructions:

1. Preheat oven to 375°F (190°C).
2. Mix softened ghee with miso paste, ginger, and garlic.
3. Cut four large squares of parchment paper. Place a trout fillet in the center of each.
4. Top each fillet with mixed vegetables and a dollop of miso butter.
5. Add a lemon slice to each packet. Season with salt and pepper.
6. Fold parchment to seal packets tightly.
7. Bake for 12-15 minutes until fish is cooked through.
8. Serve packets directly on plates, allowing diners to open them at the table.

Tip: To enhance umami, brush trout with a thin layer of miso paste before adding vegetables and butter.

Nutritional Information (per serving):

- Calories: 420
- Protein: 34g
- Fat: 28g
- Carbohydrates: 10g
- Fiber: 2g

RAINBOW TROUT AND SAUERKRAUT SKILLET WITH DILL BUTTER

Prep Time: 15 minutes
Cook Time: 20 minutes
Serves: 4

Ingredients:

- 4 wild-caught rainbow trout fillets (6 oz each)
- 2 cups organic sauerkraut, drained
- 1 organic onion, sliced
- 2 tbsp organic ghee
- 2 tbsp organic fresh dill, chopped
- 1 organic lemon, juiced
- Sea salt and black pepper to taste

Instructions:
1. In a large skillet, melt 1 tbsp ghee over medium heat. Add onion and cook until softened.
2. Add sauerkraut to the skillet and cook for 5 minutes.
3. Push sauerkraut to the sides of the skillet. Add trout fillets to the center.
4. Cook trout for 4-5 minutes per side until done.
5. In a small bowl, mix remaining ghee with dill and lemon juice.
6. Serve trout over sauerkraut, topped with dill butter.

Tip: Rinse sauerkraut before cooking if you prefer a milder flavor that won't overpower the trout.

Nutritional Information (per serving):
- Calories: 360
- Protein: 34g
- Fat: 22g
- Carbohydrates: 8g
- Fiber: 3g

CAULIFLOWER "PASTA" PUTTANESCA WITH ANCHOVY BREADCRUMBS

Prep Time: 20 minutes
Cook Time: 25 minutes
Serves: 4

Ingredients:
- For the Puttanesca:
    - 1 large head organic cauliflower, riced
    - 2 tbsp organic avocado oil
    - 4 organic garlic cloves, minced
    - 1/2 cup organic Kalamata olives, pitted and halved
    - 1/4 cup organic capers, rinsed
    - 1 can (14 oz) organic diced tomatoes, undrained
    - 1/4 cup organic fresh parsley, chopped
    - 4 anchovy fillets, minced
    - Sea salt and black pepper to taste
- For the Breadcrumbs:
    - 1/4 cup organic almond flour
    - 2 tbsp organic grated Parmesan cheese
    - 2 tbsp organic ghee, melted
    - 4 anchovy fillets, minced
    - 1 tbsp organic fresh thyme leaves

Instructions:
1. Preheat oven to 400°F (200°C).
2. For the puttanesca, heat avocado oil in a large skillet over medium heat. Sauté garlic for 1 minute until fragrant.
3. Add olives, capers, diced tomatoes, parsley, and minced anchovies. Simmer for 15 minutes, stirring occasionally.
4. Meanwhile, for the breadcrumbs, mix almond flour, Parmesan cheese, melted ghee, minced anchovies, and thyme in a bowl.
5. Spread breadcrumbs on a baking sheet and bake for 10 minutes, stirring halfway through, until golden brown and crispy.
6. While breadcrumbs bake, sauté cauliflower rice in a separate skillet with a little avocado oil for 5-7 minutes until tender.
7. Combine cauliflower rice with the puttanesca sauce. Season with salt and pepper to taste.
8. Serve topped with the crispy anchovy breadcrumbs.

Tip: Use high-quality anchovies packed in olive oil for the best flavor.

Nutritional Information (per serving):
- Calories: 310
- Protein: 16g
- Fat: 24g
- Carbohydrates: 14g
- Fiber: 6g

SEARED SCALLOPS WITH ANCHOVY-CAPER BROWN BUTTER

Prep Time: 10 minutes
Cook Time: 10 minutes
Serves: 4

Ingredients:
- 1 lb wild-caught sea scallops, patted dry
- 4 tbsp organic ghee
- 6 anchovy fillets, minced
- 2 tbsp organic capers, rinsed
- 1 tbsp organic lemon juice
- 2 tbsp organic fresh parsley, chopped
- Sea salt and black pepper to taste

Instructions:
1. Season scallops with salt and pepper.
2. Heat ghee in a large skillet over medium-high heat until melted.
3. Add scallops and sear for 2-3 minutes per side until golden brown and cooked through. Remove from skillet and set aside.
4. Reduce heat to medium and add minced anchovies to the skillet. Cook for 1 minute, stirring constantly, until they melt into the ghee.
5. Stir in capers and lemon juice. Cook for another minute until fragrant.
6. Add scallops back to the skillet and toss to coat in the sauce.
7. Serve immediately, garnished with fresh parsley.

Tip: Do not overcrowd the skillet when searing scallops. Cook in batches if necessary to ensure proper browning. Serve with a high fiber side or salad and a side of fermented vegetable to make it a complete meal.

Nutritional Information (per serving):
- Calories: 280
- Protein: 24g
- Fat: 18g
- Carbohydrates: 2g
- Fiber: 1g

ANCHOVY AND RED PEPPER PESTO ZOODLES

Prep Time: 20 minutes
Cook Time: 10 minutes
Serves: 4

Ingredients:
- 4 medium organic zucchinis, spiralized into noodles
- 6 fillets wild-caught anchovies
- 1 organic red bell pepper, roasted and peeled
- 1/4 cup organic pine nuts
- 1/4 cup organic extra-virgin olive oil
- 2 organic garlic cloves
- 1/4 cup organic Parmesan cheese (optional)
- Sea salt and black pepper to taste

Instructions:
1. In a food processor, combine anchovies, roasted red pepper, pine nuts, olive oil, garlic, and Parmesan cheese. Blend until smooth. Season with salt and pepper.
2. In a large skillet, heat a bit of olive oil over medium heat. Add zucchini noodles and sauté for 2-3 minutes until tender.
3. Stir in the anchovy-red pepper pesto and cook for another 2 minutes until heated through.
4. Serve immediately.

Tip: Avoid overcooking the zucchini noodles to prevent them from becoming mushy. They should be tender but still have a bit of a bite.

Nutritional Information (per serving):
- Calories: 280
- Protein: 8g
- Fat: 24g
- Carbohydrates: 10g, Fiber: 4g

TUNA WITH CANNELLINI BEANS

Prep Time: 10 minutes
Cook Time: 10 minutes
Serves: 4

Ingredients:

- 2 cans (5 oz each) wild-caught tuna, drained
- 1 can (15 oz) organic cannellini beans, drained and rinsed
- 1 cup organic cherry tomatoes, halved
- 1/2 cup organic red onion, finely chopped
- 1/4 cup organic fresh parsley, chopped
- 1/4 cup organic fresh basil, chopped
- 2 tbsp organic capers, drained
- 2 tbsp organic extra-virgin olive oil
- 2 tbsp organic lemon juice
- 1 organic garlic clove, minced
- Sea salt and freshly ground black pepper to taste
- Optional: 1/4 tsp organic red pepper flakes (for a touch of heat)

Instructions:

1. In a large mixing bowl, combine the drained tuna and cannellini beans. Break up the tuna into smaller pieces with a fork.
2. Add the halved cherry tomatoes, chopped red onion, parsley, basil, and capers to the bowl with the tuna and beans.
3. In a small bowl, whisk together the olive oil, lemon juice, minced garlic, sea salt, black pepper, and red pepper flakes (if using).
4. Pour the dressing over the tuna and bean mixture. Toss gently to combine, ensuring all ingredients are evenly coated.

Tip: For an added layer of flavor, you can toast the capers in a dry skillet over medium heat for 2-3 minutes until they are slightly crispy.

Nutritional Information (per serving):

- Calories: 250
- Protein: 20g
- Fat: 12g
- Carbohydrates: 18g
- Fiber: 6g

ZUCCHINI NOODLES WITH SEARED SCALLOPS AND BASIL GHEE SAUCE

Prep Time: 10 minutes
Cook Time: 10 minutes
Serves: 4

Ingredients:

- 3 large organic zucchinis, spiralized
- 1 lb wild-caught scallops
- 2 tbsp organic ghee
- 1/4 cup organic fresh basil, chopped
- 1 tbsp organic lemon juice

Instructions:

1. Sear the Scallops: Heat 1 tbsp ghee in a pan over medium-high heat. Sear scallops for 2-3 minutes on each side until golden and cooked through.
2. Make the Basil Ghee Sauce: In a small pan, melt the remaining ghee and stir in basil and lemon juice.
3. Cook the Zucchini Noodles: Lightly sauté zucchini noodles for 2-3 minutes.
4. Serve: Plate the zucchini noodles, top with seared scallops, and drizzle with basil ghee sauce.

Tip: Searing scallops quickly over high heat ensures a golden crust while keeping the inside tender.

Nutritional Information (per serving):

- Calories: 320
- Protein: 24g
- Fat: 22g
- Carbohydrates: 10g

- Fiber: 3g

GRILLED YELLOWTAIL (HAMACHI) WITH PICKLED GINGER AND GARLIC GHEE

Prep Time: 10 minutes
Cook Time: 15 minutes
Serves: 4

Ingredients:

- 4 fillets wild-caught yellowtail (hamachi)
- 2 tbsp organic ghee
- 2 cloves organic garlic, minced
- 1 tbsp organic tamari
- 1 tbsp organic lemon juice
- 1/4 cup organic pickled ginger

Instructions:

1. In a small pan, melt the ghee over low heat. Add the minced garlic and cook for 2-3 minutes until fragrant. Remove from heat and stir in the tamari and lemon juice.
2. Preheat a grill or grill pan over medium heat. Grill the yellowtail for 4-5 minutes on each side until cooked through and slightly charred. Grill the fish skin-side down first to ensure the skin crisps up nicely.
3. Drizzle the grilled yellowtail with the garlic ghee and garnish with pickled ginger.

Tip: The richness of the ghee complements the mild flavor of the yellowtail, while the pickled ginger adds a tangy, probiotic punch.

Nutritional Information (per serving):

- Calories: 370
- Protein: 32g
- Fat: 24g
- Carbohydrates: 3g
- Fiber: 0g

BUTTERFLIED LOBSTER TAILS WITH GARLIC HERB BUTTER AND PICKLED VEGETABLES

Prep Time: 15 minutes
Cook Time: 12 minutes
Serves: 4

Ingredients:

- 4 wild-caught lobster tails
- 4 tbsp organic ghee, melted
- 3 cloves organic garlic, minced
- 2 tbsp organic fresh parsley, chopped
- 2 tbsp organic lemon juice
- 1 tbsp organic olive oil
- 1 cup pickled vegetables (for a probiotic side)

Instructions:

1. Prepare the Lobster Tails: Preheat your oven to 400°F (200°C). Use kitchen shears to cut through the top of each lobster shell to butterfly them. Gently lift the lobster meat over the shell and brush with olive oil.
2. Broil the Lobster: Place the lobster tails on a baking sheet and broil for 8-10 minutes until the meat is opaque and firm.
3. Make the Garlic Herb Butter: In a small saucepan, melt the ghee and stir in garlic, parsley, and lemon juice. Simmer for 2 minutes.
4. Serve with Pickled Vegetables: Drizzle the garlic herb butter over the lobster tails and serve with a side of pickled vegetables for a refreshing, probiotic-rich contrast.
   Tip: The acidity of the pickled vegetables balances the richness of the lobster and butter.

Nutritional Information (per serving):

- Calories: 320
- Protein: 25g
- Fat: 22g
- Carbohydrates: 4g
- Fiber: 1g

VEGAN AND VEGETARIAN RECIPES

VEGETARIAN

BAKED FETA AND ZUCCHINI NOODLES

Prep Time: 15 minutes
Cook Time: 30 minutes
Serves: 4

Ingredients:

- 1 block (8 oz) organic feta cheese
- 2 pints organic cherry tomatoes
- 4 organic garlic cloves, minced
- 1/4 cup organic extra-virgin olive oil
- 1 tsp organic dried oregano
- 1/4 tsp organic red pepper flakes
- Sea salt and black pepper to taste
- 4 medium organic zucchini, spiralized into noodles
- 1/4 cup organic fresh basil leaves, torn
- 2 tbsp organic pine nuts, toasted

Instructions:

1. Preheat the oven to 400°F (200°C).
2. In a baking dish, place the feta cheese in the center and surround it with cherry tomatoes.
3. Drizzle with olive oil and sprinkle with minced garlic, oregano, red pepper flakes, sea salt, and black pepper.
4. Bake for 25-30 minutes, until the tomatoes burst and the feta is soft and golden.
5. While the feta is baking, spiralize the zucchini into noodles.
6. In a large skillet, sauté the zucchini noodles over medium heat for 2-3 minutes until just tender.
7. Remove the baking dish from the oven and immediately stir to combine the melted feta with the burst tomatoes.
8. Toss the zucchini noodles with the feta-tomato mixture.
9. Garnish with fresh basil and toasted pine nuts before serving.

Tip: To prevent watery zucchini noodles, salt them lightly and let them sit in a colander for 10 minutes before cooking. Pat dry with paper towels.

Nutritional Information (per serving):

- Calories: 350
- Protein: 10g
- Fat: 30g
- Carbohydrates: 12g
- Fiber: 4g

BLACK BEAN AND SPINACH FRITTATA WITH FERMENTED SALSA

Prep Time: 15 minutes
Cook Time: 20 minutes
Serves: 4

Ingredients:

- 8 organic, pasture-raised eggs
- 1 cup cooked organic black beans
- 2 cups organic spinach, chopped
- 1 organic onion, diced
- 2 organic garlic cloves, minced
- 2 tbsp organic ghee
- 1 tsp organic cumin
- 1/4 cup organic fresh cilantro, chopped
- Sea salt and black pepper to taste
- 1/2 cup fermented salsa

Instructions:

1. Preheat oven to 375°F (190°C).
2. In an oven-safe skillet, heat ghee over medium heat. Sauté onion and garlic until softened.
3. Add spinach and cook until wilted.
4. Whisk eggs with cumin, salt, and pepper. Stir in black beans and cilantro.
5. Pour egg mixture over vegetables in the skillet.
6. Transfer to oven and bake for 15-20 minutes until set.
7. Serve slices topped with fermented salsa.

Tip: For a fluffy frittata, whisk the eggs vigorously to incorporate air before adding them to the skillet. This is also great for breakfast as a leftover.

Nutritional Information (per serving):

- Calories: 270
- Protein: 16g
- Fat: 17g
- Carbohydrates: 13g
- Fiber: 4g

FLAXSEED AND SPINACH FRITTATA WITH ROASTED CHERRY TOMATOES AND COCONUT YOGURT DRIZZLE

Prep Time: 20 minutes
Cook Time: 25 minutes
Serves: 4

Ingredients:

- 8 organic, pasture-raised eggs
- 1/4 cup organic ground flaxseed
- 2 cups organic spinach, chopped
- 1 organic onion, diced
- 2 organic garlic cloves, minced
- 2 tbsp organic ghee
- 1 cup organic cherry tomatoes
- 1/2 cup organic coconut yogurt
- 1 tbsp organic fresh dill, chopped
- Sea salt and black pepper to taste

Instructions:

1. Preheat oven to 375°F (190°C).

2. In an oven-safe skillet, heat ghee over medium heat. Sauté onion and garlic until softened.
3. Add spinach and cook until wilted.
4. Whisk eggs with ground flaxseed, salt, and pepper.
5. Pour egg mixture over vegetables in the skillet.
6. Transfer to oven and bake for 15-20 minutes until set.
7. Meanwhile, toss cherry tomatoes with a little ghee and roast for 10-12 minutes.
8. Mix coconut yogurt with dill, salt, and pepper.
9. Serve frittata slices topped with roasted tomatoes and a drizzle of dill coconut yogurt.

Tip: Substitute Greek yogurt with coconut yogurt for a dairy-free alternative

Nutritional Information (per serving):
- Calories: 290
- Protein: 15g
- Fat: 22g
- Carbohydrates: 10g
- Fiber: 4g

LENTIL AND EGGPLANT MOUSSAKA

Prep Time: 30 minutes
Cook Time: 45 minutes
Serves: 6

Ingredients:
- 2 cups cooked organic green lentils
- 2 large organic eggplants, sliced 1/4 inch thick
- 1 organic onion, finely chopped
- 3 organic garlic cloves, minced
- 1 tbsp organic ginger, grated
- 1 can (14 oz) organic diced tomatoes
- 2 tbsp organic coconut aminos
- 1 tsp organic ground cinnamon
- 1 tsp organic ground cumin
- 1/4 cup organic extra-virgin olive oil
- 1 cup organic, full-fat, grass-fed cream
- 2 organic eggs, beaten
- 1/4 cup organic nutritional yeast
- Sea salt and black pepper to taste

Instructions:
1. Preheat oven to 375°F (190°C).
2. Brush eggplant slices with coconut oil and roast for 20 minutes.
3. In a skillet, sauté onion, garlic, and ginger in coconut oil until softened.
4. Add lentils, tomatoes, coconut aminos, cinnamon, and cumin. Simmer for 10 minutes.
5. Layer eggplant and lentil mixture in a baking dish.
6. Whisk coconut cream with eggs and nutritional yeast. Pour over the layers.
7. Bake for 30 minutes until golden and set.

Tip: Salting the eggplant slices and letting them sit for 30 minutes before roasting helps remove bitterness and excess moisture.

Nutritional Information (per serving):
- Calories: 340
- Protein: 13g
- Fat: 22g
- Carbohydrates: 25g
- Fiber: 8g

TEMPEH AND MUSHROOM "BOURGUIGNON" WITH CAULIFLOWER MASH

Prep Time: 25 minutes
Cook Time: 40 minutes
Serves: 4

Ingredients:
- 2 packages organic tempeh, cubed
- 8 oz organic cremini mushrooms, quartered
- 1 organic onion, diced
- 2 organic carrots, sliced
- 2 organic celery stalks, sliced
- 2 organic garlic cloves, minced
- 1 cup organic red wine (optional, or use extra broth)
- 2 cups organic vegetable broth
- 2 tbsp organic tomato paste
- 1 tbsp organic fresh thyme leaves
- 2 tbsp organic coconut oil
- Sea salt and black pepper to taste

For the Cauliflower Mash:
- 1 large organic cauliflower, cut into florets
- 1/4 cup organic coconut cream
- 2 tbsp organic ghee
- Sea salt and black pepper to taste

Instructions:
1. Heat oil in a large pot over medium heat. Add tempeh cubes and brown on all sides, about 5-7 minutes. Remove and set aside.
2. In the same pot, sauté onion, carrots, celery, and garlic until softened, about 5 minutes.
3. Add mushrooms and cook for another 5 minutes.
4. Pour in red wine (if using) and let it reduce by half.
5. Add vegetable broth, tomato paste, thyme, salt, and pepper. Bring to a simmer.
6. Return tempeh to the pot and simmer for 20-25 minutes until the sauce thickens.
7. Meanwhile, steam cauliflower florets until tender. Mash with coconut cream, ghee, salt, and pepper.
8. Serve tempeh bourguignon over cauliflower mash.

Tip: For a deeper flavor, marinate the tempeh in red wine and herbs for 2 hours before cooking.

Nutritional Information (per serving):
- Calories: 380
- Protein: 22g
- Fat: 24g
- Carbohydrates: 18g
- Fiber: 8g

BROCCOLI "TATER" TOTS WITH AVOCADO RANCH DIP

Prep Time: 20 minutes
Cook Time: 25 minutes
Serves: 4

Ingredients:
- 2 cups organic broccoli florets, finely chopped
- 1 cup organic cauliflower florets, finely chopped
- 1 organic pasture-raised egg, beaten
- 1/4 cup organic coconut flour
- 1/4 cup organic nutritional yeast
- 1 tsp organic garlic powder
- 1/2 tsp sea salt
- 1/4 tsp organic black pepper
- 2 tbsp organic avocado oil

For the Avocado Ranch Dip:
- 1 ripe organic avocado
- 1/4 cup organic coconut yogurt
- 1 tbsp organic fresh dill, chopped
- 1 tbsp organic fresh chives, chopped
- 1 tsp organic garlic powder
- 1 tsp organic onion powder
- Sea salt and black pepper to taste

Instructions:
1. Preheat oven to 400°F (200°C).
2. Steam broccoli and cauliflower until tender, then finely chop.
3. Mix chopped vegetables with egg, coconut flour, nutritional yeast, garlic powder, salt, and pepper.
4. Form mixture into small tots.

5. Brush tots with avocado oil and place on a baking sheet.
6. Bake for 20-25 minutes, flipping halfway through, until golden brown.
7. For the dip, blend all ingredients until smooth.
8. Serve tots hot with avocado ranch dip.

Tip: For extra crispy tots, place them under the broiler for the last 1-2 minutes of cooking.

Nutritional Information (per serving):
- Calories: 220
- Protein: 9g
- Fat: 17g
- Carbohydrates: 12g
- Fiber: 6g

EGG AND AVOCADO SALAD LETTUCE WRAPS

Prep Time: 15 minutes
Cook Time: 10 minutes
Serves: 4

Ingredients:
- 6 large organic pasture-raised eggs
- 2 large organic avocados, diced
- 1/4 cup organic coconut yogurt
- 1 organic lemon, juiced
- 1/4 cup organic fresh parsley, chopped
- Sea salt and black pepper to taste
- 8 large organic lettuce leaves (butter lettuce or romaine works well)

Instructions:
1. Place eggs in a saucepan and cover with cold water. Bring to a boil, then reduce heat and simmer for 10 minutes.
2. Drain hot water and immediately place eggs in a bowl of ice water to cool.
3. Peel eggs and chop them into small pieces.
4. In a large bowl, combine chopped eggs, diced avocados, coconut yogurt, lemon juice, parsley, salt, and pepper. Mix gently to combine.
5. Spoon the egg and avocado salad into lettuce leaves and serve immediately.

Tip: For a creamier texture, mash one of the avocados before mixing with the rest of the ingredients.

Nutritional Information (per serving):
- Calories: 350
- Protein: 14g
- Fat: 28g
- Carbohydrates: 12g
- Fiber: 8g

CAULIFLOWER "MAC" AND CHEESE

Prep Time: 15 minutes
Cook Time: 25 minutes
Serves: 4

Ingredients:
- 1 large head organic cauliflower, cut into florets
- 1 cup organic coconut milk
- 1 cup organic full-fat grass-fed cheddar cheese, shredded
- 1/4 cup organic nutritional yeast
- 2 tbsp organic full-fat grass-fed ghee
- 1 tsp organic garlic powder
- 1 tsp organic onion powder
- Sea salt and black pepper to taste
- 1/4 cup organic coconut yogurt (for a creamy texture, optional)

Instructions:
1. Preheat oven to 375°F (190°C).
2. Steam cauliflower florets until tender, about 10 minutes. Drain well and set aside.
3. In a large saucepan, melt ghee over medium heat. Stir in coconut milk, garlic powder, onion powder, salt, and pepper.

4. Gradually add shredded cheese and nutritional yeast, stirring constantly until melted and smooth.
5. If using, add coconut yogurt and mix well.
6. Combine cheese sauce with steamed cauliflower in a baking dish.
7. Bake for 15 minutes until bubbly and golden on top.
8. Let cool slightly before serving.

Tip: For added texture, top with crushed nuts or seeds before baking.

Nutritional Information (per serving):
- Calories: 350
- Protein: 14g
- Fat: 28g
- Carbohydrates: 12g
- Fiber: 4g

CELERY ROOT AND WILD MUSHROOM GRATIN

Prep Time: 25 minutes
Cook Time: 45 minutes
Serves: 6

Ingredients:
- 2 large organic celery roots, thinly sliced
- 8 oz mixed organic wild mushrooms, sliced
- 1 organic onion, thinly sliced
- 2 organic garlic cloves, minced
- 1 cup organic coconut cream
- 1/2 cup organic vegetable broth (preferably homemade, see recipe)
- 1/4 cup organic grated full-fat grass-fed Parmesan cheese (optional)
- 2 tbsp organic ghee
- 1 tbsp organic fresh thyme leaves
- Sea salt and black pepper to taste
- 1/4 cup organic almond flour

Instructions:
1. Preheat oven to 375°F (190°C).
2. In a large skillet, melt ghee over medium heat. Sauté onions and garlic until softened.
3. Add mushrooms and cook until they release their moisture and begin to brown.
4. In a bowl, mix coconut cream, broth, thyme, salt, and pepper.
5. In a greased baking dish, layer half the celery root slices, followed by the mushroom mixture, then the remaining celery root.
6. Pour the cream mixture over the layers.
7. Mix almond flour with Parmesan cheese (if using) and sprinkle over the top.
8. Cover with foil and bake for 30 minutes. Remove foil and bake for an additional 15 minutes until golden and bubbly.

Tip: Soak the celery root slices in cold water for 10 minutes before assembling to remove excess starch and prevent browning.

Nutritional Information (per serving):
- Calories: 280
- Protein: 8g
- Fat: 22g
- Carbohydrates: 16g
- Fiber: 3g

CHERRY TOMATO AND ZUCCHINI NOODLE SALAD WITH PESTO

Prep Time: 20 minutes
Cook Time: 5 minutes
Serves: 4

Ingredients:
- 2 medium organic zucchinis, spiralized into noodles
- 2 pints organic cherry tomatoes, halved
- 1/2 cup organic fresh basil leaves
- 1/4 cup organic pine nuts
- 2 organic garlic cloves

- 1/4 cup organic extra-virgin olive oil
- 2 tbsp organic lemon juice
- 1/4 cup organic grated Parmesan cheese (optional)
- Sea salt and black pepper to taste

Instructions:
1. In a large bowl, combine the spiralized zucchini noodles and halved cherry tomatoes.
2. In a food processor, blend the basil, pine nuts, garlic, olive oil, and lemon juice until a smooth pesto forms. Season with salt and pepper.
3. Toss the zucchini noodles and cherry tomatoes with the pesto until well coated.
4. Sprinkle the Parmesan cheese (if using) over the salad and serve.

Tip: For a creamier pesto, add a tablespoon of organic coconut yogurt to the food processor.

Nutritional Information (per serving):
- Calories: 270
- Protein: 8g
- Fat: 22g
- Carbohydrates: 12g
- Fiber: 4g

EGGPLANT AND GOAT CHEESE NAPOLEON

Prep Time: 20 minutes
Cook Time: 25 minutes
Serves: 4

Ingredients:
- 1 large organic eggplant, sliced into 1/4-inch rounds
- 4 oz organic goat cheese, crumbled
- 1/2 cup organic sun-dried tomatoes, packed in olive oil, drained and chopped
- 2 tbsp organic balsamic vinegar
- 2 tbsp organic extra-virgin olive oil
- Sea salt and black pepper to taste
- 1/4 cup organic fresh basil leaves

Instructions:
1. Preheat oven to 400°F (200°C).
2. Brush eggplant slices with olive oil and season with salt and pepper.
3. Arrange slices on a baking sheet and roast for 15-20 minutes, flipping halfway through, until tender and slightly browned.
4. In a small saucepan, simmer balsamic vinegar over low heat for 5-7 minutes, until it thickens slightly.
5. To assemble the napoleon, layer a slice of roasted eggplant, followed by crumbled goat cheese, chopped sun-dried tomatoes, and a basil leaf. Repeat layers.
6. Drizzle with the balsamic glaze and serve immediately.

Tip: Serve over a bed of leafy greens for added fibers.

Nutritional Information (per serving):
- Calories: 280
- Protein: 8g
- Fat: 20g
- Carbohydrates: 14g
- Fiber: 4g

RATATOUILLE WITH HERBED GOAT CHEESE

Prep Time: 20 minutes
Cook Time: 40 minutes
Serves: 4

Ingredients:
- 1 large organic eggplant, cubed
- 2 organic zucchinis, cubed
- 1 organic red bell pepper, diced
- 1 organic yellow bell pepper, diced
- 1 organic onion, diced
- 3 organic garlic cloves, minced

- 1 can (14 oz) organic diced tomatoes
- 2 tbsp organic extra-virgin olive oil
- 1 tsp organic dried thyme
- 1 tsp organic dried oregano
- Sea salt and black pepper to taste
- 4 oz organic goat cheese, crumbled
- 2 tbsp organic fresh basil, chopped

Instructions:
1. Preheat oven to 375°F (190°C).
2. In a large oven-safe pot, heat olive oil over medium heat. Sauté onion and garlic until soft.
3. Add eggplant, zucchinis, red and yellow bell peppers, diced tomatoes, thyme, oregano, salt, and pepper. Stir well.
4. Cover and transfer to the oven. Bake for 30-35 minutes until the vegetables are tender.
5. Remove from the oven and stir in crumbled goat cheese.
6. Serve hot, garnished with fresh basil.

Tip: For a richer ratatouille, roast the vegetables separately before combining them in the pot.

Nutritional Information (per serving):
- Calories: 280
- Protein: 10g
- Fat: 20g
- Carbohydrates: 20g
- Fiber: 8g

CREAMY SPINACH PIE WITH ALMOND FLOUR CRUST

Prep Time: 25 minutes
Cook Time: 40 minutes
Serves: 6
Ingredients:

For the Almond Flour Crust:
- 2 cups organic almond flour
- 1/4 cup organic coconut oil, melted
- 1 organic egg, beaten
- 1/2 tsp sea salt

For the Spinach Filling:
- 1 lb organic fresh spinach, washed and chopped
- 1 organic onion, finely chopped
- 3 organic garlic cloves, minced
- 1 cup organic coconut yogurt
- 3 organic eggs
- 1/4 cup organic fresh dill, chopped
- 1/4 cup organic nutritional yeast (optional, for a cheesy flavor)
- 2 tbsp organic coconut oil
- Sea salt and black pepper to taste

Instructions:
1. **Preheat the Oven:** Preheat your oven to 350°F (175°C).
2. **Make the Crust:**
   1. In a large bowl, combine the almond flour, melted coconut oil, beaten egg, and sea salt until a dough forms.
   2. Press the dough evenly into the bottom and up the sides of a 9-inch pie dish.
   3. Bake the crust for 10 minutes, then set aside to cool slightly.
3. **Prepare the Filling:**
   1. In a skillet, heat oil over medium heat. Add the chopped onion and garlic, and sauté until softened, about 5 minutes.
   2. Add the chopped spinach to the skillet and cook until wilted, about 3-4 minutes. Remove from heat and let cool slightly.
   3. In a large bowl, whisk together the coconut yogurt, eggs, chopped dill, nutritional yeast (if using), salt, and pepper.
   4. Stir in the cooked spinach mixture until well combined.

4. Assemble the Pie:
   1. Pour the spinach filling into the pre-baked almond flour crust.
   2. Smooth the top with a spatula.
5. Bake the Pie:
   1. Bake the pie in the preheated oven for 25-30 minutes, or until the filling is set and the top is golden brown.
   2. Allow the pie to cool for 10 minutes before slicing and serving.

Tip: For a richer flavor, you can add a handful of crumbled feta or goat cheese to the spinach mixture before baking.

Nutritional Information (per serving):
- Calories: 320
- Protein: 10g
- Fat: 26g
- Carbohydrates: 12g
- Fiber: 4g

MEDITERRANEAN PIZZA WITH ALMOND-COCONUT FLOUR CRUST

Prep Time: 20 minutes
Cook Time: 25 minutes
Serves: 4

Ingredients:
For the Crust:
- 1 1/2 cups organic almond flour
- 1/2 cup organic coconut flour
- 1/4 cup organic coconut oil, melted
- 2 organic eggs, beaten
- 1/2 tsp sea salt
- 1/4 tsp organic garlic powder
- 1/4 tsp organic dried oregano

For the Toppings:
- 1/2 cup organic marinara sauce (no added sugars)
- 1 cup organic spinach leaves
- 1/2 cup organic cherry tomatoes, halved
- 1/4 cup organic Kalamata olives, pitted and halved
- 1/4 cup organic red onion, thinly sliced
- 1/4 cup organic feta cheese, crumbled (or dairy-free feta alternative)
- 2 tbsp organic pine nuts, toasted
- 1 tbsp organic fresh basil, chopped

For Drizzling:
- 2 tbsp organic extra-virgin olive oil
- 1 tbsp organic balsamic glaze (optional)

Instructions:
1. Preheat your oven to 375°F (190°C). Line a baking sheet with parchment paper.
2. In a large bowl, combine almond flour, coconut flour, melted coconut oil, beaten eggs, sea salt, garlic powder, and dried oregano. Mix until a dough forms.

3. Transfer the dough to the prepared baking sheet and press it into a round or rectangular shape, about 1/4-inch thick.
4. Bake the crust for 10 minutes, then remove from the oven and set aside.
5. Spread the marinara sauce evenly over the pre-baked crust and layer the spinach leaves, cherry tomatoes, Kalamata olives, and red onion over the sauce. Sprinkle the crumbled feta cheese evenly over the toppings.
6. Return the pizza to the oven and bake for an additional 10-15 minutes, until the crust is golden and the toppings are heated through.
7. Remove the pizza from the oven and sprinkle with toasted pine nuts and chopped basil and drizzle with extra-virgin olive oil and balsamic glaze (if using) before serving.

Tip: For a crispier crust, you can bake the crust for an additional 5 minutes before adding the toppings.

Nutritional Information (per serving):
- Calories: 350
- Protein: 12g
- Fat: 28g
- Carbohydrates: 16g
- Fiber: 6g

DUKKAH-ROASTED CARROTS WITH GOAT CHEESE AND TOASTED ALMONDS

Prep Time: 15 minutes
Cook Time: 25 minutes
Serves: 4

Ingredients:
- 1 lb organic carrots, peeled and cut into 1-inch pieces
- 2 tbsp organic dukkah
- 2 tbsp organic avocado oil
- 1/4 cup organic goat cheese, crumbled
- 1/4 cup organic almonds, slivered and toasted
- Sea salt and black pepper to taste

Instructions:
1. Preheat oven to 400°F (200°C).
2. Toss carrots with dukkah and avocado oil. Spread on a baking sheet.
3. Roast for 20-25 minutes, until tender and slightly caramelized.
4. Transfer carrots to a serving dish and sprinkle with crumbled goat cheese and toasted almonds.

Tip: Serve with marinated grilled tempeh for a complete meal

Nutritional Information (per serving):
- Calories: 280
- Protein: 6g
- Fat: 20g
- Carbohydrates: 22g
- Fiber: 6g

VEGAN

CARROT NOODLES WITH ALMOND BUTTER SAUCE AND TOFU

Prep Time: 10 minutes
Cook Time: 15 minutes
Serves: 4

Ingredients:
- 3 large organic carrots, spiralized
- 1 block organic tofu, cubed
- 2 tbsp organic almond butter
- 1 tbsp organic coconut aminos
- 1 tbsp organic lime juice
- 1 tbsp organic sesame oil

Instructions:
1. Cook the Tofu: Heat sesame oil in a pan over medium heat. Cook tofu cubes until crispy, about 5-6 minutes. Set aside.
2. Make the Almond Butter Sauce: Whisk together almond butter, coconut aminos, and lime juice until smooth.
3. Sauté the Carrot Noodles: Lightly sauté carrot noodles for 3-4 minutes until tender.
4. Serve: Toss the noodles with almond butter sauce and top with crispy tofu.

Tip: Almond butter sauce adds a creamy, nutty flavor that pairs well with the sweetness of carrot noodles.

Nutritional Information (per serving):
- Calories: 280
- Protein: 13g
- Fat: 18g
- Carbohydrates: 18g
- Fiber: 5g

GUT-HEALING KITCHARI WITH FERMENTED VEGETABLES

Prep Time: 15 minutes
Cook Time: 30 minutes
Serves: 2

Ingredients:
- For the Kitchari:
  - 1/2 cup organic yellow split mung beans, soaked overnight
  - 1/4 cup organic cauliflower rice (grain-free alternative)
  - 1 tbsp organic ghee or coconut oil
  - 1 tsp organic cumin seeds
  - 1 tsp organic turmeric powder
  - 1 tsp organic ginger, minced
  - 1 tsp organic coriander powder
  - 1/2 tsp organic cinnamon (for warmth and sweetness)
  - 1 small organic zucchini, diced
  - 1/2 cup organic spinach, chopped
  - Sea salt to taste
  - 1/2 cup organic raw sauerkraut (unpasteurized, probiotic-rich)

Instructions:
1. Cook the Mung Beans: Rinse the soaked mung beans and cook them in a pot with 2 cups of water. Bring to a boil, then simmer for 20-25 minutes until tender.
2. Prepare the Kitchari: In a separate pan, heat ghee or coconut oil over medium heat. Add cumin seeds and toast until fragrant. Stir in ginger, turmeric, coriander, and cinnamon. Add diced zucchini and cauliflower rice. Cook for 5-7 minutes until the vegetables are tender.
3. Mix and Simmer: Add the cooked mung beans to the vegetable mixture, stirring well to combine. Simmer for another 5 minutes to let the flavors meld. Stir in the chopped spinach just before serving.
4. Serve: Spoon the kitchari into bowls and serve with a side of raw sauerkraut for a probiotic-rich boost. Garnish with fresh cilantro and a drizzle of ghee for added richness.

Nutritional Information (per serving):
- Calories: 320
- Protein: 13g
- Fat: 14g
- Carbohydrates: 38g
- Fiber: 9g

PROVENÇAL RATATOUILLE STUFFED PORTOBELLO MUSHROOMS WITH COCONUT KEFIR DRIZZLE

Prep Time: 25 minutes
Cook Time: 35 minutes
Serves: 4

Ingredients:
- 4 large organic portobello mushrooms
- 1 organic zucchini, diced
- 1 organic yellow squash, diced
- 1 organic eggplant, diced
- 1 organic red bell pepper, diced
- 1 organic yellow bell pepper, diced
- 1 organic red onion, diced
- 3 organic garlic cloves, minced
- 1/4 cup organic extra-virgin olive oil
- 1 tbsp organic herbs de Provence
- 1/4 cup organic fresh basil, chiffonade
- 1/4 cup organic coconut kefir
- Sea salt and freshly ground black pepper to taste

Instructions:
1. Preheat oven to 400°F (200°C).
2. Remove stems from mushrooms and gently scrape out gills. Brush with olive oil and season with salt and pepper.
3. In a large skillet, heat remaining olive oil. Sauté onion and garlic until fragrant.
4. Add zucchini, squash, eggplant, and bell peppers. Cook for 15 minutes, stirring occasionally.
5. Stir in herbs de Provence, salt, and pepper.
6. Fill mushroom caps with the ratatouille mixture.
7. Bake for 20-25 minutes until mushrooms are tender.
8. Garnish with fresh basil and drizzle with coconut kefir before serving.

Tip: For extra flavor, grill the mushroom caps for 2-3 minutes per side before stuffing and baking.

Nutritional Information (per serving):
- Calories: 230
- Protein: 5g
- Fat: 18g
- Carbohydrates: 18g
- Fiber: 6g

NAVY BEAN AND SPINACH STUFFED BELL PEPPERS WITH AVOCADO CREAM

Prep Time: 25 minutes
Cook Time: 30 minutes
Serves: 4

Ingredients:
- 4 large organic bell peppers, tops cut off and seeds removed
- 2 cups cooked organic navy beans
- 1 cup organic spinach, chopped
- 1 organic onion, finely chopped
- 2 organic garlic cloves, minced
- 1 tbsp organic coconut oil
- 1 tsp organic cumin

- 1 tsp organic paprika
- Sea salt and black pepper to taste
- 1 large organic avocado
- 1/4 cup coconut yogurt
- 1 tbsp organic lime juice
- 1/4 cup organic fresh cilantro, chopped

Instructions:
1. Preheat the oven to 375°F (190°C).
2. In a skillet, heat coconut oil over medium heat. Sauté onion and garlic until softened.
3. Add navy beans, spinach, cumin, paprika, salt, and pepper. Cook until spinach is wilted.
4. Stuff the bell peppers with the navy bean mixture and place in a baking dish.
5. Bake for 25-30 minutes until peppers are tender.
6. In a blender, combine avocado, coconut yogurt, lime juice, and cilantro. Blend until smooth.
7. Serve stuffed peppers with a dollop of avocado cream.

Tip: For a smoky flavor, char the bell peppers over an open flame before stuffing and baking.

Nutritional Information (per serving):
- Calories: 310
- Protein: 9g
- Fat: 18g
- Carbohydrates: 33g
- Fiber: 11g

NAVY BEAN AND MUSHROOM STUFFED ACORN SQUASH

Prep Time: 15 minutes
Cook Time: 45 minutes
Serves: 4

Ingredients:
- 2 large organic acorn squash, halved and seeded
- 2 cups cooked organic navy beans
- 1 lb organic mushrooms (any variety), chopped
- 1 organic onion, diced
- 2 organic garlic cloves, minced
- 1 tbsp organic coconut oil
- 1 tsp organic thyme
- 1 tsp organic rosemary
- Sea salt and black pepper to taste
- 1/4 cup organic fresh parsley, chopped

Instructions:
1. Preheat the oven to 400°F (200°C).
2. Rub acorn squash halves with a little coconut oil, salt, and pepper. Place cut side down on a baking sheet and roast for 30 minutes, until tender.
3. In a skillet, heat remaining coconut oil over medium heat. Sauté onion, garlic, and mushrooms until softened and browned.
4. Stir in navy beans, thyme, rosemary, salt, and pepper. Cook until heated through.
5. Remove squash from the oven and fill each half with the mushroom and navy bean mixture.
6. Return to oven and bake for an additional 10-15 minutes.
7. Garnish with fresh parsley before serving.

Tip: For a nutty flavor, sprinkle a handful of toasted pine nuts over the filling before serving.

Nutritional Information (per serving):
- Calories: 360
- Protein: 11g
- Fat: 10g
- Carbohydrates: 62g
- Fiber: 13g

CAULIFLOWER STEAKS WITH MISO TAHINI SAUCE AND PICKLED RADISH

Prep Time: 15 minutes
Cook Time: 25 minutes
Serves: 4

Ingredients:
- 1 large head organic cauliflower, cut into thick slices (steaks)
- 3 tbsp organic avocado oil
- 1 tbsp organic garlic powder
- Sea salt and freshly ground black pepper to taste
- 1/4 cup organic tahini
- 2 tbsp organic miso paste (no added sugar)
- 1 tbsp organic apple cider vinegar
- 1/4 cup water (to thin the sauce)
- 1 cup organic radishes, thinly sliced
- 1/4 cup organic rice vinegar (for pickling)

Instructions:
1. Preheat oven to 425°F (220°C).
2. Brush cauliflower steaks with avocado oil and season with garlic powder, salt, and pepper.
3. Roast cauliflower in the oven for 20-25 minutes until golden brown and tender.
4. In a bowl, whisk together tahini, miso paste, apple cider vinegar, and enough water to achieve a smooth sauce.
5. For pickled radish, combine sliced radishes and rice vinegar in a bowl. Let sit for 10 minutes.
6. Serve cauliflower steaks drizzled with miso tahini sauce and topped with pickled radish.

Tip: For extra flavor, add roasted sesame seeds on top of the cauliflower steaks before serving.

Nutritional Information (per serving):
- Calories: 240
- Protein: 5g
- Fat: 19g
- Carbohydrates: 15g
- Fiber: 5g

BLACK BEAN AND SWEET POTATO TACOS WITH AVOCADO LIME CREAM

Prep Time: 20 minutes
Cook Time: 30 minutes
Serves: 4

Ingredients:
- 2 cups cooked organic black beans
- 2 large organic sweet potatoes, peeled and diced
- 1 organic red onion, chopped
- 2 organic garlic cloves, minced
- 1 tbsp organic coconut oil
- 1 tsp organic cumin
- 1 tsp organic smoked paprika
- Sea salt and black pepper to taste
- 1 large organic avocado
- 1/4 cup coconut yogurt
- 1 organic lime, juiced
- 1/4 cup organic fresh cilantro, chopped
- 8 large organic lettuce leaves (for taco shells)
- 1/2 cup organic fermented vegetables (like sauerkraut or kimchi), drained

Instructions:
1. Preheat oven to 400°F (200°C).
2. Toss diced sweet potatoes with coconut oil, cumin, smoked paprika, salt, and pepper. Spread on a baking sheet and roast for 25-30 minutes, until tender and slightly caramelized.

3. In a skillet, sauté onion and garlic over medium heat until softened, about 5 minutes. Add black beans and cook until heated through.
4. In a blender, combine avocado, coconut yogurt, lime juice, salt, and half the cilantro. Blend until smooth to make the avocado lime cream.
5. Assemble tacos by filling lettuce leaves with roasted sweet potatoes, black beans, a dollop of avocado lime cream, and a spoonful of fermented vegetables.
6. Garnish with remaining cilantro before serving.

Tip: For extra flavor, roast the sweet potatoes until they have slightly crispy edges. This adds a delicious contrast in texture to the soft black beans and creamy avocado.

Nutritional Information (per serving):
- Calories: 380
- Protein: 9g
- Fat: 17g
- Carbohydrates: 54g
- Fiber: 14g

BLACK BEAN AND ZUCCHINI FRITTERS WITH AVOCADO CREMA

Prep Time: 20 minutes
Cook Time: 15 minutes
Serves: 4

Ingredients:
- 2 cups cooked organic black beans, mashed
- 2 medium organic zucchini, grated and squeezed dry
- 2 organic eggs, beaten
- 1/4 cup organic coconut flour
- 1 tsp organic garlic powder
- 1 tsp organic onion powder
- 2 tbsp organic avocado oil for frying
- 1 large organic avocado
- 1/4 cup organic coconut yogurt
- 1 organic lime, juiced
- Sea salt and black pepper to taste

Instructions:
1. Mix mashed beans, zucchini, eggs, coconut flour, garlic powder, and onion powder.
2. Form into small patties.
3. Heat avocado oil in a skillet over medium heat. Fry fritters for 3-4 minutes per side.
4. Blend avocado, coconut yogurt, and lime juice for the crema.
5. Serve fritters with avocado crema.

Tip: Let the batter rest for 10 minutes before forming patties to allow the coconut flour to absorb moisture.

Nutritional Information (per serving):
- Calories: 330
- Protein: 11g
- Fat: 21g
- Carbohydrates: 27g
- Fiber: 10g

VEGAN POWER BUDDHA BOWL WITH TAHINI DRESSING

Prep Time: 20 minutes
Cook Time: 30 minutes
Serves: 4

Ingredients:
- 2 cups cooked organic black beans
- 1 organic sweet potato, cubed
- 1 organic zucchini, sliced
- 1 organic red bell pepper, sliced
- 1 organic red onion, sliced
- 2 cups organic kale, chopped
- 2 tbsp organic coconut oil, melted
- 1/4 cup organic tahini
- 2 tbsp organic lemon juice
- 1 organic garlic clove, minced

- 1/4 cup water
- Sea salt and black pepper to taste

Instructions:
1. Preheat oven to 400°F (200°C).
2. Toss sweet potato, zucchini, bell pepper, and onion with melted coconut oil. Roast for 25-30 minutes.
3. Steam kale for 2-3 minutes until bright green.
4. For the dressing, whisk tahini, lemon juice, garlic, and water until smooth.
5. Assemble bowls with black beans, roasted vegetables, and kale. Drizzle with tahini dressing.

Tip: For crispier vegetables, arrange them in a single layer on the baking sheet and avoid overcrowding.

Nutritional Information (per serving):
- Calories: 380
- Protein: 12g
- Fat: 18g
- Carbohydrates: 45g
- Fiber: 13g

STUFFED SWEET POTATOES WITH FERMENTED RED CABBAGE

Prep Time: 20 minutes
Cook Time: 45 minutes
Serves: 4

Ingredients:
- 4 medium organic sweet potatoes
- 1 1/2 cups cooked organic black beans
- 1 large organic avocado, mashed
- 1/4 cup organic coconut yogurt
- 1 tbsp organic lime juice
- 1 tsp organic chili powder
- Sea salt and black pepper to taste
- 1/2 cup organic fermented red cabbage

Instructions:
1. Preheat oven to 400°F (200°C). Pierce sweet potatoes with a fork and bake for 40-45 minutes until tender.
2. In a bowl, mash the avocado and mix with black beans, coconut yogurt, lime juice, chili powder, salt, and pepper.
3. Slice the baked sweet potatoes in half lengthwise. Scoop out the flesh, leaving a thin layer attached to the skin.
4. Mash the sweet potato flesh and fold it into the black bean and avocado mixture.
5. Spoon the mixture back into the sweet potato skins.
6. Serve the stuffed sweet potatoes topped with a dollop of fermented red cabbage.

Tip: Bake the sweet potatoes a day in advance to save time on assembly.

Nutritional Information (per serving):
- Calories: 400
- Protein: 10g
- Fat: 15g
- Carbohydrates: 61g
- Fiber: 14g

CHIA AND BLACK BEAN VEGGIE BURGERS WITH AVOCADO LIME SAUCE

Prep Time: 20 minutes (plus 30 minutes chilling)
Cook Time: 15 minutes
Serves: 4

Ingredients:
- 2 cups cooked organic black beans, mashed
- 1/2 cup organic chia seeds
- 1/2 cup organic grated carrot
- 1/4 cup organic red onion, finely chopped
- 2 organic garlic cloves, minced
- 1 tsp organic ground cumin
- 1 tsp organic smoked paprika
- 2 tbsp organic coconut flour

- Sea salt and black pepper to taste
- 2 tbsp organic coconut oil
- 1 large organic avocado
- 1 organic lime, juiced
- 2 tbsp organic coconut yogurt
- 4 large organic lettuce leaves

Instructions:
1. In a bowl, mix mashed black beans, chia seeds, grated carrot, red onion, garlic, cumin, smoked paprika, coconut flour, salt, and pepper. Form into 4 patties.
2. Chill patties in the refrigerator for 30 minutes to firm up.
3. Heat coconut oil in a skillet over medium heat. Cook patties for 4-5 minutes per side until crispy and heated through.
4. In a blender, combine avocado, lime juice, and coconut yogurt until smooth. Season with salt.
5. Serve patties on lettuce leaves, topped with avocado lime sauce.

Tip: For extra flavor, add a splash of coconut aminos to the black bean mixture before forming into patties.

Nutritional Information (per serving):
- Calories: 390
- Protein: 13g
- Fat: 23g
- Carbohydrates: 38g
- Fiber: 17g

LENTIL AND WALNUT STUFFED PEPPERS WITH COCONUT-HERB SAUCE

Prep Time: 25 minutes
Cook Time: 35 minutes
Serves: 4

Ingredients:
- 1 cup organic green lentils, cooked
- 1/2 cup organic walnuts, chopped
- 4 large organic bell peppers, halved and deseeded
- 1 organic onion, diced
- 2 organic celery stalks, diced
- 2 organic garlic cloves, minced
- 1 tsp organic cumin
- 1 tsp organic paprika
- 2 tbsp organic avocado oil
- 1/2 cup organic coconut yogurt
- 1/4 cup organic fresh herbs (mix of parsley, cilantro, mint), chopped
- 1 organic lemon, juiced
- Sea salt and black pepper to taste

Instructions:
1. Preheat oven to 375°F (190°C).
2. In a skillet, heat avocado oil. Sauté onion, celery, and garlic until softened.
3. Add lentils, walnuts, cumin, and paprika. Cook for 5 minutes.
4. Stuff bell pepper halves with the lentil mixture.
5. Bake for 25-30 minutes until peppers are tender.
6. Mix coconut yogurt with herbs and lemon juice for the sauce.
7. Serve stuffed peppers with coconut-herb sauce.

Tip: For added flavor, roast the bell peppers for 10 minutes before stuffing.

Nutritional Information (per serving):
- Calories: 320
- Protein: 12g
- Fat: 18g
- Carbohydrates: 32g
- Fiber: 10g

LENTIL AND WILD MUSHROOM "RISOTTO" WITH TRUFFLE OIL AND CRISPY KALE

Prep Time: 20 minutes
Cook Time: 30 minutes
Serves: 4

Ingredients:
- 1 cup organic black lentils
- 2 cups mixed wild organic mushrooms, sliced
- 1 organic onion, finely diced
- 2 organic garlic cloves, minced
- 2 cups organic vegetable broth
- 2 tbsp organic ghee
- 1 tbsp organic truffle oil
- 1/4 cup organic nutritional yeast
- 2 cups organic kale, torn into bite-sized pieces
- 1 tbsp organic avocado oil
- Sea salt and black pepper to taste

Instructions:
1. Cook lentils in vegetable broth until tender but still firm, about 20 minutes.
2. In a large skillet, heat 1 tbsp ghee. Sauté onion and garlic until translucent.
3. Add mushrooms and cook until they release their moisture.
4. Stir in cooked lentils and remaining ghee. Simmer for 5 minutes.
5. Fold in nutritional yeast and truffle oil.
6. For crispy kale, toss kale with avocado oil and salt. Bake at 350°F (175°C) for 10-12 minutes until crisp.
7. Serve "risotto" topped with crispy kale.

Tip: For a creamier texture, purée 1/4 of the cooked lentils before adding to the skillet.

Nutritional Information (per serving):
- Calories: 300
- Protein: 9g
- Fat: 20g
- Carbohydrates: 27g
- Fiber: 9g

LENTIL AND VEGETABLE "LASAGNA" WITH BERBERE SPICE

Prep Time: 30 minutes
Cook Time: 45 minutes
Serves: 6

Ingredients:
- 2 cups cooked organic brown lentils
- 2 large organic zucchini, sliced lengthwise
- 1 large organic eggplant, sliced lengthwise
- 1 organic onion, diced
- 3 organic garlic cloves, minced
- 1 can (14 oz) organic crushed tomatoes
- 1 cup organic cashews, soaked and blended with 1/2 cup water
- 2 tbsp organic berbere spice blend (see below for homemade)
- 2 tbsp organic extra-virgin olive oil
- 1/4 cup organic fresh basil, chopped
- Sea salt and black pepper to taste

Instructions:
1. Preheat oven to 375°F (190°C).
2. Grill or roast zucchini and eggplant slices until tender.
3. In a skillet, sauté onion and garlic in avocado oil until softened.
4. Add lentils, crushed tomatoes, and berbere spice. Simmer for 10 minutes.
5. In a baking dish, layer zucchini, lentil mixture, eggplant, and cashew cream.
6. Repeat layers, ending with cashew cream on top.
7. Bake for 30 minutes until bubbly and golden.

8. Garnish with fresh basil before serving.

Tip: For a firmer "lasagna", let it rest for 10-15 minutes after baking before cutting and serving.

Make your own Berbere Spice Blend:
Ingredients:

- 2 parts red chili peppers (like arbol peppers)
- 2 parts paprika
- 1 part fenugreek seeds
- 1 part coriander seeds
- 1 part black peppercorns
- 1 part ginger
- 1/2 part cardamom pods
- 1/2 part cinnamon
- 1/4 part cloves
- 1/4 part allspice berries
- 1/4 part nutmeg
- 1/4 part garlic powder
- 1/4 part onion flakes

Instructions:
1. Toast whole spices until fragrant.
2. Let spices cool, then grind to a fine powder.
3. Mix in pre-ground spices.
4. Store in an airtight container.

Nutritional Information (per serving):
- Calories: 340
- Protein: 13g
- Fat: 18g
- Carbohydrates: 37g
- Fiber: 12g

ROASTED EGGPLANT WITH YOGURT AND FERMENTED CARROTS

Prep Time: 10 minutes
Cook Time: 25 minutes
Serves: 4

Ingredients:

- 2 large organic eggplants, halved lengthwise
- 2 tbsp organic avocado oil
- Sea salt and black pepper to taste
- 1 cup organic coconut yogurt
- 1/2 cup organic fermented carrots, finely chopped
- 2 tbsp organic fresh dill, chopped
- 1 organic lemon, zest and juice

Instructions:
1. Preheat the oven to 400°F (200°C).
2. Score the cut side of the eggplant halves in a cross-hatch pattern. Brush with avocado oil and season with salt and pepper.
3. Roast cut-side up for 25 minutes until the flesh is very tender.
4. Mix coconut yogurt with lemon zest, lemon juice, and a pinch of salt.
5. Remove eggplants from the oven, let cool slightly, then top with yogurt, fermented carrots, and fresh dill.

Tip: Scoring the eggplant helps it cook more evenly and allows it to absorb more flavor.

Nutritional Information (per serving):
- Calories: 220
- Protein: 5g
- Fat: 18g
- Carbohydrates: 12g
- Fiber: 6g

EGGPLANT AND CHICKPEA TAGINE WITH PRESERVED LEMON

Prep Time: 20 minutes
Cook Time: 40 minutes
Serves: 4

Ingredients:

- 1 large organic eggplant, cubed
- 1 can (14 oz) organic chickpeas, drained and rinsed
- 1 organic onion, diced
- 2 organic garlic cloves, minced
- 1 organic red bell pepper, diced
- 1 organic carrot, diced
- 1 can (14 oz) organic diced tomatoes
- 1 organic preserved lemon, finely chopped (preferably homemade, see recipe)
- 1 tsp organic ground cumin
- 1 tsp organic ground coriander
- 1/2 tsp organic ground cinnamon
- 2 tbsp organic extra-virgin olive oil
- Sea salt and black pepper to taste
- 1/4 cup organic fresh cilantro, chopped

Instructions:
1. Heat olive oil in a large pot over medium heat. Sauté onion, garlic, and red bell pepper until softened.
2. Add eggplant, carrot, chickpeas, diced tomatoes, preserved lemon, cumin, coriander, cinnamon, salt, and pepper. Stir well.
3. Cover and simmer for 30-35 minutes until the vegetables are tender and the flavors meld.
4. Serve hot, garnished with fresh cilantro.

Tip: For deeper flavor, cook the tagine in a traditional clay tagine pot if you have one.

Nutritional Information (per serving):
- Calories: 300
- Protein: 8g
- Fat: 14g
- Carbohydrates: 38g
- Fiber: 12g

TEMPEH STIR-FRY WITH GINGER-SESAME SAUCE

Prep Time: 15 minutes
Cook Time: 15 minutes
Serves: 4

Ingredients:

- 3 packages organic tempeh, cut into strips
- 1 organic red bell pepper, sliced
- 2 organic garlic cloves, minced
- 1 tbsp organic ginger, grated
- 2 tbsp organic coconut aminos
- 1 tbsp organic sesame oil
- 2 tbsp organic coconut oil
- 1 tbsp organic sesame seeds
- Sea salt and black pepper to taste

Instructions:
1. Heat oil in a large skillet or wok over medium-high heat. Add tempeh and cook until browned on all sides, about 3-4 minutes. Remove and set aside.
2. In the same skillet, add bell pepper, garlic, and ginger. Stir-fry for 5-7 minutes until vegetables are tender-crisp.
3. Stir in coconut aminos, sesame oil, salt, and pepper.
4. Return tempeh to the skillet and toss to combine. Cook for another 2 minutes to heat through.
5. Serve hot, garnished with sesame seeds.

Tip: For a more vibrant color and texture, blanch the tempeh slices in boiling water for 2 minutes before stir-frying.

Nutritional Information (per serving):
- Calories: 350, Protein: 18g, Fat: 22g, Carbohydrates: 10g, Fiber: 3g

TEMPEH AND SWEET POTATO HASH WITH FERMENTED CHILI PASTE

Prep Time: 20 minutes
Cook Time: 20 minutes
Serves: 4

Ingredients:

- 1 block (8 oz) organic tempeh, crumbled
- 2 large organic sweet potatoes, peeled and diced
- 1 organic red onion, diced
- 2 organic garlic cloves, minced
- 1 organic red bell pepper, diced
- 2 tbsp organic coconut oil
- Sea salt and black pepper to taste
- 2 tbsp organic fermented chili paste (such as gochujang)

For Serving:

- 1/4 cup organic coconut yogurt
- 1/4 cup organic fresh cilantro, chopped

Instructions:

1. In a large skillet, heat oil over medium heat. Add diced sweet potatoes and cook for 10 minutes until tender.
2. Add crumbled tempeh, red onion, garlic, and bell pepper. Cook for another 5-7 minutes until vegetables are softened.
3. Stir in fermented chili paste, salt, and pepper. Cook for another 2 minutes until heated through.
4. Serve hot, topped with a dollop of coconut yogurt and chopped cilantro.

Tip: For extra flavor, roast the sweet potatoes in the oven at 400°F (200°C) for 15-20 minutes before adding them to the skillet.

Nutritional Information (per serving):

- Calories: 400
- Protein: 16g
- Fat: 24g
- Carbohydrates: 36g
- Fiber: 8g

TEMPEH "TUNA" SALAD LETTUCE WRAPS

Prep Time: 15 minutes
Cook Time: 10 minutes
Serves: 4

Ingredients:

- 8 oz organic tempeh, crumbled
- 1/2 cup organic celery, finely chopped
- 1/4 cup organic red onion, finely chopped
- 2 tbsp organic mayonnaise (preferably homemade, see recipe)
- 1 tbsp organic lemon juice
- 1 tbsp organic dill pickle relish
- 1/2 tsp organic Dijon mustard
- Sea salt and black pepper to taste
- 8 large organic lettuce leaves (butter lettuce or romaine)

Instructions:

1. Steam crumbled tempeh for 10 minutes, then let cool.
2. In a bowl, combine steamed tempeh, celery, red onion, mayonnaise, lemon juice, dill pickle relish, Dijon mustard, salt, and pepper. Mix well.
3. Spoon the tempeh "tuna" salad into lettuce leaves and serve.

Tip: For a more pronounced "tuna" flavor, add a teaspoon of kelp granules or dulse flakes to the tempeh mixture.

Nutritional Information (per serving):

- Calories: 280
- Protein: 14g
- Fat: 20g
- Carbohydrates: 8g
- Fiber: 3g

KONJAC RICE SUSHI ROLLS WITH AVOCADO AND FERMENTED VEGETABLES

Prep Time: 25 minutes
Cook Time: 0 minutes
Serves: 4

Ingredients:

- 1 package (14 oz) organic konjac rice, rinsed and drained
- 4 sheets organic nori
- 1 large organic avocado, sliced
- 1 cup organic shredded carrots
- 1 cup organic cucumber, julienned
- 1/2 cup organic fermented vegetables (such as sauerkraut or kimchi)
- 2 tbsp organic coconut aminos
- 1 tbsp organic rice vinegar
- 1 tbsp organic sesame seeds

Instructions:

1. In a bowl, mix konjac rice with coconut aminos and rice vinegar.
2. Place a sheet of nori on a bamboo sushi mat. Spread a thin layer of the seasoned konjac rice over the nori, leaving a 1-inch border at the top.
3. Arrange avocado slices, shredded carrots, cucumber, and fermented vegetables along the bottom edge of the rice.
4. Roll the sushi tightly using the bamboo mat, sealing the edge with a bit of water.
5. Repeat with the remaining ingredients.
6. Slice the sushi rolls into bite-sized pieces and sprinkle with sesame seeds before serving.

Tip: For a more cohesive roll, press the konjac rice firmly onto the nori before adding the fillings.

Nutritional Information (per serving):

- Calories: 250
- Protein: 4g
- Fat: 12g
- Carbohydrates: 28g
- Fiber: 10g

LIMA BEAN CASSOULET WITH ZUCCHINI AND BUTTERNUT SQUASH

Prep Time: 20 minutes
Cook Time: 45 minutes
Serves: 4

Ingredients:
For the Cassoulet:

- 1 cup dried organic lima beans (or 2 cups cooked), soaked overnight and drained
- 1 medium organic butternut squash, peeled and cubed
- 2 medium organic zucchinis, sliced
- 1 large organic onion, diced
- 3 organic garlic cloves, minced
- 1 organic carrot, peeled and diced
- 1 organic celery stalk, diced
- 4 cups organic vegetable broth
- 1 can (14 oz) organic diced tomatoes
- 2 tbsp organic tomato paste
- 2 tbsp organic extra-virgin olive oil
- 1 tbsp organic fresh thyme leaves
- 1 tbsp organic fresh rosemary, chopped
- 2 bay leaves
- Sea salt and black pepper to taste

For Topping:

- 1/4 cup organic almond flour
- 2 tbsp organic pine nuts, toasted
- 2 tbsp organic fresh parsley, chopped

Instructions:

1. If using dried lima beans, rinse and soak them overnight. Drain and rinse before using. If using cooked lima beans, ensure they are drained and ready.
2. Heat olive oil in a large pot or Dutch oven over medium heat. Add the diced onion, carrot, and celery. Sauté until softened, about 5-7 minutes.
3. Add the minced garlic, butternut squash, and zucchini. Cook for another 3-4 minutes.
4. Stir in the soaked lima beans, diced tomatoes, tomato paste, vegetable broth, thyme, rosemary, bay leaves, salt, and pepper.
5. Bring the mixture to a boil, then reduce the heat and simmer for 35-40 minutes, or until the lima beans and vegetables are tender. If using pre-cooked lima beans, add them in the last 15 minutes of cooking.
6. In a small bowl, mix almond flour, toasted pine nuts, and chopped parsley.
7. Remove the bay leaves from the cassoulet and discard, then sprinkle the almond flour topping over the cassoulet before serving for a bit of crunch and extra flavor.

Tip: For a deeper flavor, you can roast the butternut squash cubes in the oven at 400°F (200°C) for 20 minutes before adding them to the cassoulet.

Nutritional Information (per serving):

- Calories: 380
- Protein: 12g
- Fat: 18g
- Carbohydrates: 46g
- Fiber: 12g

HEART-HEALTHY AND HEART-WARMING SOUPS, CURRIES, AND STEWS

We all need comfort and warmth from our food sometimes, but unfortunately, we don't easily identify comfort food with healthy foods. These comforting soups, curries, and stews are nutritionally balanced and exceptionally delicious.

HIGH-PROTEIN SOUPS, STEWS, AND CURRIES

MINESTRONE-STYLE SOUP WITH MEATBALLS

Prep Time: 30 minutes
Cook Time: 40 minutes **Total Time:** 1 hour 10 minutes
Serves: 6

Soup Ingredients:

- 6 cups organic chicken or beef bone broth
- 2 organic zucchini, diced
- 1 organic yellow squash, diced
- 1 organic red bell pepper, diced
- 1 organic onion, diced
- 3 organic garlic cloves, minced
- 2 tbsp organic extra-virgin olive oil
- 1 tsp sea salt
- 1/2 tsp organic black pepper
- 1/4 cup organic fresh basil leaves, torn
- 1/4 cup organic fermented vegetables (like sauerkraut or kimchi), chopped

Meatball Ingredients:

- 1 lb organic, grass-fed ground beef
- 1/4 cup organic almond flour
- 1/4 cup organic grated Parmesan cheese
- 1 organic egg, beaten
- 1 tsp organic Italian seasoning (see below for homemade)
- 1/2 tsp sea salt
- 1/4 tsp organic black pepper

Instructions:

1. In a large bowl, mix together the meatball ingredients until well combined. Form into 1-inch meatballs and set aside.
2. In a large pot, heat avocado oil over medium heat. Add onion and garlic, and cook until softened, about 5 minutes.
3. Stir in zucchini, yellow squash, bell pepper, salt, and black pepper. Cook for 5 minutes, stirring occasionally.
4. Pour in bone broth and bring to a simmer. Carefully add the meatballs to the soup and simmer, partially covered, for 25 minutes or until meatballs are cooked through and vegetables are tender.
5. Remove from heat and stir in fresh basil and fermented vegetables.
6. Ladle soup into bowls, ensuring each serving includes meatballs and vegetables.

Tips:

- For a spicier soup, add a pinch of organic red pepper flakes or cayenne pepper.
- Grate Parmesan cheese over each serving for added flavor and richness.
- Bone broth and grass-fed beef provide gut-healing nutrients and satiating protein, while low-carb vegetables

offer fiber and micronutrients. Fermented vegetables add beneficial probiotics for gut health.

Nutritional Information (per serving):
- Calories: 350
- Protein: 25g
- Fat: 22g
- Carbohydrates: 12g
- Fiber: 3g

HOMEMADE ITALIAN SEASONING

Prep Time: 10 minutes
Serves: 12-15 servings

Ingredients:
- 2 parts dried basil
- 2 parts dried oregano
- 2 parts dried parsley
- 1 part dried rosemary
- 1 part dried thyme
- 1 part garlic powder
- Optional: 1/2 part red pepper flakes

Instructions:
1. Combine all ingredients in a bowl and mix well.
2. Store in an airtight container in a cool, dry place for up to 6 months.

CREAMY CAULIFLOWER SOUP WITH CRISPY PANCETTA AND SAGE

Prep Time: 20 minutes
Cook Time: 30 minutes
Serves: 4

Soup Ingredients:
- 1 large organic cauliflower head, chopped
- 4 cups organic chicken bone broth
- 1 cup organic full-fat coconut milk
- 1 organic onion, chopped
- 3 organic garlic cloves, minced
- 2 tbsp organic grass-fed ghee
- 1 tsp sea salt
- 1/2 tsp organic black pepper
- 1/4 tsp organic nutmeg

Topping Ingredients:
- 4 oz organic, pasture-raised pancetta, diced
- 1 tbsp organic avocado oil
- 1/4 cup organic sage leaves
- 1/4 cup organic fermented vegetables (like sauerkraut or kimchi), chopped

Instructions:
1. In a large pot, melt ghee over medium heat. Add onion and garlic, and cook until softened, about 5 minutes.
2. Stir in cauliflower, salt, black pepper, and nutmeg. Cook for 5 minutes, stirring occasionally.
3. Pour in chicken broth and bring to a boil. Reduce heat to low and simmer, partially covered, for 20 minutes or until cauliflower is tender.
4. While the soup simmers, prepare the toppings. In a skillet, heat avocado oil over medium heat. Add pancetta and cook until crispy, about 5 minutes. Remove with a slotted spoon and set aside.
5. In the same skillet, fry sage leaves until crispy, about 1 minute. Remove and set aside.
6. Remove soup from heat and stir in coconut milk. Using an immersion blender, puree the soup until smooth and creamy.
7. Ladle soup into bowls and top with crispy pancetta, fried sage leaves, and fermented vegetables.

Tips:
- For a vegetarian version, omit pancetta and use organic vegetable broth instead of chicken broth.

- Roast the cauliflower before adding to the soup for a deeper, nuttier flavor.
- Coconut milk and ghee provide satiating, anti-inflammatory healthy fats, while cauliflower offers fiber and micronutrients. Fermented vegetables add beneficial probiotics for gut health.

Nutritional Information (per serving):
- Calories: 356
- Protein: 12 g
- Fat: 30 g
- Carbohydrates: 15 g
- Fiber: 4 g

MEXICAN CHICKEN TORTILLA-LESS SOUP

Prep Time: 20 minutes
Cook Time: 30 minutes
Serves: 6

Ingredients:
- 1 lb organic, pasture-raised chicken breasts, cut into bite-sized pieces
- 4 cups organic chicken bone broth
- 1 can (14 oz) organic, fire-roasted diced tomatoes
- 1 organic red bell pepper, diced
- 1 organic jalapeno pepper, seeded and minced
- 1 organic onion, diced
- 3 organic garlic cloves, minced
- 2 tbsp organic avocado oil
- 2 tsp organic ground cumin
- 1 tsp organic smoked paprika
- 1 tsp sea salt
- 1/2 tsp organic black pepper
- 1/4 cup organic chopped cilantro
- 1 organic avocado, diced
- 1 organic lime, juiced
- Optional: organic sour cream or coconut yogurt for garnish

Instructions:
1. In a large pot or Dutch oven, heat avocado oil over medium heat. Add onion, garlic, and jalapeno, and cook until softened, about 5 minutes.
2. Stir in chicken, cumin, smoked paprika, salt, and black pepper. Cook until chicken is no longer pink, about 5 minutes.
3. Pour in chicken broth and fire-roasted tomatoes. Bring the mixture to a boil, then reduce heat to low and simmer for 10 minutes.
4. Add bell pepper and simmer until tender, about 5 minutes.
5. Remove from heat and stir in cilantro, avocado, and lime juice.
6. Ladle into bowls, garnish with a dollop of sour cream or coconut yogurt (if desired), and serve hot.

Tips:
- For a spicier soup, leave some of the jalapeno seeds in or add a pinch of organic cayenne pepper.
- Serve with a side of organic, grain-free tortilla chips or crushed pork rinds for added crunch.
- Avocado and sour cream or coconut yogurt provide healthy fats and a creamy texture, while bell peppers and tomatoes offer antioxidants and fiber.

Nutritional Information (per serving):
- Calories: 250
- Protein: 22 g
- Fat: 15 g
- Carbohydrates: 10 g
- Fiber: 4 g

PROBIOTIC GREEK LEMON CHICKEN SOUP (AVGOLEMONO)

Prep Time: 15 minutes
Cook Time: 25 minutes
Serves: 4

Ingredients:

- 6 cups organic chicken bone broth
- 1 lb organic, pasture-raised chicken breasts, cut into bite-sized pieces
- 1 cup organic cauliflower rice
- 1/2 cup organic full-fat coconut milk
- 3 organic eggs
- 1/4 cup organic lemon juice
- 2 tbsp organic avocado oil
- 1 organic onion, diced
- 3 organic garlic cloves, minced
- 1 tsp sea salt
- 1/2 tsp organic black pepper
- 1/4 cup organic chopped dill
- 1/4 cup organic fermented vegetables (like sauerkraut or kimchi), chopped

Instructions:

1. In a large pot, heat avocado oil over medium heat. Add onion and garlic, and cook until softened, about 5 minutes.
2. Stir in chicken, salt, and black pepper. Cook until chicken is no longer pink, about 5 minutes.
3. Pour in chicken broth and bring to a simmer. Cook for 10 minutes.
4. Add cauliflower rice and simmer until tender, about 5 minutes.
5. In a separate bowl, whisk together eggs, coconut milk, and lemon juice.
6. Gradually ladle 1 cup of the hot broth into the egg mixture, whisking constantly to temper the eggs.
7. Slowly pour the tempered egg mixture back into the pot, stirring constantly. Cook over low heat until slightly thickened, about 2 minutes.
8. Remove from heat and stir in dill and fermented vegetables.
9. Ladle into bowls and serve hot.

Tips:

- For a creamier soup, use organic, full-fat coconut cream instead of coconut milk.
- Serve with a side of organic, steamed spinach or kale for added fiber and nutrients.
- Cauliflower rice provides a low-carb, fiber-rich alternative to traditional rice, while eggs and coconut milk offer satiating protein and healthy fats. Fermented vegetables add beneficial probiotics for gut health.

Nutritional Information (per serving):

- Calories: 320
- Protein: 30 g
- Fat: 18 g
- Carbohydrates: 10 g
- Fiber: 2 g

INDIAN BUTTER CHICKEN SOUP

Prep Time: 20 minutes
Cook Time: 35 minutes
Serves: 6

Ingredients:

- 1 1/2 lbs organic, pasture-raised chicken thighs, cut into bite-sized pieces
- 1 can (14 oz) organic, full-fat coconut milk
- 2 cups organic chicken bone broth
- 1 organic onion, diced
- 3 organic garlic cloves, minced
- 1 tbsp organic grated ginger
- 2 tbsp organic grass-fed ghee or butter
- 2 tbsp organic tomato paste
- 1 tbsp organic garam masala
- 1 tsp organic ground cumin
- 1 tsp organic ground turmeric
- 1 tsp sea salt
- 1/2 tsp organic black pepper
- 1/4 cup organic chopped cilantro
- 1 organic lime, juiced

Instructions:

1. In a large pot or Dutch oven, melt ghee or butter over medium heat. Add onion, garlic, and ginger, and cook until softened, about 5 minutes.
2. Stir in chicken, garam masala, cumin, turmeric, salt, and black pepper. Cook until chicken is no longer pink, about 5 minutes.
3. Add tomato paste and cook until fragrant, about 1 minute.
4. Pour in coconut milk and chicken broth. Bring the mixture to a boil, then reduce heat to low and simmer for 15 minutes.
5. Remove from heat and stir in cilantro and lime juice.
6. Ladle into bowls and serve hot.

Tips:

- For a spicier soup, add sliced organic jalapenos or a pinch of organic cayenne pepper.
- Serve with a side of organic, roasted cauliflower florets or zucchini noodles for added texture and fiber.
- Coconut milk and ghee provide satiating, anti-inflammatory healthy fats, while tomato paste and spices offer antioxidants and anti-inflammatory compounds.

Nutritional Information (per serving):

- Calories: 410
- Protein: 30 g
- Fat: 30 g
- Carbohydrates: 8 g
- Fiber: 2 g

THAI GREEN CURRY CHICKEN SOUP

Prep Time: 20 minutes
Cook Time: 30 minutes
Serves: 6

Ingredients:

- 1 lb organic, pasture-raised chicken thighs, cut into bite-sized pieces
- 1 can (14 oz) organic, full-fat coconut milk
- 2 cups organic chicken bone broth
- 2 organic zucchini, spiralized or julienned
- 1 organic red bell pepper, thinly sliced
- 1 cup organic bamboo shoots
- 1/2 cup organic Thai basil leaves
- 2 tbsp organic green curry paste
- 2 tbsp organic fish sauce
- 2 tbsp organic avocado oil
- 1 tbsp organic grated ginger
- 1 tbsp organic grated lemongrass
- 1 organic lime, juiced
- 1 tsp sea salt

Instructions:

1. In a large pot or Dutch oven, heat avocado oil over medium heat. Add chicken and cook until browned, about 5 minutes.
2. Stir in green curry paste, ginger, and lemongrass. Cook until fragrant, about 1 minute.
3. Pour in coconut milk and chicken broth. Bring the mixture to a boil, then reduce heat to low and simmer for 10 minutes.

4. Add zucchini noodles, bell pepper, bamboo shoots, fish sauce, and salt. Simmer until vegetables are tender-crisp, about 5 minutes.
5. Remove from heat and stir in Thai basil and lime juice.
6. Ladle into bowls and serve hot.

Tips:

- For a spicier soup, add sliced organic Thai chili peppers or a pinch of organic cayenne pepper.
- Garnish with additional Thai basil leaves, lime wedges, and chopped organic roasted peanuts for added texture and flavor.
- Zucchini noodles provide a low-carb, fiber-rich alternative to traditional rice noodles, while coconut milk and avocado oil offer satiating, anti-inflammatory healthy fats.

Nutritional Information (per serving):

- Calories: 350
- Protein: 25 g
- Fat: 26 g
- Carbohydrates: 10 g
- Fiber: 3 g

BEEF BONE BROTH SOUP WITH KELP NOODLES

Prep Time: 15 minutes
Cook Time: 8-24 hours (for broth), 30 minutes (for soup)
Serves: 6

Ingredients:

- 3 lbs grass-fed beef bones
- 1 organic onion, quartered
- 2 organic carrots, chopped
- 2 organic celery stalks, chopped
- 2 organic garlic cloves, crushed
- 1 tbsp organic apple cider vinegar
- 1 tbsp organic ginger, sliced
- 1 package organic kelp noodles
- 1/2 lb grass-fed beef sirloin, thinly sliced
- 2 organic eggs, beaten
- 1 cup organic spinach
- 1/4 cup organic green onions, chopped
- 1 sheet organic nori, crumbled

Instructions:

1. For broth: Simmer bones, vegetables, vinegar, and ginger in water for 8-24 hours.
2. Strain broth and return to pot.
3. Add kelp noodles and sliced beef to simmering broth.
4. Slowly pour in beaten eggs, stirring gently.
5. Add spinach and cook until wilted.
6. Serve topped with green onions and crumbled nori.

Tip: Roast the bones before simmering for a deeper flavor.

Nutritional Information (per serving):

- Calories: 300
- Protein: 30 g
- Fat: 15 g
- Carbohydrates: 8 g
- Fiber: 2 g

BROCCOLI AND BACON "POTATO" SOUP

Prep Time: 15 minutes
Cook Time: 25 minutes
Serves: 4

Ingredients:

- 4 cups organic broccoli florets
- 1 large organic cauliflower head, cut into florets
- 4 slices organic pasture-raised bacon, diced
- 1 organic onion, diced
- 2 organic garlic cloves, minced
- 3 cups organic chicken bone broth

- 1/2 cup organic full-fat, grass-fed cream
- 1 tbsp organic ghee
- 1 tsp organic dried thyme
- Sea salt and black pepper to taste
- 1/4 cup organic chives, chopped

Instructions:

1. In a large pot, cook bacon until crispy. Remove and set aside, leaving the fat in the pot.
2. Sauté onion and garlic in the bacon fat until softened.
3. Add cauliflower, broccoli, bone broth, and thyme. Simmer for 15-20 minutes until vegetables are tender.
4. Use an immersion blender to puree the soup until smooth.
5. Stir in coconut cream and ghee. Season with salt and pepper.
6. Serve topped with crispy bacon bits and chopped chives.

Tip: For a smoother texture, strain the soup through a fine-mesh sieve after blending. Serve with sauerkraut for a probiotic side or topping.

Nutritional Information (per serving):

- Calories: 280
- Protein: 12g
- Fat: 22g
- Carbohydrates: 15g
- Fiber: 5g

EGG AND VEGETABLE "NOODLE" SOUP WITH BONE BROTH

Prep Time: 15 minutes
Cook Time: 25 minutes
Serves: 4

Ingredients:

- 4 organic, pasture-raised eggs
- 4 cups organic bone broth
- 2 organic zucchini, spiralized
- 1 cup organic shiitake mushrooms, sliced
- 2 organic carrots, julienned
- 2 organic garlic cloves, minced
- 1 tbsp organic ginger, grated
- 2 tbsp organic coconut aminos
- 1 tbsp organic coconut oil
- 1/4 cup organic green onions, chopped
- 1/4 cup organic cilantro, chopped

Instructions:

1. In a large pot, bring bone broth to a simmer. Add garlic and ginger, cook for 5 minutes.
2. Add carrots and mushrooms, simmer for 5 more minutes.
3. Add zucchini noodles and coconut aminos, cook for 2-3 minutes until tender.
4. Carefully crack eggs into the simmering broth, poach for 3-4 minutes until whites are set but yolks are still runny.
5. Remove from heat, drizzle with oil.
6. Serve in bowls, garnished with green onions and cilantro.

Tip: For perfectly poached eggs, create a gentle whirlpool in the broth before adding the eggs.

Nutritional Information (per serving):

- Calories: 220
- Protein: 16g
- Fat: 14g
- Carbohydrates: 12g
- Fiber: 3g

GRASS-FED BEEF MASSAMAN CURRY WITH FERMENTED COCONUT YOGURT

Prep Time: 35 minutes
Cook Time: 1 hour 30 minutes
Serves: 6

Ingredients:

- 2 lbs organic, grass-fed beef chuck, cut into 1-inch cubes
- 1 can (14 oz) organic, full-fat coconut milk
- 1 cup organic beef bone broth
- 1 organic onion, chopped
- 3 organic garlic cloves, minced
- 2 organic sweet potatoes, peeled and cut into 1-inch cubes
- 1/2 cup organic fermented coconut yogurt
- 2 tbsp organic avocado oil
- 2 tbsp organic Massaman curry paste
- 1 tbsp organic fish sauce
- 1 tsp organic grated ginger
- 1 tsp sea salt
- 1/2 tsp organic black pepper
- 1/4 cup organic fresh cilantro, chopped
- 1/4 cup organic roasted, unsalted peanuts, chopped

Instructions:

1. In a large, heavy-bottomed pot or Dutch oven, heat avocado oil over medium-high heat. Add beef cubes and cook, stirring occasionally, until browned on all sides, about 8-10 minutes.
2. Reduce heat to medium and add onion, garlic, and ginger to the pot. Cook until onion is softened and translucent, about 5 minutes.
3. Stir in Massaman curry paste and cook until fragrant, about 1 minute.
4. Pour in coconut milk, bone broth, fish sauce, salt, and black pepper. Bring the mixture to a simmer, then reduce heat to low and cover the pot.
5. Simmer the curry, stirring occasionally, for 1 hour or until beef is tender.
6. Add sweet potato cubes to the pot and continue to simmer, uncovered, until sweet potatoes are tender, about 20-25 minutes.
7. Remove from heat and stir in fermented coconut yogurt.
8. Garnish with chopped cilantro and roasted peanuts.
9. Serve the curry hot, alone or over a bed of organic cauliflower rice or zucchini noodles.

Tips:

- For a richer flavor, marinate the beef cubes in a mixture of fish sauce, grated ginger, and minced garlic for 30 minutes before cooking.
- Add organic kaffir lime leaves or lemongrass stalks to the curry for a more authentic Thai flavor.

Nutritional Information (per serving):

- Calories: 590
- Protein: 35 g
- Fat: 42 g
- Carbohydrates: 20 g
- Fiber: 4 g

BEEF AND BONE BROTH OSSO BUCO

Prep Time: 20 minutes
Cook Time: 3 hours
Serves: 4

Ingredients:

- 4 grass-fed beef shanks
- 2 tbsp ghee
- 1 medium onion, chopped
- 2 medium carrots, chopped

- 2 cups organic bone broth
- 1 cup organic diced tomatoes
- 1 tsp fresh thyme
- 1 tsp fresh rosemary
- Sea salt and black pepper to taste

Instructions:

1. Sear the Beef Shanks: Heat ghee in a large pot. Sear the beef shanks on both sides, about 8-10 minutes. Remove from the pot.
2. Sauté the Vegetables: Add onions and carrots to the pot, cooking for 5 minutes until softened.
3. Simmer the Stew: Add bone broth, diced tomatoes, thyme, and rosemary. Return the beef shanks to the pot. Simmer on low heat for 3 hours, until the meat is tender and falling off the bone.
4. Season & Serve: Season with salt and pepper before serving.

Tip: Bone broth enhances the stew's richness while adding collagen and gelatin, making the broth nutritious and flavorful. Slow-cooking ensures the meat is tender and flavorful.

Nutritional Information (per serving):

- Calories: 650
- Protein: 50 g
- Fat: 45 g
- Carbohydrates: 10 g
- Fiber: 2 g

WEST AFRICAN PEANUT STEW WITH GRASS-FED BEEF AND SPINACH

Prep Time: 15 minutes
Cook Time: 45 minutes
Serves: 4

Ingredients:

- 1 lb organic grass-fed beef chuck, cubed
- 2 tbsp organic coconut oil
- 1 large organic onion, diced
- 2 cloves organic garlic, minced
- 1-inch piece organic fresh ginger, minced
- 1/4 cup organic peanut butter (unsweetened)
- 1 tbsp organic tomato paste (no added sugar)
- 4 cups organic beef broth
- 2 cups organic spinach
- 1 tbsp organic fresh cilantro, chopped

Instructions:

1. Brown the Beef: Heat coconut oil in a large pot over medium heat. Brown the beef on all sides for about 5 minutes, then remove from the pot and set aside.
2. Sauté the Aromatics: In the same pot, add the onions, garlic, and ginger. Sauté for 5 minutes until softened and fragrant. Add the tomato paste and cook for another 2 minutes.
3. Simmer the Stew: Add the beef back to the pot along with the peanut butter and beef broth. Bring to a boil, then reduce the heat and simmer for 35 minutes, stirring occasionally.
4. Add Spinach and Serve: Stir in the spinach and cook for another 5 minutes until wilted. Garnish with fresh cilantro and serve hot.

   Tip: The peanut butter adds richness to the stew, while the spinach adds a fresh, slightly bitter contrast.

Nutritional Information (per serving):

- Calories: 550
- Protein: 40 g
- Fat: 38 g
- Carbohydrates: 12 g
- Fiber: 3 g

FISH SOUPS, STEWS, AND CURRIES

BOUILLABAISSE-INSPIRED FISH STEW WITH SAFFRON CAULIFLOWER RICE AND FERMENTED GARLIC

Prep Time: 30 minutes
Cook Time: 40 minutes
Serves: 6

Ingredients:
- 1.5 lbs mixed wild-caught fish (such as cod, halibut, and sea bass), cut into chunks
- 1/2 lb wild-caught shrimp, peeled and deveined
- 1 organic fennel bulb, sliced
- 2 organic leeks, white and light green parts only, sliced
- 3 organic tomatoes, diced
- 4 organic garlic cloves, minced
- 1 organic orange, zested
- 1 tsp organic saffron threads
- 2 cups organic fish or shellfish stock
- 1/4 cup organic extra-virgin olive oil
- 1 large organic cauliflower, riced
- 2 tbsp organic ghee
- 1/4 cup fermented garlic cloves, minced
- Sea salt and freshly ground black pepper to taste

Instructions:
1. In a large pot, heat olive oil and sauté fennel and leeks until softened.
2. Add tomatoes, garlic, orange zest, and saffron. Cook for 5 minutes.
3. Pour in stock and simmer for 15 minutes.
4. Add fish chunks and shrimp, cooking for another 5-7 minutes until just done.
5. Meanwhile, sauté cauliflower rice in ghee until tender. Season with salt and pepper.
6. Serve the stew over saffron cauliflower rice, topped with minced fermented garlic.

Tip: For an authentic touch, serve with a side of homemade rouille made with fermented garlic and coconut yogurt.

Nutritional Information (per serving):
- Calories: 420
- Protein: 40 g
- Fat: 20 g
- Carbohydrates: 20 g
- Fiber: 5 g

JJIGAE-INSPIRED SEAFOOD STEW WITH DAIKON NOODLES

Prep Time: 20 minutes
Cook Time: 30 minutes
Serves: 4

Ingredients:
- 1 lb mixed wild-caught seafood (shrimp, white fish, squid)
- 1 organic daikon radish, spiralized
- 1 organic zucchini, diced
- 1 organic onion, sliced
- 2 organic garlic cloves, minced
- 1 tbsp organic ginger, grated
- 4 cups organic seafood or bone broth
- 2 tbsp organic red pepper flakes
- 1 tbsp organic fish sauce
- 2 tbsp organic coconut oil
- 1 organic egg per serving
- 1/4 cup organic green onions, chopped
- 1/4 cup organic cilantro, chopped

Instructions:
1. Heat coconut oil in a large pot. Sauté onion, garlic, and ginger until fragrant.
2. Add broth, red pepper flakes, and fish sauce. Bring to a simmer.
3. Add zucchini and cook for 5 minutes.
4. Add seafood and cook until just done, about 5 minutes.
5. In a separate pan, quickly sauté daikon noodles until tender.
6. Serve stew over daikon noodles, topped with a poached egg, green onions, and cilantro.

Tip: For extra umami, add a sheet of crushed nori seaweed to the broth.

Nutritional Information (per serving):
- Calories: 350
- Protein: 32 g
- Fat: 20 g
- Carbohydrates: 12 g
- Fiber: 4 g

BRAZILIAN SHRIMP STEW (MOQUECA)

Prep Time: 20 minutes
Cook Time: 30 minutes
Serves: 4

Ingredients:
- 1 lb wild-caught jumbo shrimp, peeled and deveined
- 1 can (14 oz) organic, full-fat coconut milk
- 1 cup organic chicken bone broth
- 1 organic red bell pepper, sliced
- 1 organic yellow bell pepper, sliced
- 1 organic onion, sliced
- 3 organic garlic cloves, minced
- 2 tbsp organic tomato paste
- 2 tbsp organic lime juice
- 2 tbsp organic avocado oil
- 1 tbsp organic smoked paprika
- 1 tsp organic ground cumin
- 1 tsp sea salt
- 1/2 tsp organic red pepper flakes
- 1/4 cup organic chopped cilantro

Instructions:
1. In a large pot or Dutch oven, heat avocado oil over medium heat. Add onion and garlic, and cook until softened, about 5 minutes.
2. Stir in bell peppers, tomato paste, smoked paprika, cumin, salt, and red pepper flakes. Cook until fragrant, about 2 minutes.
3. Pour in coconut milk and chicken broth. Bring the mixture to a boil, then reduce heat to low and simmer for 10 minutes.
4. Add shrimp and simmer until cooked through, about 5 minutes.
5. Remove from heat and stir in lime juice and cilantro.
6. Ladle into bowls and serve hot.

Tips:
- For a heartier stew, add sliced organic zucchini or cauliflower florets along with the shrimp.
- Serve over a bed of organic cauliflower rice or sautéed greens for added fiber and nutrients.
- Coconut milk and avocado oil provide satiating, anti-inflammatory healthy fats, while bell peppers and tomato paste offer antioxidants and vitamin C.

Nutritional Information (per serving):
- Calories: 400
- Protein: 30 g

- Fat: 28 g
- Carbohydrates: 12 g
- Fiber: 3 g

SICILIAN-STYLE SWORDFISH STEW WITH CAPERS & TOMATOES

Prep Time: 10 minutes
Cook Time: 30 minutes
Serves: 4

Ingredients:
- 1 lb wild-caught swordfish, cut into chunks
- 2 tbsp olive oil
- 1 medium onion, diced
- 2 cloves garlic, minced
- 1 cup organic diced tomatoes
- 1/2 cup organic vegetable broth (preferably homemade, see recipe)
- 2 tbsp capers, drained
- 1/4 cup green olives, halved
- 1 tsp fresh oregano, chopped
- 1/4 tsp red pepper flakes (optional for heat)
- 1 tbsp fresh parsley, chopped (for garnish)
- Sea salt and black pepper to taste

Instructions:
1. Sauté the Aromatics: Heat olive oil in a large pot over medium heat. Add onions and sauté until softened, about 5 minutes. Add garlic and cook for 1 more minute.
2. Simmer the Tomatoes and Broth: Stir in the diced tomatoes, vegetable broth, capers, and olives. Simmer for 10 minutes to allow the flavors to develop.
3. Cook the Swordfish: Add the swordfish chunks to the pot. Simmer for 10-12 minutes, until the fish is cooked through but still tender.
4. Finish with Fresh Herbs: Stir in fresh oregano and red pepper flakes (if using). Garnish with parsley before serving.

Tip: Swordfish is a firm, meaty fish that holds up well in stews. Capers and olives add a briny contrast to the sweetness of the tomatoes, creating a balanced, savory dish.

Nutritional Information (per serving):
- Calories: 320
- Protein: 35 g
- Fat: 15 g
- Carbohydrates: 10 g
- Fiber: 3 g

CREAMY LEEK AND SALMON SOUP WITH COCONUT MILK

Prep Time: 15 minutes
Cook Time: 30 minutes
Serves: 4

Ingredients:
- 2 large organic leeks, white and light green parts only, sliced
- 1 lb wild-caught salmon, skinned and cubed
- 1 organic cauliflower head, chopped
- 2 organic garlic cloves, minced
- 1 can (14 oz) organic full-fat coconut milk
- 2 cups organic bone broth
- 2 tbsp organic ghee
- 1 tbsp organic fresh dill, chopped
- Sea salt and black pepper to taste
- 2 tbsp organic lemon juice

Instructions:
1. In a large pot, melt ghee over medium heat. Add leeks and garlic, sauté until softened, about 5 minutes.

2. Add cauliflower and bone broth. Bring to a boil, then reduce heat and simmer for 15 minutes until cauliflower is tender.
3. Blend the soup until smooth using an immersion blender or regular blender.
4. Stir in coconut milk and bring back to a simmer.
5. Add salmon cubes and cook for 5-7 minutes until salmon is cooked through.
6. Stir in dill, lemon juice, salt, and pepper.
7. Serve hot, garnished with extra dill if desired.

Tip: For a more intense leek flavor, reserve some of the sautéed leeks before blending and add them back to the soup at the end.

Nutritional Information (per serving):
- Calories: 420
- Protein: 28g
- Fat: 32g
- Carbohydrates: 12g
- Fiber: 4g

EAST AFRICAN COCONUT FISH STEW (SAMAKI WA NAZI)

Prep Time: 15 minutes
Cook Time: 20 minutes
Serves: 4

Ingredients:
- 4 fillets wild-caught white fish (such as tilapia or snapper)
- 2 tbsp organic coconut oil
- 1 large organic onion, sliced
- 2 cloves organic garlic, minced
- 1-inch piece organic fresh ginger, minced
- 1 cup organic coconut milk
- 2 tbsp organic tomato paste (no added sugar)
- 1 tbsp organic turmeric powder
- 1 tbsp organic lime juice
- 1/4 cup organic fresh cilantro, chopped

Instructions:
1. Heat coconut oil in a large pot over medium heat. Sauté the onions, garlic, and ginger for 5 minutes until softened and fragrant.
2. Stir in the turmeric and tomato paste. Cook for 2 minutes to allow the flavors to blend. Gently cook the turmeric to bring out its earthy flavor without overpowering the dish.
3. Pour in the coconut milk and bring to a simmer. Add the fish fillets and lime juice. Cook for 10 minutes until the fish is tender and cooked through.
4. Garnish the stew with fresh cilantro and serve.
   Tip: The creamy coconut milk balances the spice, while lime juice adds brightness to the rich fish stew.

Nutritional Information (per serving):
- Calories: 350
- Protein: 30 g
- Fat: 24 g
- Carbohydrates: 8 g
- Fiber: 2 g

GREEN COCONUT CURRY WITH GRILLED SHRIMP AND FERMENTED VEGETABLES

Prep Time: 30 minutes
Cook Time: 20 minutes
Serves: 4

Ingredients:
- 1 lb wild-caught jumbo shrimp, peeled and deveined
- 1 can (14 oz) organic, full-fat coconut milk
- 1 cup organic chicken or vegetable bone broth
- 2 cups organic mixed vegetables (such as bell peppers, zucchini, and eggplant), sliced
- 1/2 cup organic fermented vegetables (like sauerkraut or kimchi), chopped
- 2 tbsp organic green curry paste

- 2 tbsp organic avocado oil
- 1 tbsp organic fish sauce
- 1 tbsp organic lime juice
- 1 tsp organic grated ginger
- 1 tsp sea salt
- 1/4 cup organic fresh Thai basil leaves, torn

Instructions:
1. In a large skillet or wok, heat 1 tablespoon of avocado oil over medium-high heat. Add shrimp and cook, stirring occasionally, until pink and cooked through, about 3-4 minutes. Remove from the skillet and set aside.
2. In the same skillet, heat the remaining tablespoon of avocado oil over medium heat. Add green curry paste and ginger, stirring until fragrant, about 1 minute.
3. Pour in coconut milk and bone broth, stirring to combine. Bring the mixture to a simmer.
4. Add mixed vegetables and salt to the skillet. Simmer until vegetables are tender-crisp, about 5-7 minutes.
5. Stir in fish sauce, lime juice, fermented vegetables, and cooked shrimp. Cook for an additional 2 minutes to heat through.
6. Remove from heat and garnish with torn Thai basil leaves.
7. Serve the curry hot, alone or over a bed of organic cauliflower rice.

Tips:
- For a spicier curry, add organic red chili peppers or a pinch of organic cayenne pepper.
- Grill the shrimp for added smoky flavor and attractive char marks.
- Coconut milk and avocado oil provide satiating, anti-inflammatory healthy fats, while mixed vegetables offer fiber and micronutrients. Fermented vegetables add beneficial probiotics for gut health.

Nutritional Information (per serving):
- Calories: 420
- Protein: 30 g
- Fat: 28 g
- Carbo: 15 g
- Fiber: 4 g

ROMANESCO AND PRAWN CURRY WITH COCONUT YOGURT

Prep Time: 15 minutes
Cook Time: 25 minutes
Serves: 4

Ingredients:
- 1 medium organic Romanesco, cut into florets
- 1 lb wild-caught prawns, peeled and deveined
- 1 organic onion, diced
- 3 organic garlic cloves, minced
- 1 tbsp organic ginger, grated
- 1 can (14 oz) organic full-fat coconut milk
- 2 tbsp organic curry powder
- 2 tbsp organic coconut oil
- Sea salt and black pepper to taste
- 1/4 cup organic coconut yogurt
- 1/4 cup organic fresh cilantro, chopped

Instructions:
1. Heat coconut oil in a large skillet over medium heat. Sauté onion, garlic, and ginger until fragrant.
2. Add curry powder and cook for another minute.

3. Stir in coconut milk and bring to a simmer. Add Romanesco florets and cook for 10 minutes.
4. Add prawns and cook for an additional 5 minutes until they're pink and cooked through.
5. Season with salt and pepper to taste.
6. Serve hot, topped with a dollop of coconut yogurt and sprinkled with fresh cilantro.

Tip: For a more complex flavor, toast whole spices like cumin and coriander seeds before grinding and adding to the curry.

Nutritional Information (per serving):
- Calories: 420
- Protein: 24g
- Fat: 32g
- Carbohydrates: 14g
- Fiber: 5g

CREAMY ARTICHOKE AND SPINACH SOUP WITH SARDINES

Prep Time: 15 minutes
Cook Time: 30 minutes
Serves: 4

Ingredients:
- 1 tbsp organic olive oil
- 1 medium organic onion, diced
- 2 cloves organic garlic, minced
- 2 cups organic spinach, chopped
- 1 cup organic artichoke hearts, chopped
- 4 cups organic vegetable broth
- 1/2 cup organic coconut milk
- 2 cans (4 oz each) wild-caught sardines, drained and flaked
- 1 tbsp organic lemon juice
- 1 tbsp organic fresh parsley, chopped (for garnish)
- Sea salt and pepper to taste
- Optional topping: 2 tbsp organic sauerkraut or fermented veggies

Instructions:
1. Sauté the Onion and Garlic: Heat the olive oil in a large pot over medium heat. Add the diced onion and minced garlic, cooking for 4-5 minutes until softened.
2. Cook the Vegetables: Add the spinach and artichoke hearts to the pot, sautéing for 3-4 minutes until the spinach is wilted.
3. Simmer the Soup: Add the vegetable broth and bring the mixture to a boil. Reduce heat and simmer for 15 minutes until the artichokes are tender.
4. Blend the Soup: Use an immersion blender to puree the soup until creamy. Stir in the coconut milk, lemon juice, sea salt, and pepper.
5. Add the Sardines: Gently stir in the flaked sardines and heat through for 2-3 minutes.
6. Serve and Garnish: Serve the soup hot, garnished with parsley. Add sauerkraut or fermented veggies for a probiotic boost.

Tip: Sardines add a rich, briny flavor and a boost of omega-3s, pairing beautifully with the creamy texture of artichokes and spinach.

Nutritional Information (per serving):
- Calories: 380
- Protein: 22 g
- Fat: 28 g
- Carbohydrates: 10 g
- Fiber: 4 g

VEGETARIAN/VEGAN SOUPS, CURRIES, AND STEWS

CARROT-GINGER SOUP WITH COCONUT YOGURT SWIRL

Prep Time: 15 minutes
Cook Time: 30 minutes
Serves: 4

Ingredients:

- 1 lb organic carrots, peeled and chopped
- 1 medium organic onion, diced
- 3 organic garlic cloves, minced
- 1 tbsp organic ginger, grated
- 4 cups organic vegetable broth
- 1 can (14 oz) organic coconut milk
- 2 tbsp organic coconut oil
- Sea salt and black pepper to taste
- 1/4 cup organic coconut yogurt for garnish
- 1 tbsp organic fresh cilantro, chopped for garnish

Instructions:

1. In a large pot, heat coconut oil over medium heat. Sauté onion, garlic, and ginger until softened, about 5 minutes.
2. Add chopped carrots and vegetable broth. Bring to a boil, then reduce heat and simmer for 20 minutes, until the carrots are tender.
3. Use an immersion blender to purée the soup until smooth (or blend in batches in a countertop blender).
4. Stir in the coconut milk, salt, and pepper. Simmer for another 5 minutes.
5. Serve hot, garnished with a swirl of coconut yogurt and a sprinkle of fresh cilantro.

Tip: For extra depth of flavor, roast the carrots in the oven at 400°F (200°C) for 20 minutes before adding them to the soup.

Nutritional Information (per serving):

- Calories: 280
- Protein: 4g
- Fat: 22g
- Carbohydrates: 22g
- Fiber: 6g

CREAMY PEA SOUP WITH CRISPY TOFU AND MINT

Prep Time: 25 minutes
Cook Time: 30 minutes
Serves: 4

Soup
Ingredients:

- 2 lbs organic frozen peas
- 4 cups organic vegetable broth
- 1 cup organic full-fat coconut milk
- 1 organic onion, chopped
- 3 organic garlic cloves, minced
- 2 tbsp organic coconut oil
- 1 tsp sea salt
- 1/2 tsp organic black pepper

Topping Ingredients:

- 1 block (14 oz) organic, non-GMO extra-firm tofu, drained and cubed
- 1 tbsp organic avocado oil
- 1 tsp sea salt
- 1/2 tsp organic smoked paprika
- 1/4 cup organic fresh mint leaves, chopped
- 1/4 cup organic fermented peas or other fermented vegetables, chopped

Instructions:

1. In a large pot, heat coconut oil over medium heat. Add onion and garlic, and cook until softened, about 5 minutes.

2. Stir in frozen peas, salt, and black pepper. Cook for 5 minutes, stirring occasionally.
3. Pour in vegetable broth and bring to a boil. Reduce heat to low and simmer, partially covered, for 15 minutes or until peas are tender.
4. While the soup simmers, prepare the crispy tofu. Preheat the oven to 400°F. Toss tofu cubes with avocado oil, salt, and smoked paprika. Arrange in a single layer on a baking sheet lined with parchment paper. Bake until crispy and golden, about 25 minutes, flipping halfway through. Remove and set aside.
5. Remove soup from heat and stir in coconut milk. Using an immersion blender, puree the soup until smooth and creamy.
6. Ladle soup into bowls and top with crispy tofu, fresh mint, and fermented peas or vegetables.

Tips:

- For a brighter green color, blanch the peas in boiling water for 1 minute before adding them to the soup.
- Add a squeeze of fresh lemon juice to the soup before serving for a bright, tangy note.
- Coconut milk and avocado oil provide satiating, anti-inflammatory healthy fats, while peas offer plant-based protein, fiber, and micronutrients. Fermented vegetables add beneficial probiotics for gut health.

Nutritional Information (per serving):

- Calories: 480
- Protein: 20 g
- Fat: 30 g
- Carbohydrates: 40 g
- Fiber: 10 g

CREAMY ASPARAGUS SOUP WITH SOFT TOFU CROUTONS AND DILL

Prep Time: 25 minutes
Cook Time: 30 minutes
Serves: 4

Soup Ingredients:

- 2 lbs organic asparagus, trimmed and chopped
- 4 cups organic vegetable broth
- 1 cup organic full-fat coconut milk
- 1 organic onion, chopped
- 3 organic garlic cloves, minced
- 2 tbsp organic coconut oil
- 1 tsp sea salt
- 1/2 tsp organic black pepper

Topping Ingredients:

- 1 block (14 oz) organic, non-GMO soft tofu, drained and cubed
- 1 tbsp organic avocado oil
- 1 tsp sea salt
- 1/4 tsp organic garlic powder
- 1/4 cup organic fresh dill, chopped
- 1/4 cup organic fermented vegetables (like sauerkraut or kimchi), chopped

Instructions:

1. In a large pot, heat coconut oil over medium heat. Add onion and garlic, and cook until softened, about 5 minutes.
2. Stir in asparagus, salt, and black pepper. Cook for 5 minutes, stirring occasionally.
3. Pour in vegetable broth and bring to a boil. Reduce heat to low and simmer, partially covered, for 15 minutes or until asparagus is tender.

4. While the soup simmers, prepare the tofu croutons. Preheat the oven to 400°F. Toss tofu cubes with avocado oil, salt, and garlic powder. Arrange in a single layer on a baking sheet lined with parchment paper. Bake until crispy and golden, about 20 minutes, flipping halfway through. Remove and set aside.
5. Remove soup from heat and stir in coconut milk. Using an immersion blender, puree the soup until smooth and creamy.
6. Ladle soup into bowls and top with crispy tofu croutons, fresh dill, and fermented vegetables.

Tips:

- For a more intense asparagus flavor, reserve a few asparagus tips to use as a garnish.
- Add a squeeze of fresh lemon juice to the soup before serving for a bright, tangy note.
- Coconut milk and avocado oil provide satiating, anti-inflammatory healthy fats, while asparagus offers fiber, vitamin K, and micronutrients. Fermented vegetables add beneficial probiotics for gut health.

Nutritional Information (per serving):

- Calories: 350
- Protein: 12 g
- Fat: 26 g
- Carbohydrates: 20 g
- Fiber: 6 g

SILKEN TOFU SOUP WITH SPINACH AND GINGER

Prep Time: 10 minutes
Cook Time: 15 minutes
Serves: 4

Ingredients:

- 12 oz silken tofu, cubed
- 1 tbsp coconut oil
- 1 medium onion, thinly sliced
- 2 cloves garlic, minced
- 1 tbsp fresh ginger, grated
- 4 cups organic vegetable broth
- 2 cups organic spinach, chopped
- 1 tbsp coconut aminos (soy sauce alternative)
- Juice of 1 lime
- Sea salt and black pepper to taste

Instructions:

1. Sauté the Aromatics: In a large pot, heat coconut oil over medium heat. Add onion, garlic, and ginger. Sauté for 3-4 minutes until softened and fragrant.
2. Add Broth and Simmer: Pour in the vegetable broth and coconut aminos, then bring to a simmer.
3. Add Spinach and Tofu: Add the chopped spinach and cubed silken tofu. Simmer for 5 minutes until the spinach is wilted and the tofu is heated through.
4. Finish with Lime Juice: Stir in lime juice and season with salt and pepper before serving.

Tip: Silken tofu has a delicate texture that melts into the soup, creating a smooth, creamy broth without the need for added cream or thickening agents. The ginger and lime add a fresh, zesty contrast to the richness of the tofu.

Nutritional Information (per serving):

- Calories: 150
- Protein: 6 g
- Fat: 10 g
- Carbohydrates: 10 g
- Fiber: 2 g

CREAMY SPINACH SOUP WITH TEMPEH BACON BITS AND CHIVES

Prep Time: 25 minutes
Cook Time: 35 minutes
Serves: 4

Soup Ingredients:

- 2 lbs organic spinach
- 4 cups organic vegetable broth
- 1 cup organic full-fat coconut milk
- 1 organic onion, chopped
- 3 organic garlic cloves, minced
- 2 tbsp organic coconut oil
- 1 tsp sea salt
- 1/2 tsp organic black pepper
- 1/4 tsp organic nutmeg

Topping Ingredients:

- 8 oz organic, non-GMO tempeh, thinly sliced
- 2 tbsp organic coconut aminos
- 1 tbsp organic avocado oil
- 1 tsp organic smoked paprika
- 1/2 tsp sea salt
- 1/4 cup organic fresh chives, chopped
- 1/4 cup organic fermented vegetables (like sauerkraut or kimchi), chopped

Instructions:

1. In a large pot, heat coconut oil over medium heat. Add onion and garlic, and cook until softened, about 5 minutes.
2. Stir in spinach, salt, black pepper, and nutmeg. Cook until spinach wilts, about 5 minutes.
3. Pour in vegetable broth and bring to a boil. Reduce heat to low and simmer, partially covered, for 15 minutes.
4. While the soup simmers, prepare the tempeh bacon bits. In a bowl, whisk together coconut aminos, avocado oil, smoked paprika, and salt. Add tempeh slices and toss to coat. Arrange in a single layer on a baking sheet lined with parchment paper. Bake at 400°F until crispy, about 20 minutes, flipping halfway through. Remove, let cool, and crumble into bits.
5. Remove soup from heat and stir in coconut milk. Using an immersion blender, puree the soup until smooth and creamy.
6. Ladle soup into bowls and top with tempeh bacon bits, fresh chives, and fermented vegetables.

Tips:

- For a creamier texture, add a peeled, diced potato to the soup before simmering.
- Use a combination of baby spinach and mature spinach for a more complex flavor profile.
- Coconut milk and avocado oil provide satiating, anti-inflammatory healthy fats, while spinach offers fiber, vitamin A, and iron. Fermented vegetables add beneficial probiotics for gut health.

Nutritional Information (per serving):

- Calories: 320
- Protein: 15 g
- Fat: 22 g
- Carbohydrates: 16 g
- Fiber: 5 g

CREAMY TOMATO SOUP WITH CRISPY CHICKPEAS AND BASIL

Prep Time: 25 minutes
Cook Time: 35 minutes
Serves: 4

Soup Ingredients:

- 2 lbs organic tomatoes, chopped
- 4 cups organic vegetable broth
- 1 cup organic full-fat coconut milk
- 1 organic onion, chopped
- 3 organic garlic cloves, minced
- 2 tbsp organic coconut oil
- 1 tsp sea salt
- 1/2 tsp organic black pepper
- 1/4 tsp organic cayenne pepper (optional)

Topping Ingredients:

- 1 can (15 oz) organic chickpeas, drained and rinsed
- 1 tbsp organic avocado oil
- 1 tsp sea salt
- 1/2 tsp organic smoked paprika
- 1/4 cup organic fresh basil leaves, torn
- 1/4 cup organic fermented vegetables (like sauerkraut or kimchi), chopped

Instructions:

1. In a large pot, heat coconut oil over medium heat. Add onion and garlic, and cook until softened, about 5 minutes.
2. Stir in tomatoes, salt, black pepper, and cayenne (if using). Cook for 5 minutes, stirring occasionally.
3. Pour in vegetable broth and bring to a boil. Reduce heat to low and simmer, partially covered, for 25 minutes.
4. While the soup simmers, prepare the crispy chickpeas. Preheat the oven to 400°F. Pat chickpeas dry with a clean kitchen towel. Toss with avocado oil, salt, and smoked paprika. Arrange in a single layer on a baking sheet lined with parchment paper. Bake until crispy, about 30 minutes, shaking the pan halfway through. Remove and set aside.
5. Remove soup from heat and stir in coconut milk. Using an immersion blender, puree the soup until smooth and creamy.
6. Ladle soup into bowls and top with crispy chickpeas, fresh basil, and fermented vegetables.

Tips:

- For a smoky flavor, roast the tomatoes before adding them to the soup.
- Add a dollop of organic, unsweetened coconut yogurt for a tangy, creamy finish.
- Coconut milk and avocado oil provide satiating, anti-inflammatory healthy fats, while tomatoes offer lycopene and vitamin C. Chickpeas provide plant-based protein and fiber, and fermented vegetables add beneficial probiotics for gut health.

Nutritional Information (per serving):

- Calories: 350
- Protein: 10 g
- Fat: 22 g
- Carbohydrates: 30 g
- Fiber: 8 g

CREAMY BROCCOLI SOUP WITH CRISPY PROSCIUTTO AND PUMPKIN SEEDS

Prep Time: 20 minutes
Cook Time: 30 minutes
Serves: 4

Soup Ingredients:

- 2 lbs organic broccoli, chopped (stems and florets)
- 4 cups organic chicken bone broth
- 1 cup organic full-fat coconut milk
- 1 organic onion, chopped
- 3 organic garlic cloves, minced
- 2 tbsp organic grass-fed butter
- 1 tsp sea salt
- 1/2 tsp organic black pepper

Topping Ingredients:

- 4 oz organic, pasture-raised prosciutto, thinly sliced
- 1/4 cup organic pumpkin seeds
- 1 tbsp organic avocado oil
- 1/4 cup organic chopped chives
- 1/4 cup organic fermented vegetables (like sauerkraut or kimchi), chopped

Instructions:

1. In a large pot, melt butter over medium heat. Add onion and garlic, and cook until softened, about 5 minutes.
2. Stir in broccoli, salt, and black pepper. Cook for 5 minutes, stirring occasionally.
3. Pour in chicken broth and bring to a boil. Reduce heat to low and simmer, partially covered, for 20 minutes or until broccoli is tender.
4. While the soup simmers, prepare the toppings. Preheat the oven to 400°F. Arrange prosciutto slices on a baking sheet lined with parchment paper. Bake until crispy, about 10 minutes. Remove and set aside.
5. In a small skillet, toast pumpkin seeds over medium heat until lightly golden and fragrant, about 5 minutes. Remove and set aside.
6. Remove soup from heat and stir in coconut milk. Using an immersion blender, puree the soup until smooth and creamy.
7. Ladle soup into bowls and top with crispy prosciutto, toasted pumpkin seeds, chives, and fermented vegetables.

Tips:

- For a vegan version, use organic vegetable broth, omit prosciutto, and replace butter with coconut oil.
- Roast the broccoli before adding to the soup for a deeper, more complex flavor.
- Coconut milk and butter provide satiating, anti-inflammatory healthy fats, while broccoli offers fiber, vitamin C, and micronutrients. Fermented vegetables add beneficial probiotics for gut health.

Nutritional Information per serving):

- Calories: 400
- Protein: 15 g
- Fat: 32 g
- Carbohydrates: 14 g
- Fiber: 5 g

PROBIOTIC MISO MUSHROOM SOUP

Prep Time: 15 minutes
Cook Time: 20 minutes
Serves: 4

Ingredients:

- 8 cups organic mushroom broth
- 1 lb organic mixed mushrooms (shiitake, oyster, enoki, etc.), sliced
- 1/2 cup organic white miso paste
- 1/2 cup organic coconut milk
- 2 organic green onions, sliced
- 2 tbsp organic coconut oil
- 1 tbsp organic grated ginger
- 1 tbsp organic coconut aminos
- 1 tsp organic toasted sesame oil
- 1/4 cup organic chopped cilantro
- 1/4 cup organic fermented vegetables (like kimchi or sauerkraut), chopped

Instructions:
1. In a large pot, heat coconut oil over medium heat. Add ginger and cook until fragrant, about 1 minute.
2. Stir in mushrooms and cook until softened, about 5 minutes.
3. Pour in mushroom broth and bring to a simmer. Cook for 10 minutes.
4. In a small bowl, whisk together miso paste and 1/2 cup of the hot broth until smooth. Stir the mixture back into the pot.
5. Remove from heat and stir in coconut milk, coconut aminos, sesame oil, cilantro, and fermented vegetables.
6. Ladle into bowls, garnish with green onions, and serve hot.

Tips:
- For a spicier soup, add sliced organic jalapenos or a pinch of organic red pepper flakes.
- Serve with a side of organic kelp noodles or spiralized daikon radish for added texture and fiber.
- Miso paste and fermented vegetables provide beneficial probiotics for gut health, while mushrooms offer immune-boosting compounds and umami flavor.

Nutritional Information (per serving):
- Calories: 250
- Protein: 6 g
- Fat: 18 g
- Carbohydrates: 18 g
- Fiber: 3 g

CREAMY MUSHROOM SOUP WITH CRISPY SHIITAKE CHIPS AND THYME

Prep Time: 25 minutes
Cook Time: 35 minutes
Serves: 4

Soup Ingredients:
- 1 1/2 lbs organic mixed mushrooms (shiitake, oyster, cremini), sliced
- 4 cups organic mushroom or chicken bone broth
- 1 cup organic full-fat coconut milk
- 1 organic onion, chopped
- 3 organic garlic cloves, minced
- 2 tbsp organic grass-fed ghee
- 1 tsp sea salt
- 1/2 tsp organic black pepper
- 1/4 cup organic coconut aminos

Topping Ingredients:
- 1/2 lb organic shiitake mushrooms, sliced
- 1 tbsp organic avocado oil
- 1 tsp sea salt
- 1/4 cup organic fresh thyme leaves
- 1/4 cup organic fermented vegetables (like sauerkraut or kimchi), chopped

Instructions:
1. In a large pot, melt ghee over medium heat. Add onion and garlic, and cook until softened, about 5 minutes.
2. Stir in mixed mushrooms, salt, and black pepper. Cook until mushrooms release their liquid and start to brown, about 10 minutes.
3. Pour in broth and coconut aminos. Bring to a boil, then reduce heat to low and simmer, partially covered, for 20 minutes.
4. While the soup simmers, prepare the shiitake chips. Preheat the oven to 300°F. Toss shiitake slices with avocado oil and salt. Arrange in a single layer on a baking sheet lined with parchment paper. Bake until crispy, about 30 minutes, flipping halfway through. Remove and set aside.
5. Remove soup from heat and stir in coconut milk. Using an immersion blender, puree the soup until smooth and creamy.
6. Ladle soup into bowls and top with crispy shiitake chips, fresh thyme leaves, and fermented vegetables.

Tips:
- For a richer flavor, add a splash of organic dry white wine to the mushrooms before pouring in the broth.
- Use a variety of mushrooms for a complex, umami-rich soup.
- Coconut milk and ghee provide satiating, anti-inflammatory healthy fats, while mushrooms offer immune-boosting compounds and fiber. Fermented vegetables add beneficial probiotics for gut health.

Nutritional Information (per serving):
- Calories: 350
- Protein: 10 g
- Fat: 28 g
- Carbohydrates: 18 g
- Fiber: 5 g

CELERY ROOT AND LEEK SOUP WITH FERMENTED SAUERKRAUT

Prep Time: 15 minutes
Cook Time: 30 minutes
Serves: 4

Ingredients:
- 2 large organic celery roots, peeled and diced
- 2 organic leeks, white and light green parts only, chopped
- 4 cups organic vegetable broth
- 1 can (14 oz) organic coconut milk
- 2 tbsp organic ghee
- 1 tsp organic ground nutmeg
- 1/2 cup organic sauerkraut
- Sea salt and black pepper to taste
- 1/4 cup organic fresh chives, chopped

Instructions:
1. In a large pot, melt ghee over medium heat. Sauté leeks until softened, about 5 minutes.
2. Add diced celery root, vegetable broth, and nutmeg. Bring to a boil, then reduce heat and simmer for 20 minutes until celery root is tender.
3. Blend the soup until smooth using an immersion blender or regular blender.
4. Stir in coconut milk and heat through.
5. Serve the soup hot, garnished with sauerkraut and fresh chives.

Tip: For a richer flavor, roast the celery root and leeks in the oven before adding them to the soup.

Nutritional Information (per serving):
- Calories: 320
- Protein: 4g
- Fat: 24g
- Carbohydrates: 24g
- Fiber: 7g

NAVY BEAN AND ROASTED VEGETABLE SOUP WITH HERB-INFUSED GHEE

Prep Time: 20 minutes
Cook Time: 45 minutes
Serves: 6

Ingredients:
- 2 cups organic navy beans, soaked overnight and cooked until tender
- 2 organic sweet potatoes, peeled and cubed
- 2 organic parsnips, peeled and cubed
- 1 organic red onion, quartered
- 4 cloves organic garlic, peeled
- 2 tbsp organic avocado oil

- 6 cups organic vegetable or bone broth
- 2 organic bay leaves
- 1 tsp organic ground cumin
- 1 tsp organic smoked paprika
- Sea salt and freshly ground black pepper to taste
- 1/4 cup organic ghee
- 2 tbsp mixed organic fresh herbs (such as thyme, rosemary, and sage), finely chopped
- 1/4 cup organic sauerkraut, for serving

Instructions:
1. Preheat oven to 425°F (220°C).
2. Toss sweet potatoes, parsnips, onion, and garlic with avocado oil. Spread on a baking sheet and roast for 25-30 minutes, until vegetables are tender and caramelized.
3. In a large pot, combine roasted vegetables, cooked navy beans, broth, bay leaves, cumin, and smoked paprika. Bring to a boil, then simmer for 15 minutes.
4. Remove bay leaves. Use an immersion blender to partially blend the soup, leaving some chunks for texture.
5. In a small saucepan, melt ghee over low heat. Add fresh herbs and infuse for 5 minutes.
6. Serve soup topped with a drizzle of herb-infused ghee and a spoonful of sauerkraut.

Tip: To add depth to the soup's flavor, deglaze the roasting pan with a splash of broth after removing the vegetables, and add this flavorful liquid to the soup pot.

Nutritional Information (per serving):
- Calories: 350
- Protein: 10 g
- Fat: 16 g
- Carbohydrates: 45 g
- Fiber: 10 g

CAULIFLOWER AND LENTIL CURRY

Prep Time: 15 minutes
Cook Time: 30 minutes
Serves: 4

Ingredients:
- 1 head organic cauliflower, cut into florets
- 1 cup organic green lentils, cooked
- 1 organic onion, diced
- 3 organic garlic cloves, minced
- 1 tbsp organic ginger, grated
- 1 can organic coconut milk
- 2 tbsp organic curry powder
- 1 tbsp organic coconut oil
- Sea salt to taste
- 1/4 cup organic fresh cilantro, chopped

Instructions:
1. Heat coconut oil in a large pot. Sauté onion, garlic, and ginger until fragrant.
2. Add cauliflower and curry powder, stirring to coat.
3. Pour in coconut milk and simmer for 15 minutes.
4. Stir in cooked lentils and simmer for another 10 minutes.
5. Garnish with fresh cilantro before serving.

Tip: For a creamier texture, blend half the cauliflower before adding the lentils.

Nutritional Information (per serving):
- Calories: 320
- Protein: 14g
- Fat: 18g
- Carbohydrates: 32g
- Fiber: 14g

LENTIL AND SPINACH CURRY WITH COCONUT CHUTNEY

Prep Time: 20 minutes
Cook Time: 30 minutes
Serves: 4

Ingredients:
- 1 cup cooked organic lentils
- 1 lb organic spinach, chopped
- 1 organic onion, diced
- 3 organic garlic cloves, minced
- 1 tbsp organic grated ginger
- 1 tsp organic ground cumin
- 1 tsp organic ground coriander
- 1/2 tsp organic ground turmeric
- 1/4 tsp organic cayenne pepper (or to taste)
- 1 can (13.5 oz) organic coconut milk
- 2 tbsp organic coconut oil
- Sea salt and black pepper to taste
- 1/2 cup organic coconut yogurt
- 1/4 cup organic fresh cilantro, chopped
- 1 organic lime, juiced

Instructions:
1. In a large pot, heat coconut oil over medium heat. Sauté onion, garlic, and ginger until fragrant, about 2-3 minutes.
2. Add cumin, coriander, turmeric, and cayenne. Cook for 1 minute to toast the spices.
3. Stir in coconut milk and lentils. Bring to a simmer and cook for 10 minutes.
4. Add spinach and cook until wilted, about 5 more minutes.
5. Season with salt and pepper to taste.
6. For the chutney, mix coconut yogurt, cilantro, and lime juice.
7. Serve the lentil curry topped with the coconut chutney.

Tip: To balance the flavors, start with a smaller amount of cayenne and adjust to your desired level of heat.

Nutritional Information (per):
- Calories: 380
- Protein: 12 g
- Fat: 28 g
- Carbohydrates: 25 g
- Fiber: 8 g

LENTIL AND SWEET POTATO CURRY

Prep Time: 15 minutes
Cook Time: 30 minutes
Serves: 4

Ingredients:
- 2 cups cooked organic red lentils
- 1 large organic sweet potato, cubed
- 1 organic red bell pepper, sliced
- 1 organic onion, diced
- 2 organic garlic cloves, minced
- 1 tbsp organic ginger, grated
- 1 can (14 oz) organic coconut milk
- 2 tbsp organic red curry paste
- 1 tbsp organic za'atar spice blend
- 2 tbsp organic coconut oil
- 1/4 cup organic fresh cilantro, chopped
- 1/4 cup organic fresh mint, chopped
- Sea salt to taste

Instructions:
1. In a large pot, heat coconut oil over medium heat. Sauté onion, garlic, and ginger until fragrant.
2. Add sweet potato and bell pepper, cook for 5 minutes.
3. Stir in red curry paste and za'atar, cook for 1 minute.

4. Add coconut milk and simmer for 15 minutes until sweet potato is tender.
5. Stir in lentils and cook for another 5 minutes.
6. Garnish with fresh cilantro and mint before serving.

Tip: For a smoother curry, blend half the lentils before adding to the pot.

Nutritional Information (per serving):
- Calories: 420
- Protein: 14 g
- Fat: 22 g
- Carbohydrates: 45 g
- Fiber: 10 g

TEMPEH AND VEGETABLE CURRY WITH COCONUT CREAM

Prep Time: 20 minutes
Cook Time: 30 minutes
Serves: 4

Ingredients:
- 8 oz organic tempeh, cubed
- 1 organic onion, diced
- 2 organic garlic cloves, minced
- 1 tbsp organic ginger, grated
- 1 organic red bell pepper, diced
- 1 cup organic broccoli florets
- 1 can (14 oz) organic full-fat coconut milk
- 2 tbsp organic curry powder
- 2 tbsp organic coconut oil
- Sea salt and black pepper to taste
- 1/4 cup organic fresh cilantro, chopped

Instructions:
1. Heat coconut oil in a large skillet over medium heat. Add onion, garlic, and ginger, and sauté until fragrant.
2. Add tempeh cubes and cook until lightly browned.
3. Stir in curry powder and cook for another minute.
4. Add bell pepper, broccoli, and coconut milk. Bring to a simmer and cook for 15-20 minutes until vegetables are tender.
5. Season with salt and pepper to taste.
6. Serve hot, garnished with fresh cilantro.

Tip: For a richer flavor, toast the curry powder in a dry pan before adding it to the curry.

Nutritional Information (per serving):
- Calories: 400
- Protein: 20g
- Fat: 30g
- Carbohydrates: 16g
- Fiber: 6g

POWER SALAD RECIPES

SEAFOOD

NICOISE-STYLE SALAD WITH GRILLED TUNA AND KOMBUCHA VINAIGRETTE

Prep Time: 25 minutes
Cook Time: 10 minutes
Serves: 4

Ingredients:
- 4 wild-caught tuna steaks (6 oz each)
- 1 lb organic green beans, trimmed
- 4 organic eggs
- 2 cups organic cherry tomatoes, halved
- 1 organic cucumber, sliced
- 1/2 cup organic Kalamata olives
- 1/4 cup organic capers
- 1 organic red onion, thinly sliced
- 4 cups organic mixed salad greens
- 2 tbsp organic avocado oil

For the vinaigrette:
- 1/4 cup organic extra-virgin olive oil
- 2 tbsp unflavored kombucha
- 1 tbsp organic Dijon mustard
- 1 organic garlic clove, minced
- 1 tsp organic herbs de Provence
- Sea salt and freshly ground black pepper to taste

Instructions:
1. Boil green beans until crisp-tender, then chill in ice water.
2. Soft boil eggs for 6-7 minutes, then chill in ice water. Peel and halve.
3. Whisk together all vinaigrette ingredients.

4. Grill tuna steaks in avocado oil for 2-3 minutes per side for medium-rare.
5. Arrange salad greens on plates. Top with green beans, tomatoes, cucumber, olives, capers, and red onion.
6. Slice tuna and arrange on top of the salad with halved eggs.
7. Drizzle with kombucha vinaigrette before serving.

Tip: For perfectly grilled tuna, ensure your grill is very hot before adding the fish. This will give you nice grill marks while keeping the inside tender.

Nutritional Information (per serving):
- Calories: 550, Protein: 45 g, Fat: 35 g, Carbohydrates: 20 g, Fiber: 6 g

MEDITERRANEAN NAVY BEAN AND WILD SALMON SALAD

Prep Time: 20 minutes
Cook Time: 15 minutes (for beans if using dried)
Serves: 4

Ingredients:

- 2 cups cooked organic navy beans (if using dried, soak overnight and cook until tender)
- 12 oz wild-caught salmon fillet
- 2 cups organic mixed salad greens
- 1 organic cucumber, diced
- 1 organic bell pepper, diced
- 1/4 cup organic Kalamata olives, pitted and halved
- 1/4 cup organic red onion, finely sliced
- 2 tbsp organic capers, drained
- 1/4 cup organic extra virgin olive oil
- 2 tbsp organic lemon juice
- 1 tsp organic Dijon mustard
- 1 clove organic garlic, minced
- 1 tsp organic dried oregano
- Sea salt and freshly ground black pepper to taste
- 1/4 cup organic fermented vegetables (like sauerkraut or kimchi), for serving

Instructions:

1. Preheat oven to 400°F (200°C). Season salmon with salt and pepper, then bake for 12-15 minutes until just cooked through. Let cool, then flake into large pieces.
2. In a large bowl, combine navy beans, mixed greens, cucumber, bell pepper, olives, red onion, and capers.
3. In a small bowl, whisk together olive oil, lemon juice, Dijon mustard, garlic, oregano, salt, and pepper to make the dressing.
4. Gently fold the flaked salmon into the salad mixture.
5. Drizzle the dressing over the salad and toss gently to combine.
6. Serve with a side of fermented vegetables.

Tip: To enhance the flavor of the navy beans, cook them with a bay leaf, a clove of garlic, and a strip of organic lemon zest. Remove these aromatics before adding the beans to the salad.

Nutritional Information (per serving):

- Calories: 500
- Protein: 35 g
- Fat: 28 g
- Carbohydrates: 30 g
- Fiber: 8 g

MEDITERRANEAN SARDINE AND AVOCADO SALAD

Prep Time: 15 minutes
Cook Time: 0 minutes
Serves: 4

Ingredients:

- 2 cans (4 oz each) wild-caught sardines in olive oil, drained
- 2 large organic avocados, diced
- 1 cup organic cherry tomatoes, halved
- 1/4 cup organic red onion, finely chopped
- 1/4 cup organic Kalamata olives, pitted and halved
- 1/4 cup organic fresh parsley, chopped
- 2 tbsp organic extra-virgin olive oil
- 1 organic lemon, juiced
- Sea salt and black pepper to taste

Instructions:

1. In a large bowl, combine avocados, cherry tomatoes, red onion, Kalamata olives, and parsley.
2. Gently fold in the sardines, being careful not to break them up too much.
3. Drizzle with olive oil and lemon juice. Season with salt and pepper.

4. Toss gently to combine and serve immediately.

Tip: For extra flavor, marinate the sardines in lemon juice and olive oil for 10 minutes before adding them to the salad.

Nutritional Information (per serving):

- Calories: 320
- Protein: 18g
- Fat: 26g
- Carbohydrates: 10g
- Fiber: 7g

SARDINE AND AVOCADO SALAD WITH LEMON-TAHINI DRESSING

Prep Time: 20 minutes
Cook Time: 0 minutes
Serves: 4

Ingredients:

- 2 cans (4 oz each) wild-caught sardines in olive oil, drained and flaked
- 2 large organic avocados, diced
- 4 cups organic mixed greens (arugula, spinach, and kale)
- 1/4 cup organic red onion, thinly sliced
- 1/4 cup organic sunflower seeds
- Sea salt and black pepper to taste

For the Lemon-Tahini Dressing:

- 1/4 cup organic tahini
- 1/4 cup organic lemon juice
- 2 tbsp organic extra-virgin olive oil
- 1 organic garlic clove, minced
- 2 tbsp water
- Sea salt and black pepper to taste

Instructions:

1. In a blender, blend all dressing ingredients until smooth. Adjust seasoning as needed.
2. In a large bowl, combine mixed greens, diced avocado, flaked sardines, red onion, and sunflower seeds.
3. Drizzle the lemon-tahini dressing over the salad and toss gently to combine.
4. Serve immediately.

Tip: For added texture, lightly toast the sunflower seeds before adding them to the salad.

Nutritional Information (per serving):

- Calories: 400
- Protein: 20g
- Fat: 34g
- Carbohydrates: 10g
- Fiber: 6g

ROASTED BROCCOLI SALAD WITH ANCHOVY VINAIGRETTE AND TOASTED ALMONDS

Prep Time: 15 minutes
Cook Time: 20 minutes
Serves: 4

Ingredients:

- 1 lb organic broccoli florets
- 2 tbsp organic avocado oil
- Sea salt and black pepper to taste
- 1/4 cup organic slivered almonds
- **For the Vinaigrette:**
  - 1/4 cup organic extra-virgin olive oil
  - 2 tbsp organic red wine vinegar
  - 4 anchovy fillets, minced
  - 1 organic garlic clove, minced
  - 1 tsp organic Dijon mustard

Instructions:

1. Preheat oven to 400°F (200°C).

2. Toss broccoli florets with avocado oil, salt, and pepper. Spread on a baking sheet and roast for 15-20 minutes until tender and slightly charred.
3. Meanwhile, toast almonds in a dry skillet over medium heat for 3-5 minutes until fragrant and lightly browned.
4. For the vinaigrette, whisk together olive oil, red wine vinegar, minced anchovies, garlic, and Dijon mustard until well combined.
5. Transfer roasted broccoli to a bowl. Pour vinaigrette over warm broccoli and toss to coat.
6. Top with toasted almonds and serve.

Tip: For a more intense roasted flavor, broil the broccoli for the last 2-3 minutes of cooking.

Nutritional Information (per serving):
- Calories: 280
- Protein: 8g
- Fat: 24g
- Carbohydrates: 12g
- Fiber: 6g

FENNEL AND CITRUS SALAD WITH SHRIMP AND AVOCADO

Prep Time: 20 minutes **Cook Time:** 5 minutes **Serves:** 4

Ingredients:
- 2 organic fennel bulbs, thinly sliced
- 1 organic grapefruit, segmented
- 1 organic orange, segmented
- 1 lb organic, wild-caught shrimp, peeled and deveined
- 1 organic avocado, diced
- 1/4 cup organic fresh mint, chopped
- 2 tbsp organic extra-virgin olive oil
- 1 tbsp organic lemon juice
- Sea salt and black pepper to taste

Instructions:
1. In a large bowl, combine fennel slices, grapefruit segments, orange segments, and mint.
2. In a skillet, heat olive oil over medium heat. Sauté shrimp for 3-4 minutes until pink and cooked through. Season with salt and pepper.
3. Gently toss the shrimp and diced avocado with the fennel mixture.
4. Drizzle with lemon juice and olive oil. Season with salt and pepper to taste.
5. Serve immediately.

Tip: Use a mandoline to thinly slice the fennel for a delicate texture.

Nutritional Information (per serving):
- Calories: 340
- Protein: 24g
- Fat: 24g
- Carbohydrates: 14g
- Fiber: 6g

ARUGULA SALAD WITH CALAMARI, ZUCCHINI, AND BALSAMIC

Prep Time: 20 minutes
Cook Time: 10 minutes
Serves: 4

Ingredients:
For the Salad:
- 6 cups organic arugula
- 1 lb wild-caught calamari, cleaned and cut into rings
- 2 medium organic zucchinis, spiralized or thinly sliced
- 1/2 cup organic cherry tomatoes, halved
- 1/4 cup organic red onion, thinly sliced
- 1/4 cup organic fresh basil leaves, chopped
- 1/4 cup organic pine nuts, toasted

For the Dressing:
- 1/4 cup organic extra-virgin olive oil
- 2 tbsp organic balsamic vinegar
- 1 tbsp organic lemon juice
- 1 tsp organic Dijon mustard
- 1 organic garlic clove, minced
- Sea salt and freshly ground black pepper to taste

Instructions:
1. Heat 1 tbsp of the olive oil in a skillet over medium-high heat. Add the calamari rings and cook for 2-3 minutes on each side until they are opaque and cooked through. Season with salt and pepper. Remove from heat and set aside.
2. In the same skillet, add another 1 tbsp of olive oil. Add the spiralized or thinly sliced zucchini and sauté for 2-3 minutes until just tender. Remove from heat and allow to cool slightly.
3. In a large bowl, combine the arugula, cherry tomatoes, red onion, and basil.
4. In a small bowl, whisk together the remaining olive oil, balsamic vinegar, lemon juice, Dijon mustard, minced garlic, salt, and pepper until well combined.
5. Assemble the Salad by the cooked calamari and sautéed zucchini to the salad bowl.
6. Pour the dressing over the salad and toss gently to combine and sprinkle with toasted pine nuts.

Tip: For added flavor, you can marinate the calamari in a mixture of olive oil, lemon juice, garlic, and herbs for 30 minutes before cooking.

Nutritional Information (per serving):
- Calories: 320
- Protein: 20g
- Fat: 22g
- Carbohydrates: 12g
- Fiber: 4g

MACKEREL WITH FENNEL AND CITRUS SALAD

Prep Time: 10 minutes
Cook Time: 8 minutes
Serves: 2

Ingredients:
- 2 fillets wild-caught mackerel
- 1 small organic fennel bulb, thinly sliced
- 1 organic orange, segmented
- 1 tbsp organic olive oil
- 1 tbsp organic lemon juice
- 1 tbsp organic fresh dill, chopped
- 1 tbsp organic apple cider vinegar

Instructions:
1. In a bowl, combine sliced fennel, orange segments, lemon juice, olive oil, and apple cider vinegar. Toss well and let it marinate while you cook the fish.
2. Heat a pan over medium heat and cook the mackerel fillets skin-side down for about 4 minutes. Flip and cook for another 3-4 minutes until the flesh is opaque and flakes easily with a fork. Cooking the mackerel skin-side down first crisps up the skin while keeping the fish moist.
3. Plate the mackerel with the fennel and citrus salad on the side. Garnish with fresh dill and serve immediately.
   Tip: Thinly slice the fennel using a mandoline for a crisp, even texture that complements the softness of the orange.

Nutritional Information (per serving):
- Calories: 400
- Protein: 30 g
- Fat: 28 g
- Carbohydrates: 12 g
- Fiber: 4 g

MEAT

GRILLED CHICKEN SALAD WITH RASPBERRY VINAIGRETTE

Prep Time: 20 minutes
Cook Time: 10 minutes
Serves: 4

Ingredients:
- 1 lb organic, pasture-raised chicken breasts
- 5 cups organic mixed greens (arugula, spinach, and kale)
- 1 cup organic raspberries
- 1 organic avocado, sliced
- 1/4 cup organic walnuts, toasted
- 1/4 cup organic feta cheese, crumbled (optional)
- 2 tbsp organic extra-virgin olive oil
- Sea salt and black pepper to taste

For the Vinaigrette:
- 1/2 cup organic raspberries
- 1/4 cup organic extra-virgin olive oil
- 2 tbsp organic apple cider vinegar
- 1 tsp organic Dijon mustard
- Sea salt and black pepper to taste

Instructions:
1. Preheat grill to medium-high heat.
2. Season chicken breasts with salt and pepper. Grill for 5-6 minutes per side, or until fully cooked. Let rest for 5 minutes before slicing.
3. In a blender, combine all vinaigrette ingredients and blend until smooth. Adjust seasoning as needed.
4. In a large bowl, combine mixed greens, raspberries, avocado, walnuts, and feta cheese.
5. Top with sliced grilled chicken and drizzle with raspberry vinaigrette before serving.

Tip: For extra flavor, marinate the chicken in a bit of the vinaigrette for 30 minutes before grilling.

Nutritional Information (per serving):
- Calories: 480
- Protein: 32g
- Fat: 35g
- Carbohydrates: 18g
- Fiber: 8g

DUKKAH-SPICED CHICKEN SALAD WITH AVOCADO AND COCONUT YOGURT DRESSING

Prep Time: 20 minutes
Cook Time: 20 minutes
Serves: 4

Ingredients:
- 1 lb organic, pasture-raised chicken breast, cooked and shredded
- 1/2 cup organic celery, diced
- 1/4 cup organic red onion, diced
- 1 large organic avocado, diced
- 2 tbsp organic dukkah
- Sea salt and black pepper to taste

For the Dressing:
- 1/2 cup organic coconut yogurt
- 1 tbsp organic lemon juice
- 1 tsp organic Dijon mustard

Instructions:
1. In a large bowl, combine shredded chicken, celery, red onion, avocado, and dukkah. Season with salt and pepper.
2. In a small bowl, whisk together coconut yogurt, lemon juice, and Dijon mustard to make the dressing.

3. Pour dressing over the chicken salad and toss gently to combine.
4. Serve immediately or chill for 30 minutes before serving.

Tip: For a creamier dressing, blend the avocado with the other dressing ingredients until smooth.

Nutritional Information (per serving):
- Calories: 360
- Protein: 30g
- Fat: 22g
- Carbohydrates: 10g
- Fiber: 4g

JICAMA AND CHICKEN SALAD WITH APPLE CIDER VINAIGRETTE

Prep Time: 20 minutes
Cook Time: 10 minutes
Serves: 4

Ingredients:
- 2 cups organic cooked chicken breast, shredded
- 1 medium organic jicama, peeled and julienned
- 1 organic apple, thinly sliced
- 1/4 cup organic red onion, thinly sliced
- 4 cups organic mixed salad greens
- 1/4 cup organic walnuts, toasted and chopped

For the Apple Cider Vinaigrette:
- 1/4 cup organic extra-virgin olive oil
- 2 tbsp organic apple cider vinegar
- 1 tbsp organic Dijon mustard
- 1 organic garlic clove, minced
- Sea salt and black pepper to taste

Instructions:
1. In a large bowl, combine shredded chicken, jicama, apple slices, red onion, and mixed salad greens.
2. In a small bowl, whisk together olive oil, apple cider vinegar, Dijon mustard, minced garlic, salt, and pepper to make the vinaigrette.
3. Pour the vinaigrette over the salad and toss gently to combine.
4. Top with toasted walnuts and serve immediately.

Tip: For added flavor, marinate the cooked chicken in a bit of the vinaigrette for 15 minutes before adding it to the salad.

Nutritional Information (per serving):
- Calories: 320
- Protein: 24g
- Fat: 20g
- Carbohydrates: 16g
- Fiber: 8g

BROCCOLI SALAD WITH BACON AND AVOCADO DRESSING

Prep Time: 20 minutes
Cook Time: 10 minutes
Serves: 4

Ingredients:
- 4 cups organic broccoli florets
- 6 slices organic, pasture-raised bacon, cooked and crumbled
- 1/4 cup organic red onion, finely chopped
- 1/4 cup organic sunflower seeds
- 1/2 cup organic coconut yogurt
- 1 large organic avocado
- 1 organic lemon, juiced
- Sea salt and black pepper to taste

Instructions:
1. In a large bowl, combine broccoli florets, crumbled bacon, red onion, and sunflower seeds.
2. In a blender, blend coconut yogurt, avocado, lemon juice, salt, and pepper until smooth.
3. Pour the dressing over the broccoli mixture and toss to combine.
4. Chill in the refrigerator for at least 30 minutes before serving.

Tip: For added texture, lightly blanch the broccoli florets in boiling water for 1-2 minutes, then immediately transfer to ice water to retain their crunch and vibrant color.

Nutritional Information (per serving):
- Calories: 420
- Protein: 18g
- Fat: 34g
- Carbohydrates: 14g
- Fiber: 8g

KOHLRABI AND PROSCIUTTO SALAD WITH AVOCADO DRESSING

Prep Time: 15 minutes
Cook Time: 0 minutes
Serves: 4

Ingredients:
- 2 medium organic kohlrabi, peeled and thinly sliced
- 4 oz organic prosciutto, thinly sliced
- 2 cups organic mixed salad greens
- 1/4 cup organic walnuts, toasted and chopped
- 1/4 cup organic fresh mint leaves, torn

For the Avocado Dressing:
- 1 ripe organic avocado
- 1/4 cup organic extra-virgin olive oil
- 2 tbsp organic apple cider vinegar
- 1 organic garlic clove, minced
- Sea salt and black pepper to taste

Instructions:
1. Using a mandoline or sharp knife, slice the kohlrabi very thinly.
2. Arrange kohlrabi slices, prosciutto, and salad greens on serving plates.
3. For the dressing, blend avocado, olive oil, apple cider vinegar, garlic, salt, and pepper until smooth.
4. Drizzle the avocado dressing over the salad.
5. Top with toasted walnuts and torn mint leaves.

Tip: For a more tender texture, lightly salt the kohlrabi slices and let them sit for 10 minutes before assembling the salad. Rinse and pat dry before using.

Nutritional Information (per serving):
- Calories: 320
- Protein: 12g
- Fat: 28g
- Carbohydrates: 10g
- Fiber: 5g

BEEF LIVER AND POMEGRANATE SALAD

Prep Time: 15 minutes
Cook Time: 10 minutes
Serves: 4

Ingredients:
- 1 lb organic, grass-fed beef liver, thinly sliced
- 1 tbsp organic extra-virgin olive oil
- 4 cups organic mixed greens (such as arugula, spinach, and kale)
- 1 cup organic pomegranate seeds
- 1/4 cup organic walnuts, toasted and chopped
- 1/4 cup organic red onion, thinly sliced
- 2 tbsp organic extra-virgin olive oil
- 1 tbsp organic apple cider vinegar
- 1 tbsp organic lemon juice
- Sea salt and freshly ground black pepper to taste

Instructions:
1. Heat oil in a large skillet over medium-high heat.
2. Add the liver slices and cook for about 3-4 minutes per until browned and cooked through. Remove from heat and set aside.
3. In a large bowl, combine mixed greens, pomegranate seeds, toasted walnuts, and red onion.
4. In a small bowl, whisk together olive oil, apple cider vinegar, lemon juice, salt, and pepper.
5. Slice the cooked liver into bite-sized pieces and add to the salad.

Tip: For a more intense flavor marinate the liver slices in pomegranate juice and herbs for 30 minutes before cooking.

Nutritional Information (per serving):
- Calories: 350
- Protein: 20g
- Fat: 24g
- Carbohydrates: 14g
- Fiber: 4g

GRILLED ASPARAGUS AND CHICKEN SALAD WITH PROBIOTIC GARLIC-TAHINI DRESSING

Prep Time: 15 minutes
Cook Time: 15 minutes
Serves: 4

Ingredients:
- **For the Salad:**
  - 1 bunch organic asparagus, trimmed
  - 2 organic, free-range chicken breasts, grilled and sliced
  - 2 tbsp organic avocado oil (for grilling)
  - 4 cups organic mixed greens (arugula, spinach, Romaine)
  - 1/4 cup organic pumpkin seeds, toasted
  - 1/2 organic cucumber, sliced thinly
  - 1/4 cup organic cherry tomatoes, halved
- **For the Probiotic Garlic-Tahini Dressing:**
  - 2 tbsp organic tahini
  - 2 tbsp organic coconut yogurt (unsweetened, probiotic-rich)
  - 1 tbsp organic lemon juice
  - 1 clove organic garlic, minced
  - 1 tbsp organic apple cider vinegar (unpasteurized)
  - 1 tbsp organic olive oil
  - Sea salt & pepper to taste

Instructions:
1. **Grill the Chicken and Asparagus:** Preheat a grill to medium-high heat. Brush the chicken breasts and asparagus with avocado oil, and season with salt and pepper. Grill the chicken for 6-8 minutes per side, until fully cooked (internal temperature should reach 165°F). Grill the asparagus for 3-4 minutes per side until tender and slightly charred. Let the chicken rest before slicing.
2. **Prepare the Dressing:** In a small bowl, whisk together tahini, coconut yogurt, lemon juice, garlic, apple cider vinegar, olive oil, salt, and pepper until smooth.
3. **Assemble the Salad:** In a large bowl, toss the mixed greens, grilled asparagus (cut into bite-sized pieces), cucumber slices, cherry tomatoes, and toasted pumpkin seeds. Top with the sliced grilled chicken.
4. **Dress the Salad:** Drizzle the probiotic garlic-tahini dressing over the salad and toss gently. Serve immediately for a nutrient-dense, high-protein meal.

Nutritional Information (per serving):
- Calories: 450
- Protein: 35 g
- Fat: 30 g
- Carbohydrates: 12 g, Fiber: 5 g

GRAIN-FREE CAESAR SALAD WITH ALMOND CROUTONS AND PROBIOTIC DRESSING

Prep Time: 15 minutes
Cook Time: 10 minutes (for croutons)
Serves: 4

Ingredients:
- For the Salad:
  - 1 large head organic Romaine lettuce, chopped
  - 1/4 cup organic Parmesan cheese, shaved (optional)
  - 1/2 cup organic almond croutons (recipe below)
- For the Almond Croutons:
  - 1/2 cup organic almond flour
  - 1 tbsp organic ghee or coconut oil, melted
  - 1 tsp organic garlic powder
  - 1/2 tsp organic Italian seasoning
  - Sea salt & pepper to taste
- For the Probiotic Caesar Dressing:
  - 1/2 cup organic coconut yogurt (unsweetened, probiotic-rich)
  - 1 tbsp organic Dijon mustard (no added sugar)
  - 2 tbsp organic lemon juice
  - 1 clove organic garlic, minced
  - 2 tbsp organic olive oil
  - 2 organic anchovy fillets (optional, for umami flavor)
  - Sea salt & pepper to taste

Instructions:
1. Prepare the Almond Croutons: Preheat the oven to 350°F (175°C). In a bowl, mix the almond flour, melted ghee or coconut oil, garlic powder, Italian seasoning, salt, and pepper. Form into small bite-sized pieces and place on a baking sheet. Bake for 8-10 minutes until golden and crispy.
2. Make the Probiotic Caesar Dressing: In a small bowl, whisk together the coconut yogurt, Dijon mustard, lemon juice, garlic, olive oil, and anchovy fillets (if using). Season with salt and pepper to taste. Refrigerate for 10 minutes to allow the flavors to meld.
3. Assemble the Salad: In a large bowl, toss the chopped Romaine lettuce with the dressing. Top with shaved Parmesan (optional) and almond croutons. Serve immediately for a crunchy, creamy Caesar salad with a probiotic twist!

Nutritional Information (per serving):
- Calories: 320
- Protein: 10 g
- Fat 26 g
- Carbohydrates: 10 g
- Fiber: 4 g

VEGETARIAN AND VEGAN

NAVY BEAN SALAD WITH AVOCADO AND FERMENTED VEGETABLES

Prep Time: 20 minutes
Cook Time: 0 minutes
Serves: 4

Ingredients:
- 2 cups cooked organic navy beans
- 1 large organic avocado, diced
- 1 organic cucumber, diced
- 1 cup organic cherry tomatoes, halved
- 1/2 cup organic red bell pepper, diced
- 1/4 cup organic red onion, finely chopped
- 1/2 cup organic fermented vegetables (like sauerkraut or kimchi), drained
- 2 tbsp organic extra-virgin olive oil
- 2 tbsp organic apple cider vinegar
- 1 tbsp organic fresh lemon juice
- Sea salt and black pepper to taste
- 1/4 cup organic fresh cilantro, chopped

Instructions:
1. In a large bowl, combine navy beans, avocado, cucumber, cherry tomatoes, red bell pepper, and red onion.
2. Add the fermented vegetables to the bowl.
3. In a small bowl, whisk together olive oil, apple cider vinegar, lemon juice, salt, and pepper.
4. Pour the dressing over the salad and toss gently to combine.
5. Garnish with fresh cilantro before serving.

Tip: To keep the avocado from browning, add it just before serving and toss gently to preserve its texture.

Nutritional Information (per serving):
- Calories: 350
- Protein: 10 g
- Fat: 20 g
- Carbohydrates: 30 g
- Fiber: 10 g

MEDITERRANEAN LENTIL AND ROASTED VEGETABLE SALAD WITH TAHINI DRESSING

Prep Time: 20 minutes
Cook Time: 30 minutes
Serves: 4

Ingredients:
- 2 cups cooked organic lentils
- 1 organic eggplant, cubed
- 1 organic zucchini, cubed
- 1 organic red bell pepper, cubed
- 1 organic red onion, sliced
- 3 tbsp organic extra-virgin olive oil
- 1/4 cup organic tahini
- 2 tbsp organic lemon juice
- 1 organic garlic clove, minced
- 2 tbsp water
- 1/4 cup organic fresh parsley, chopped
- Sea salt and black pepper to taste

Instructions:
1. Preheat oven to 400°F (200°C).
2. Toss the eggplant, zucchini, bell pepper, and onion with 2 tbsp oil on a baking sheet. Roast for 25-30 minutes, stirring halfway, until vegetables are tender and caramelized.
3. In a small bowl, whisk together the tahini, lemon juice, garlic, remaining 1 tbsp oil, water, salt, and pepper to make the dressing.
4. In a large bowl, combine the roasted vegetables and cooked lentils. Drizzle with the tahini dressing and toss to coat.
5. Garnish with fresh parsley before serving.

Tip: For a more intense flavor, roast the vegetables until they develop some charred edges. Serve with some fermented vegetables for a probiotic side or fermented chilis for an extra spicy kick.

Nutritional Information (per serving):
- Calories: 420
- Protein: 16 g
- Fat: 24 g
- Carbohydrates: 40 g, Fiber: 12 g

AVOCADO AND BEET SALAD WITH LEMON-TAHINI DRESSING

Prep Time: 20 minutes
Cook Time: 20 minutes
Serves: 4

Ingredients:
- 3 organic beets, roasted and cubed
- 2 large organic avocados, diced
- 1 organic red onion, thinly sliced
- 1/4 cup organic fresh parsley, chopped
- 1/4 cup organic raw pumpkin seeds

For the Lemon-Tahini Dressing:
- 1/4 cup organic tahini
- 1/4 cup organic lemon juice
- 2 tbsp organic extra-virgin olive oil
- 1 organic garlic clove, minced
- 2 tbsp water
- Sea salt and black pepper to taste

Instructions:
1. Preheat oven to 400°F (200°C). Roast the beets until tender, about 20 minutes. Let cool, then peel and cube.
2. In a large bowl, combine roasted beets, diced avocado, red onion, and parsley.
3. In a small bowl, whisk together the tahini, lemon juice, olive oil, garlic, and water. Season with salt and pepper.
4. Drizzle the lemon-tahini dressing over the salad and gently toss to coat.
5. Sprinkle the pumpkin seeds on top before serving.

Tip: For a more vibrant color, use a mix of red and golden beets.

Nutritional Information (per serving):
- Calories: 380
- Protein: 8g
- Fat: 30g
- Carbohydrates: 24g
- Fiber: 10g

WALNUT, BEET, AND AVOCADO SALAD WITH COCONUT YOGURT DRESSING

Prep Time: 20 minutes
Cook Time: 40 minutes (for roasting beets)
Serves: 4

Ingredients:
- 3 organic beets, roasted, peeled, and diced
- 2 large organic avocados, diced
- 4 cups organic baby spinach
- 1/2 cup organic walnuts, toasted and chopped
- 1/4 cup organic red onion, thinly sliced

For the Dressing:
- 1/2 cup organic coconut yogurt
- 2 tbsp organic lemon juice
- 1 tbsp organic extra-virgin olive oil
- 1 organic garlic clove, minced
- Sea salt and black pepper to taste

Instructions:
1. Preheat oven to 400°F (200°C). Wrap beets in foil and roast for 40 minutes until tender. Let cool, then peel and dice.
2. In a large bowl, combine roasted beets, diced avocados, spinach, walnuts, and red onion.
3. For the dressing, whisk together coconut yogurt, lemon juice, olive oil, garlic, salt, and pepper.
4. Drizzle the dressing over the salad and toss gently to combine.
5. Serve immediately.

Tip: To peel roasted beets easily, rub them with a paper towel while they are still warm.

Nutritional Information (per serving):
- Calories: 350
- Protein: 7g
- Fat: 29g
- Carbohydrates: 20g
- Fiber: 9g

GREEN BEAN AND ALMONDINE SALAD WITH LEMON-DIJON DRESSING

Prep Time: 15 minutes
Cook Time: 10 minutes
Serves: 4

Ingredients:
- 2 cups organic green beans, trimmed
- 1/4 cup organic almonds, sliced and toasted
- 1/4 cup organic red onion, thinly sliced
- 1/4 cup organic fresh parsley, chopped

For the Lemon-Dijon Dressing:
- 1/4 cup organic extra-virgin olive oil
- 2 tbsp organic lemon juice
- 1 tbsp organic Dijon mustard
- 1 organic garlic clove, minced
- Sea salt and black pepper to taste

Instructions:
1. Bring a pot of salted water to a boil. Blanch green beans for 2-3 minutes until tender-crisp. Immediately transfer to an ice bath to stop the cooking process.
2. In a bowl, whisk together olive oil, lemon juice, Dijon mustard, minced garlic, salt, and pepper to make the dressing.
3. Drain and pat dry the green beans. Toss with toasted almonds, red onion, and parsley.
4. Drizzle with lemon-Dijon dressing and toss to coat.
5. Serve immediately.

Tip: For added flavor, grill the green beans for a few minutes after blanching.

Nutritional Information (per serving):
- Calories: 220
- Protein: 4g
- Fat: 18g
- Carbohydrates: 12g
- Fiber: 4g

OKRA AND TOMATO SALAD WITH LEMON-HERB DRESSING

Prep Time: 15 minutes
Cook Time: 10 minutes
Serves: 4

Ingredients:
- 1 lb organic okra, trimmed and blanched
- 2 cups organic cherry tomatoes, halved
- 1/4 cup organic red onion, thinly sliced
- 1/4 cup organic fresh parsley, chopped
- 1/4 cup organic fresh basil, chopped

For the Lemon-Herb Dressing:
- 1/4 cup organic extra-virgin olive oil
- 2 tbsp organic lemon juice
- 1 organic garlic clove, minced
- 1 tbsp organic fresh oregano, chopped
- Sea salt and black pepper to taste

Instructions:
1. Bring a pot of salted water to a boil. Add okra and blanch for 2-3 minutes until tender-crisp. Drain and immediately transfer to an ice bath to stop the cooking process.
2. In a bowl, whisk together olive oil, lemon juice, garlic, oregano, salt, and pepper to make the dressing.
3. Combine blanched okra, cherry tomatoes, red onion, parsley, and basil in a large bowl.
4. Drizzle with lemon-herb dressing and toss to coat.
5. Serve immediately.

Tip: Grill the okra after blanching for a smoky flavor and added texture.

Nutritional Information (per serving):
- Calories: 200
- Protein: 4g
- Fat: 16g
- Carbohydrates: 12g
- Fiber: 5g

KONJAC NOODLE SALAD WITH GINGER-MISO DRESSING

Prep Time: 20 minutes
Cook Time: 0 minutes
Serves: 4

Ingredients:
- 1 package (14 oz) organic konjac noodles, rinsed and drained
- 1 cup organic red cabbage, shredded
- 1 cup organic carrots, julienned
- 1 cup organic cucumber, julienned
- 1/4 cup organic green onions, sliced
- 1/4 cup organic fresh cilantro, chopped

For the Ginger-Miso Dressing:
- 2 tbsp organic white miso paste2 tbsp organic rice vinegar
- 1 tbsp organic ginger, grated
- 1 tbsp organic coconut aminos
- 1 tbsp organic sesame oil
- 1/4 cup organic avocado oil
- Sea salt to taste

Instructions:
1. In a large bowl, combine konjac noodles, red cabbage, carrots, cucumber, green onions, and cilantro.
2. In a small bowl, whisk together miso paste, rice vinegar, grated ginger, coconut aminos, sesame oil, avocado oil, and salt to make the dressing.
3. Pour the dressing over the salad and toss to combine.
4. Serve chilled.

Tip: For an extra burst of flavor, garnish the salad with toasted sesame seeds or crushed peanuts.

Nutritional Information (per serving):
- Calories: 280
- Protein: 4g
- Fat: 24g
- Carbohydrates: 14g
- Fiber: 6g

GOOD ENERGY MEAL-PREP RECIPES

One of the main reasons we default to processed and ultra-processed foods is their sheer convenience—they're everywhere, easy to grab, and fit into our busy schedules. With packed days and little time to cook, it can feel overwhelming to eat whole, unprocessed, low-carb meals consistently. But the truth is, setting yourself up for success doesn't require endless time or effort. It's all about a little thoughtful meal prep. By planning ahead, you'll have nutritious options at the ready for those days when cooking isn't an option or you simply don't feel like it. Instead of reaching for a processed protein bar, imagine grabbing a homemade energy ball packed with healthy fats. Instead of buying a plastic-wrapped, ultra-processed wrap, you could pull out a pre-made coconut flatbread from your freezer, ready to fill with fresh, whole ingredients.

I've included fermented foods—which are a must-have in your pantry—and simple low-carb swaps for grain-based recipes. You'll also find high-protein, healthy-fat dips and snacks that will keep you satisfied and energized without compromising on health.

FERMENTED FOODS

Fermented foods are a fundamental part of the Good Energy Diet. I would recommend integrating their preparation in your weekly meal prep. I always have 2-3 fermented vegetables on end and a few fermented sauces to add to my dishes. I am particularly partial to pickled onions, fermented jalapenos, and fermented garlic which can be easily integrated in savory dishes. Sauerkraut and other fermented vegetables make for excellent sides. Find your favorites and have fun with spices!

The following tables will help you ferment any vegetable the way you like it.

FERMENTING VEGETABLES IN BRINE

Prep Time: 20-30 minutes
Fermentation Time: 3-14 days (refer to the table below for specific vegetables)
Serves: Varies depending on the quantity of vegetables used

Ingredients:
- **Vegetables of your choice** (refer to the table below)
- **Non-iodized sea salt or Himalayan pink salt:** Use a kitchen scale for precise measurements
- **Filtered Water:** Ensure it's chlorine-free, as chlorine can inhibit fermentation.
- **Optional Flavorings** (refer to the table below)

Equipment:
- Clean glass jar or fermentation crock

- Weight (smaller jar filled with water, fermentation weight, etc.)
- Cheesecloth or a clean kitchen towel
- Rubber band or twine

Instructions:

1. **Prepare Vegetables:** Wash thoroughly and trim any undesirable parts. Cut or shred according to the table below.
2. **Create Brine:**
   o **Standard Brine (2-3%):** Dissolve 1-2 tablespoons of salt per quart of filtered water. Stir until salt is fully dissolved.
   o **Stronger Brine (3-5%):** For cucumbers and peppers, dissolve 2.5-3.5 tablespoons of salt per quart of filtered water.
3. **Pack the Jar:**
   o **Tightly pack** the vegetables into the jar, leaving about 1 inch of headspace at the top.
   o **Add optional flavorings** according to the table below.
   o **For cabbage:** Massage the shredded cabbage with salt until it releases its juices before packing. This helps create a natural brine and ensures proper fermentation.
4. **Pour Brine:**
   o **Submerge:** Pour the brine over the vegetables, ensuring they are completely submerged.
   o **Top Off:** If needed, add more filtered water to completely cover the vegetables.

5. **Weigh Down:**
   o **Ensure Submersion:** Place a weight on top of the vegetables to keep them submerged beneath the brine. This prevents them from being exposed to air and developing mold.
   o **Weight Options:** Use a smaller jar filled with water, a fermentation weight, or a zip-top bag filled with brine to keep the vegetables submerged
6. **Cover:** Cover the jar with cheesecloth or a clean kitchen towel and secure it with a rubber band or twine. This allows gases to escape during fermentation while preventing dust and insects from entering
7. **Ferment:**
   o **Ideal Temperature:** Place the jar in a cool, dark place with a consistent temperature between 60-75°F (15-24°C). Avoid direct sunlight or extreme temperature fluctuations
   o **Fermentation Time:** Refer to the table below for specific fermentation times for each vegetable
8. **Monitor and Taste:** Check the ferment daily. You should see bubbles forming, indicating active fermentation. Taste the vegetables periodically to gauge the flavor development.
9. **Store:** Once the vegetables have reached your desired level of fermentation, transfer them to airtight containers and store them in the refrigerator. Fermented vegetables can last for several months when properly refrigerated

Vegetable	Fermentation Time (Days)	Preferred Salt Concentration (%)	Preferred Cutting	Spices & Flavorings	Key Micronutrients	Nutritional Information (per 1/2 cup serving, approx.)	Technical Tips
Cabbage (Sauerkraut)	7-21	2-3%	Thinly shredded	Caraway seeds, juniper berries, garlic, dill seeds	Vitamin C, Vitamin K2	Calories: 27, Protein: 1g, Fat: 0g, Carbs: 6g, Fiber: 4g	Use a mandoline or sharp knife for even shreds. Pound cabbage to release juices before adding brine.
Carrots	7-14	2-3%	Julienned, grated, or coins	Garlic, ginger, dill seeds, turmeric	Vitamin A, Potassium	Calories: 25, Protein: 1g, Fat: 0g, Carbs: 6g, Fiber: 3g	Blanch carrots briefly (1-2 minutes) before fermenting for a crisper texture.
Beets	7-14	2-3%	Thinly sliced, grated, or cubed	Bay leaf, star anise, garlic, ginger	Folate, Manganese	Calories: 35, Protein: 1g, Fat: 0g, Carbs: 8g, Fiber: 2g	Wear gloves when handling beets to avoid staining. Roasting beets beforehand can add depth of flavor.
Radishes	3-7	2-3%	Thinly sliced or whole	Dill, garlic, black peppercorns, chili flakes	Vitamin C, Potassium	Calories: 10, Protein: 1g, Fat: 0g, Carbs: 2g, Fiber: 1g	Use a mix of radish varieties for a colorful ferment. Smaller radishes can be left whole, while larger ones should be sliced.
Cucumbers (Pickles)	3-7	3-5%	Whole, spears, or sliced	Dill, garlic, mustard seeds, grape leaves, coriander seeds	Vitamin K, Potassium	Calories: 11, Protein: 0g, Fat: 0g, Carbs: 3g, Fiber: 1g	Use pickling cucumbers for a crispier texture. Add grape leaves or oak leaves to help maintain crispness.
Green Beans	5-10	2-3%	Trimmed, whole or cut	Garlic, dill, chili flakes, bay leaves	Vitamin K, Vitamin C	Calories: 20, Protein: 1g, Fat: 0g, Carbs: 4g, Fiber: 2g	Blanch green beans briefly (1-2 minutes) before fermenting to preserve color and texture.
Asparagus	3-5	2-3%	Trimmed, whole spears	Lemon zest, tarragon, black peppercorns	Vitamin K, Folate	Calories: 13, Protein: 1.5g, Fat: 0g, Carbs: 2g, Fiber: 1.5g	Choose firm asparagus spears for best results. Blanching is optional but can help retain color.
Cauliflower	5-7	2-3%	Florets or grated	Turmeric, cumin, coriander seeds, garlic	Vitamin C, Vitamin K	Calories: 15, Protein: 1g, Fat: 0g, Carbs: 3g, Fiber: 2g	Blanch cauliflower briefly (1-2 minutes) for a crisper texture. Grating provides a finer texture, similar to rice.
Brussels Sprouts	5-7	2-3%	Halved or quartered	Garlic, ginger, caraway seeds, apple slices	Vitamin C, Vitamin K	Calories: 28, Protein: 2g, Fat:	Score the base of each sprout to aid in brine penetration. Apple slices can

Vegetable	Time	Salt %	Cut	Flavorings	Key Compounds	Nutrition	Notes
						Og, Carbs: 5g, Fiber: 3g	add sweetness and complexity.
Peppers (Jalapeños, etc.)	7-14	3-5%	Slit or whole	Garlic, onions, herbs (cilantro, oregano)	Vitamin C, Capsaicin	Calories: 17, Protein: 1g, Fat: 0g, Carbs: 4g, Fiber: 2g	Wear gloves when handling hot peppers. Adjust fermentation time based on desired heat level. Slitting peppers allows for better brine penetration and faster fermentation.
Onions	5-10	2-3%	Sliced or whole, peeled	Bay leaves, peppercorns, juniper berries	Quercetin, Vitamin C	Calories: 22, Protein: 1g, Fat: 0g, Carbs: 5g, Fiber: 1g	Choose small onions for whole fermentation or slice larger ones. Whole onions ferment more slowly and retain a firmer texture.
Garlic	3-4 weeks	3-5%	Peeled whole cloves	No additional spices needed	Allicin, Manganese	Calories: 4, Protein: 0.2g, Fat: 0g, Carbs: 1g, Fiber: 0.1g	Use fresh, firm garlic cloves for best results. Fermented garlic develops a mellower flavor compared to raw garlic.
Green Tomatoes	7-14	2-3%	Sliced or quartered	Mustard seeds, dill, garlic, chili flakes (optional)	Vitamin C, Potassium	Calories: 22, Protein: 1g, Fat: 0g, Carbs: 5g, Fiber: 2g	Choose firm, unripe green tomatoes for pickling. Add chili flakes for a spicy kick.
Additional Vegetables							
Summer Squash	3-5	2-3%	Sliced or cubed	Dill, garlic, turmeric	Vitamin C, Potassium	Calories: 16, Protein: 1g, Fat: 0g, Carbs: 3g, Fiber: 1g	Choose firm squash varieties like zucchini or yellow squash.
Turnips	7-14	2-3%	Cubed or matchsticks	Caraway seeds, bay leaves, garlic	Vitamin C, Potassium	Calories: 28, Protein: 1g, Fat: 0g, Carbs: 6g, Fiber: 3g	Peel turnips before fermenting. Add a small piece of ginger for a subtle zing.
Kohlrabi	5-7	2-3%	Cubed or matchsticks	Dill seeds, garlic, black peppercorns	Vitamin C, Potassium	Calories: 27, Protein: 2g, Fat: 0g, Carbs: 6g, Fiber: 3g	Peel kohlrabi before fermenting. Its mild flavor pairs well with various spices.
Celery	3-5	2-3%	Chopped stalks	Celery seeds, black peppercorns, garlic	Vitamin K, Potassium	Calories: 6, Protein: 0.3g, Fat: 0g, Carbs: 1g, Fiber: 1g	Use celery stalks and leaves for a flavorful ferment.
Fennel	5-7	2-3%	Thinly sliced bulbs	Fennel seeds, orange zest, black peppercorns	Vitamin C, Potassium	Calories: 27, Protein: 1.5g, Fat: 0g, Carbs: 6g, Fiber: 3g	Fennel adds a unique anise-like flavor to ferments.
Rutabaga	7-14	2-3%	Cubed or matchsticks	Caraway seeds, mustard seeds, garlic	Vitamin C, Potassium	Calories: 35, Protein: 1g, Fat: 0g, Carbs: 8g, Fiber: 3g	Peel rutabaga before fermenting. Its earthy flavor pairs well with bold spices.

VEGETABLES FERMENTED IN THEIR OWN JUICES (SALT-MASSAGED)

Prep Time: 20-30 minutes
Fermentation Time: 3-7 days (refer to the table below for specific vegetables)
Serves: Varies depending on the quantity of vegetables used

Ingredients:
- **Vegetables of your choice** (refer to the table below)
- **Non-iodized sea salt or Himalayan pink salt**
- **Optional Flavorings** (refer to the table below)

Equipment:
- Clean glass jar or fermentation crock
- Weight (smaller jar filled with water, fermentation weight, etc.)
- Cheesecloth or a clean kitchen towel
- Rubber band or twine

Instructions:

1. **Prepare Vegetables:** Wash thoroughly, remove any undesirable parts, and cut or shred according to the table below.
2. **Salt Massage:**
   - **Weigh Vegetables:** Use a kitchen scale to accurately measure the weight of your prepared vegetables.
   - **Calculate Salt:** Use the recommended salt amount per pound of vegetables from the table below.
   - **Massage:** Sprinkle the salt over the vegetables and massage them gently but firmly for several minutes until they soften and release their juices. You can also let them sit with the salt for 30 minutes to an hour, allowing the salt to draw out moisture naturally.
3. **Pack the Jar:**
   - **Tightly pack** the salted vegetables into the jar, pressing down to release any trapped air bubbles. Ensure the vegetables are completely submerged in their own juices. If there isn't

enough liquid to cover them, add a small amount of filtered water.
   - ○ **Add optional flavorings** according to the table below.
4. **Weigh Down:**
   - ○ **Ensure Submersion:** Place a weight on top of the vegetables to keep them submerged beneath their juices.
   - ○ **Weight Options:** Use a smaller jar filled with water, a fermentation weight, or a zip-top bag filled with brine to keep the vegetables submerged.
5. **Cover:**
   - ○ **Breathable Cover:** Cover the jar with cheesecloth or a clean kitchen towel and secure it with a rubber band or twine. This allows gases to escape during fermentation while preventing dust and insects from entering

6. **Ferment:**
   - ○ **Ideal Temperature:** Place the jar in a cool, dark place with a consistent temperature between 60-75°F (15-24°C). Avoid direct sunlight or extreme temperature fluctuations
   - ○ **Fermentation Time:** Refer to the table below for specific fermentation times for each vegetable
7. **Monitor and Taste:** Check the ferment daily. You should see bubbles forming, indicating active fermentation. Taste the vegetables periodically to gauge the flavor development.
8. **Store:**
   - ○ **Refrigerate:** Once the vegetables have reached your desired level of fermentation, transfer them to airtight containers and store them in the refrigerator. Fermented vegetables can last for several months when properly refrigerated

VEGETABLES FERMENTED IN THEIR OWN JUICES (SALT-MASSAGED)

Vegetable	Fermentation Time (Days)	Salt Amount (per pound of vegetables)	Preferred Cutting	Spices & Flavorings	Key Micronutrients	Nutritional Information (per 1/2 cup serving, approx.)	Technical Tips
Green Cabbage (Kimchi)	3-7	1-2 tablespoons	Quartered then coarsely chopped	Garlic, ginger, gochugaru, fish sauce (optional), daikon radish, scallions	Vitamin C, Vitamin K, Probiotics	Calories: 20, Protein: 1g, Fat: 0g, Carbs: 4g, Fiber: 2g	Massage cabbage thoroughly until it becomes pliable and releases its juices. Use a non-reactive container (glass or ceramic) for fermentation.
Napa Cabbage (Kimchi)	3-7	1-2 tablespoons	Quartered then coarsely chopped	Similar to green cabbage kimchi but can be milder	Vitamin C, Vitamin K, Probiotics	Calories: 15, Protein: 1g, Fat: 0g, Carbs: 3g, Fiber: 2g	Napa cabbage is more delicate, so handle with care during massaging.
Kale	3-5	1 tablespoon	De-stemmed and coarsely chopped or shredded	Garlic, ginger, red pepper flakes, nutritional yeast	Vitamin K, Vitamin C, Calcium	Calories: 30, Protein: 3g, Fat: 0g, Carbs: 6g, Fiber: 3g	Massage kale thoroughly to release juices and soften leaves. You can also add a small amount of grated carrot or apple to help release more liquid.
Collard Greens	3-5	1 tablespoon	De-stemmed and coarsely chopped or shredded	Garlic, ginger, apple cider vinegar, smoked paprika	Vitamin K, Vitamin C, Calcium	Calories: 25, Protein: 2g, Fat: 0g, Carbs: 5g, Fiber: 2g	Similar to kale, but collard greens may require slightly longer massaging due to their thicker leaves.
Zucchini	3-5	1 tablespoon	Grated	Dill, mint, garlic, lemon zest	Vitamin C, Potassium	Calories: 10, Protein: 1g, Fat: 0g, Carbs: 2g, Fiber: 1g	Squeeze out excess moisture after salting to prevent a watery ferment. You can also add a small amount of grated carrot or apple to help release more liquid.
Radishes	3-5	1 tablespoon	Thinly sliced or grated	Dill, garlic, black peppercorns	Vitamin C, Potassium	Calories: 10, Protein: 1g, Fat: 0g, Carbs: 2g, Fiber: 1g	Choose a variety of radishes for a colorful ferment.
Green Onions (Scallions)	3-5	1 tablespoon	Chopped into 1-inch pieces	Ginger, garlic, chili flakes	Vitamin K, Vitamin C	Calories: 15, Protein: 1g, Fat: 0g, Carbs: 3g, Fiber: 1g	Massage the green onions gently to avoid bruising.

QUICK PICKLES (REFRIGERATOR PICKLES)

Prep Time: 10-15 minutes
Refrigerator Time: 30 minutes - 2 weeks (refer to the table above for specific vegetables)
Serves: Varies depending on the quantity of vegetables used

Ingredients:
- Vegetables of your choice (refer to the table above)
- Vinegar (white, apple cider, rice vinegar, or red wine vinegar)
- Water
- Salt
- Sugar (optional)
- Optional Flavorings (refer to the table above)

Equipment:
- Clean glass jar
- Saucepan

Instructions:
1. **Prepare Vegetables:** Wash and chop the vegetables according to the preferred cutting method mentioned in the table.
2. **Prepare Brine:** In a saucepan, combine vinegar, water, salt, and sugar (if using). Bring to a boil, stirring until the salt and sugar dissolve. Remove from heat and let cool completely.
3. **Pack the Jar:** Tightly pack the vegetables into the jar, leaving about 1/2 inch of headspace at the top. Add any optional flavorings.
4. **Pour Brine:** Pour the cooled brine over the vegetables, ensuring they are completely submerged.
5. **Seal and Refrigerate:** Seal the jar tightly and refrigerate for at least the minimum time specified in the table above. The pickles will continue to develop flavor over time.

Technical Tips & Considerations:
- **Vinegar Choice:** The type of vinegar you use will significantly impact the flavor of your pickles. Experiment with different vinegars to find your favorites.
- **Salt Selection:** Use non-iodized salt, as iodine can interfere with the pickling process and cause discoloration.
- **Sugar (Optional):** Sugar is traditionally used in quick pickles to balance the acidity of the vinegar. However, you can omit it or use a natural sweetener like honey or maple syrup in moderation.
- **Flavor Infusion:** Add spices and herbs to the brine for additional flavor complexity. Common additions include dill, garlic, mustard seeds, peppercorns, and bay leaves.
- **Crispness:** To ensure crisp pickles, use fresh, firm vegetables and avoid overcooking them if blanching. Adding a grape leaf or a pinch of alum to the brine can also help maintain crispness.
- **Storage:** Quick pickles should be stored in the refrigerator and consumed within a few weeks for optimal flavor and texture.

Vegetable	Preparation Time	Refrigerator Time	Preferred Cutting	Brine Ingredients (per 1 cup of vinegar)	Key Micronutrients	Nutritional Information (per 1/2 cup serving, approx.)	Technical Tips
Cucumbers	15 minutes	1-2 hours (minimum), up to 2 weeks	Sliced, spears, or whole	1 cup vinegar (white or apple cider), 1/2 cup water, 1 tablespoon salt, 1 tablespoon sugar (optional)	Vitamin K, Potassium	Calories: 15-20 (depending on sugar content), Protein: 0g, Fat: 0g, Carbs: 4-5g, Fiber: 1g	Use pickling cucumbers for best results. For crispier pickles, add a grape leaf or a pinch of alum to the brine.
Onions	10 minutes	30 minutes (minimum), up to 1 week	Thinly sliced or rings	1 cup vinegar (white or red wine), 1/4 cup water, 1 tablespoon salt, 1 teaspoon sugar (optional)	Vitamin C, Quercetin	Calories: 20-25 (depending on sugar content), Protein: 0g, Fat: 0g, Carbs: 5-6g, Fiber: 1g	Use red onions for a vibrant color or white/yellow onions for a milder flavor.
Radishes	10 minutes	30 minutes (minimum), up to 1 week	Thinly sliced or whole	1 cup vinegar (rice vinegar or apple cider), 1/4 cup water, 1 tablespoon salt, 1 teaspoon sugar (optional)	Vitamin C, Potassium	Calories: 10-15 (depending on sugar content), Protein: 1g, Fat: 0g, Carbs: 2-3g, Fiber: 1g	Use a mix of radish varieties for a colorful pickle.
Green Beans	15 minutes	1 hour (minimum), up to 2 weeks	Trimmed, whole or cut	1 cup vinegar (white or apple cider), 1/2 cup water, 1 tablespoon salt, 1 tablespoon sugar (optional)	Vitamin K, Vitamin C	Calories: 20-25 (depending on sugar content), Protein: 1g, Fat: 0g, Carbs: 4-5g, Fiber: 2g	Blanch green beans briefly before pickling to preserve color and texture.
Asparagus	15 minutes	1 hour (minimum), up to 2 weeks	Trimmed, whole spears	1 cup vinegar (white or rice vinegar), 1/2 cup water, 1 tablespoon salt, 1 teaspoon sugar (optional)	Vitamin K, Folate	Calories: 15-20 (depending on sugar content), Protein: 2g, Fat: 0g, Carbs: 3-4g, Fiber: 2g	Choose firm asparagus spears for best results. Blanching is optional but can help retain color.
Bell Peppers	15 minutes	1 hour (minimum), up to 2 weeks	Sliced or strips	1 cup vinegar (white or apple cider), 1/2 cup water, 1 tablespoon salt, 1 tablespoon sugar (optional)	Vitamin C, Vitamin A	Calories: 20-25 (depending on sugar content), Protein: 1g, Fat: 0g, Carbs: 5-6g, Fiber: 2g	Use a mix of colorful bell peppers for a vibrant pickle.

INDIAN-STYLE PICKLES (ACHAR)

Prep Time: 30-45 minutes
Fermentation Time: 7-14 days (refer to the table above for specific vegetables/fruits)
Serves: Varies depending on the quantity of vegetables/fruits used

Ingredients:

- Vegetables or fruits of your choice (refer to the table above)
- Mustard oil or sesame oil
- Spices: Mustard seeds, fenugreek seeds, turmeric powder, chili powder, salt
- Optional Flavorings: Asafoetida (hing), ginger, garlic

Equipment:

- Clean glass jar
- Saucepan

Instructions:

1. **Prepare Vegetables/Fruits:** Wash, peel (if necessary), and cut the vegetables/fruits according to the preferred cutting method mentioned in the table.
2. **Sun-dry (Optional):** For certain pickles like mango or lemon, spread the cut pieces on a clean cloth and sun-dry them for a few hours to remove excess moisture.
3. **Prepare Spice Mix:** In a dry skillet, roast the mustard seeds and fenugreek seeds until fragrant. Let them cool, then grind them into a coarse powder. Combine this powder with turmeric, chili powder, and salt.
4. **Mix with Oil:** Heat the mustard oil or sesame oil in a saucepan until it reaches its smoking point. Let it cool slightly, then add the spice mix and any optional flavorings like asafoetida, ginger, or garlic.
5. **Pack the Jar:** Tightly pack the vegetables/fruits into the jar, leaving about 1 inch of headspace at the top
6. **Pour Oil Mixture:** Pour the cooled oil-spice mixture over the vegetables/fruits, ensuring they are completely submerged.
7. **Seal and Ferment:** Seal the jar tightly and let it ferment in a cool, dark place for 7-14 days, or until the pickles develop a tangy flavor and aroma

Technical Tips & Considerations:

- **Oil Selection:** Mustard oil is traditionally used in Indian pickles for its pungent flavor and preservative qualities. However, you can substitute it with sesame oil if preferred.
- **Spice Blending:** Roasting the mustard and fenugreek seeds before grinding enhances their flavor and aroma. Adjust the amount of chili powder based on your desired spice level.
- **Sun-drying:** Sun-drying helps remove excess moisture from the vegetables/fruits, preventing spoilage and promoting a longer shelf life for the pickles
- **Sterilization:** Ensure all equipment and jars are clean and sterilized before use to prevent contamination and unwanted microbial growth.
- **Airtight Storage:** Once the pickles are fermented, store them in airtight containers in the refrigerator to maintain their flavor and quality.

Vegetable/Fruit	Fermentation Time (Days)	Oil Type	Spices & Flavorings	Key Micronutrients	Nutritional Information (per 1/4 cup serving, approx.)	Technical Tips
Mango	7-14	Mustard oil	Mustard seeds, fenugreek seeds, turmeric, chili powder, salt	Vitamin C, Vitamin A	Calories: 80-100, Protein: 1g, Fat: 7-9g, Carbs: 5-7g, Fiber: 2-3g	Use raw, unripe mangoes for a tart flavor. Sun-dry the mango pieces for a more intense flavor and longer shelf life.
Lemon	7-14	Sesame oil	Mustard seeds, fenugreek seeds, turmeric, chili powder, salt	Vitamin C, Potassium	Calories: 60-80, Protein: 0g, Fat: 6-8g, Carbs: 3-5g, Fiber: 1-2g	Use whole lemons, cut into wedges or slices. Remove the seeds before pickling.
Lime	7-14	Sesame oil	Mustard seeds, fenugreek seeds, turmeric, chili powder, salt	Vitamin C, Potassium	Calories: 50-70, Protein: 0g, Fat: 5-7g, Carbs: 2-4g, Fiber: 1-2g	Use whole limes, cut into wedges or slices. Remove the seeds before pickling.
Green Chili Peppers	7-14	Mustard oil	Mustard seeds, fenugreek seeds, turmeric, salt	Vitamin C, Capsaicin	Calories: 30-40, Protein: 1g, Fat: 3-4g, Carbs: 2-3g, Fiber: 1-2g	Slit the chili peppers lengthwise to allow the spices to penetrate. Wear gloves when handling hot peppers.
Mixed Vegetables	7-14	Mustard oil	Mustard seeds, fenugreek seeds, turmeric, chili powder, salt	Varies depending on vegetables used	Varies depending on vegetables used	Choose a variety of vegetables like carrots, cauliflower, green beans, and onions. Cut them into bite-sized pieces.
Eggplant	7-14	Mustard oil	Mustard seeds, fenugreek seeds, turmeric, chili powder, salt, asafoetida (hing)	Potassium, Fiber	Calories: 60-80, Protein: 1g, Fat: 6-8g, Carbs: 3-5g, Fiber: 2-3g	Cut eggplant into small cubes or long strips. Salt and squeeze out excess moisture before adding to the spice mixture.
Cauliflower	7-14	Mustard oil	Mustard seeds, fenugreek seeds, turmeric, chili powder, salt	Vitamin C, Vitamin K	Calories: 40-50, Protein: 1g, Fat: 4-5g, Carbs: 2-3g, Fiber: 1-2g	Cut cauliflower into small florets. Blanch briefly before adding to the spice mixture.
Green Beans	7-14	Mustard oil	Mustard seeds, fenugreek seeds, turmeric, chili powder, salt	Vitamin K, Vitamin C	Calories: 30-40, Protein: 1g, Fat: 3-4g, Carbs: 2-3g, Fiber: 1-2g	Trim the ends of green beans and leave them whole or cut into smaller pieces.
Onions	7-14	Mustard oil	Mustard seeds, fenugreek seeds, turmeric, chili powder, salt	Quercetin, Vitamin C	Calories: 50-60, Protein: 1g, Fat: 5-6g, Carbs: 3-4g, Fiber: 1-2g	Use small onions or pearl onions for pickling whole. For larger onions, slice them thinly or cut into rings.

FERMENTED CAULIFLOWER WITH GARLIC AND DILL

Prep Time: 15 minutes
Fermentation Time: 5-7 days
Serves: Makes 1 quart jar

Ingredients:
- 1 medium organic cauliflower, cut into florets
- 3 cloves organic garlic, crushed
- 1 tbsp organic fresh dill, chopped
- 1 tbsp Himalayan salt
- 2 cups filtered water

Instructions:
1. Prepare the Cauliflower: Sterilize a quart jar. Pack the cauliflower florets tightly in the jar with the crushed garlic and dill.
2. Make the Brine: Dissolve the salt in the filtered water to make a brine. Pour over the cauliflower, ensuring it's fully submerged. Use a fermentation weight if necessary.
3. Ferment: Seal the jar loosely and leave at room temperature for 5-7 days, checking for bubbles. Once the cauliflower tastes tangy, store it in the fridge.

Tip: Fermented cauliflower makes a crunchy, tangy snack and pairs perfectly with roasted meats or salads.

Nutritional Information (per 1/2 cup serving):
- Calories: 25
- Protein: 2g
- Fat: 0g
- Carbohydrates: 5g
- Fiber: 2g

FERMENTED GINGER CARROTS

Prep Time: 10 minutes
Fermentation Time: 5-7 days
Serves: Makes 1 pint jar

Ingredients:
- 4 large organic carrots, peeled and julienned
- 1 tbsp organic fresh ginger, grated
- 1 tbsp Himalayan salt
- 2 cups filtered water

Instructions:
1. Prepare the Carrots: Sterilize the jar. Pack the julienned carrots tightly into the jar, mixing in the grated ginger.
2. Make the Brine: Dissolve the salt in filtered water to create the brine. Pour it over the carrots, ensuring they're submerged.
3. Ferment: Seal the jar loosely and leave at room temperature for 5-7 days. Check for bubbles and taste after 5 days. Once fermented, store in the fridge.

Tip: Fermented ginger carrots add a bright, tangy flavor to salads, grain-free wraps, or grilled fish dishes.

Nutritional Information (per 1/4 cup serving):
- Calories: 10 kcal
- Protein: 0g
- Fat: 0g
- Carbohydrates: 3g
- Fiber: 1g

KIMCHI (SPICY FERMENTED VEGETABLES)

Prep Time: 30 minutes
Fermentation Time: 1-2 weeks
Serves: Makes 1 quart jar

Ingredients:
- 1 medium organic Napa cabbage, chopped
- 1 organic carrot, julienned
- 1 organic daikon radish, julienned
- 3 cloves organic garlic, minced
- 1-inch piece organic fresh ginger, grated
- 2 tbsp Korean red pepper flakes (adjust to taste)
- 2 tbsp Himalayan salt
- 2 cups filtered water

Instructions:
1. Prepare the Vegetables: Massage the chopped cabbage with 1 tbsp salt and let it sit for 1-2 hours to release its water. Rinse the cabbage and drain.
2. Mix the Vegetables: Combine the cabbage with carrots, daikon, garlic, ginger, and red pepper flakes. Mix well.
3. Pack and Ferment: Pack the mixture tightly into a sterilized quart jar. Pour enough brine (2 cups filtered water + 1 tbsp salt) to submerge the vegetables. Let it ferment for 1-2 weeks at room temperature.
4. Store: Once fermented to your taste, store it in the fridge.

Tip: Kimchi adds heat and tang to any dish. Serve it with eggs, grilled meats, or use as a side for stir-fries.

Nutritional Information (per 1/4 cup serving):
- Calories: 20
- Protein: 1g
- Fat: 0g
- Carbohydrates: 4g
- Fiber: 2g

FERMENTED GREEN BEANS WITH MUSTARD SEEDS

Prep Time: 15 minutes
Fermentation Time: 7-10 days
Serves: Makes 1 quart jar

Ingredients:
- 1 lb organic green beans, trimmed
- 2 cloves organic garlic, crushed
- 1 tsp organic mustard seeds
- 1 tbsp Himalayan salt
- 2 cups filtered water

Instructions:
1. Prepare the Green Beans: Sterilize a quart jar. Pack the green beans tightly into the jar, layering them with garlic and mustard seeds.
2. Make the Brine: Dissolve the salt in filtered water. Pour the brine over the green beans, ensuring they're fully submerged.
3. Ferment: Seal the jar loosely and let it sit at room temperature for 7-10 days. Check daily for bubbles and release any built-up gases. Once fermented to your taste, store in the fridge.

Tip: These tangy green beans are a perfect accompaniment to grilled meats or grain-free salads.

Nutritional Information (per 1/4 cup serving):
- Calories: 15 kcal
- Protein: 1g
- Fat: 0g
- Carbohydrates: 3g
- Fiber: 1g

FERMENTED RED CABBAGE WITH CARAWAY SEEDS

Prep Time: 10 minutes
Fermentation Time: 2-4 weeks
Serves: Makes 1 quart jar

Ingredients:
- 1 medium organic red cabbage, shredded
- 1 tbsp Himalayan salt
- 1 tsp organic caraway seeds

Instructions:
1. Massage the Cabbage: In a large bowl, massage the shredded cabbage with salt for 5-10 minutes until it releases its liquid.
2. Pack the Jar: Pack the cabbage tightly into a sterilized jar, pressing it down until the brine rises above the cabbage. Sprinkle caraway seeds between layers.
3. Ferment: Seal the jar loosely and leave it at room temperature for 2-4 weeks. Check daily to ensure the cabbage remains submerged. Store in the fridge after fermentation.

Tip: Fermented red cabbage with caraway seeds is perfect as a tangy side for roasted meats or sausages.

Nutritional Information (per 1/4 cup serving):
- Calories: 15
- Protein: 1g
- Fat: 0g
- Carbohydrates: 3g
- Fiber: 1g

FERMENTED JALAPEÑO HOT SAUCE

Prep Time: 10 minutes
Fermentation Time: 1-2 weeks
Serves: Makes 1 pint jar

Ingredients:
- 10 organic jalapeños, sliced
- 3 cloves organic garlic, crushed
- 1 tbsp Himalayan salt
- 2 cups filtered water
- 1/4 cup organic apple cider vinegar (optional, for a tangy finish)

Instructions:
1. Prepare the Jalapeños: Sterilize a pint jar. Pack the jalapeño slices and garlic into the jar.
2. Make the Brine: Dissolve the salt in filtered water. Pour the brine over the jalapeños.
3. Ferment: Seal the jar loosely and ferment at room temperature for 1-2 weeks. Check daily and release any gas that builds up. After fermentation, blend the mixture into a smooth sauce and add vinegar if desired.
4. Store: Store in the fridge for up to 6 months.

Tip: This fermented hot sauce adds a spicy, probiotic kick to any dish, including eggs, tacos, and grilled meats.

Nutritional Information (per 1 tsp serving):
- Calories: 2
- Protein: 0g
- Fat: 0g
- Carbohydrates: 1g
- Fiber: 0g

DILL PICKLES

Prep Time: 15 minutes
Fermentation Time: 1-2 weeks
Serves: Makes 1 quart jar

Ingredients:
- 6-8 small organic cucumbers
- 2 cloves organic garlic, crushed
- 1 tbsp Himalayan salt
- 2 cups filtered water
- 1 tbsp organic fresh dill

Instructions:
1. Prepare the Cucumbers: Sterilize a quart jar. Pack the cucumbers tightly into the jar along with garlic and dill.
2. Make the Brine: Dissolve the salt in filtered water. Pour the brine over the cucumbers, ensuring they're fully submerged.
3. Ferment: Seal the jar loosely and let it ferment at room temperature for 1-2 weeks. Check daily to release any built-up gases.
4. Store: Once fermented to your liking, store in the fridge.

Tip: These crisp, tangy pickles make a great probiotic snack or a side for sandwiches and salads.

Nutritional Information (per 1 pickle):
- Calories: 5 kcal
- Protein: 0g
- Fats: 0g
- Carbohydrates: 1g
- Fiber: 0g

PRESERVED LEMONS

Prep Time: 10 minutes
Fermentation Time: 4-6 weeks
Serves: Makes 1 quart jar

Ingredients:
- 6-8 medium organic lemons
- 1/4 cup Himalayan salt (no additives)
- 1/2 cup organic lemon juice
- 1 tbsp organic black peppercorns
- 3-4 organic bay leaves
- 1 cinnamon stick (optional, for warmth)

Instructions:
1. Sterilize the Jar: Boil the quart jar and its lid for 10 minutes to sterilize.
2. Prepare the Lemons: Scrub the lemons under warm water. Cut each lemon lengthwise into quarters, but leave them connected at the base (so they open like a flower).
3. Salt the Lemons: Rub each lemon generously with salt, making sure the inside and outside are coated. Press the salted lemons into the sterilized jar, layering them with bay leaves, peppercorns, and cinnamon.
4. Add Lemon Juice: Pack the lemons tightly and add the freshly squeezed lemon juice to cover the lemons completely. If needed, add more juice until the lemons are fully submerged.
5. Seal and Ferment: Seal the jar tightly and leave it at room temperature for 4-6 weeks, shaking it occasionally to distribute the salt and juice. Once done, store in the fridge.

Tip: The flavor of preserved lemons intensifies over time. After fermenting, they can be finely chopped and added to sauces, salads, and roasted meats for a tangy, umami boost.

Nutritional Information (per 1 tbsp serving):
- Calories: 5 kcal
- Protein: 0g
- Fat: 0g
- Carbohydrates: 1g
- Fiber: 0g

PICKLED RED ONIONS

Prep Time: 10 minutes
Fermentation Time: 2-4 days
Serves: Makes 1 pint jar

Ingredients:
- 2 medium organic red onions, thinly sliced
- 1 cup organic apple cider vinegar (raw, with "mother")
- 1/2 cup water
- 1 tsp Himalayan salt
- 1 tsp organic mustard seeds
- 1/2 tsp organic black peppercorns

Instructions:
1. Sterilize the Jar: Boil the pint jar and its lid for 10 minutes.
2. Pack the Onions: Layer the thinly sliced onions in the jar, packing them tightly.
3. Make the Brine: In a small saucepan, combine apple cider vinegar, water, salt, mustard seeds, and peppercorns. Heat just until the salt dissolves (do not boil).
4. Pour the Brine: Pour the brine over the onions, making sure they're fully submerged. Seal the jar and leave it at room temperature for 2-4 days to ferment slightly. Store in the fridge once pickled.

Tip: Use these pickled onions to add crunch and tang to salads, grilled meats, or sandwiches.

Nutritional Information (per 1 tbsp serving):
- Calories: 5 kcal
- Protein: 0g
- Fat: 0g
- Carbohydrates: 1g
- Fiber: 0g

FERMENTED JALAPEÑOS

Prep Time: 10 minutes
Fermentation Time: 7-10 days
Serves: Makes 1 pint jar

Ingredients:

- 8-10 organic jalapeños, sliced
- 2 tbsp Himalayan salt
- 2 cups filtered water
- 1 clove organic garlic, crushed (optional)

Instructions:

1. Prepare the Jalapeños: Slice the jalapeños and pack them tightly into a sterilized jar.
2. Make the Brine: Dissolve the salt in filtered water to make the brine. Pour the brine over the jalapeños, making sure they are fully submerged.
3. Ferment: Seal the jar loosely and let it sit at room temperature for 7-10 days. Check daily and release any built-up gas. Once fermented, store in the fridge.

Tip: Use these spicy, probiotic-packed jalapeños in salads, tacos, or as a topping for burgers and grilled meats.

Nutritional Information (per 1 slice serving):

- Calories: 2 kcal
- Protein: 0g
- Fat: 0g
- Carbohydrates: 0g
- Fiber: 0g

FERMENTED TOMATO SALSA

Prep Time: 15 minutes
Fermentation Time: 3-5 days
Serves: 10 (salsa portions)

Ingredients:

- 4 large organic tomatoes, chopped
- 1 small organic red onion, diced
- 2 cloves organic garlic, minced
- 1-2 organic jalapeños, diced (optional, for heat)
- 1/4 cup organic fresh cilantro, chopped
- 1 tbsp organic sea salt
- 2 cups filtered water (to create the brine)

Instructions:

1. Prepare the Vegetables:
   In a clean jar, combine chopped tomatoes, red onion, garlic, jalapeños, and cilantro.
2. Create the Brine:
   Dissolve sea salt in filtered water. Pour the brine over the vegetables until they are fully submerged. Use a fermentation weight to keep the veggies below the liquid.
3. Ferment the Salsa:
   Cover the jar with a breathable cloth or a fermentation lid and let it ferment at room temperature for 3-5 days. Check daily for bubbling and adjust the liquid level if needed.

4. Serve:
   Once the salsa has developed a tangy flavor, store it in the refrigerator for up to 2 weeks.
   Tip: The fermentation process adds a savory umami depth to the tomatoes, making this salsa more complex than fresh versions. The slight acidity balances perfectly with grilled meats or roasted vegetables.

Nutritional Information (per serving):

- Calories: 10
- Protein: 0g
- Fat: 0g
- Carbohydrates: 2g
- Fiber: 1g

FERMENTED PINEAPPLE SALSA

Prep Time: 20 minutes
Fermentation Time: 2-3 days
Serves: 10 (salsa portions)

Ingredients:

- 2 cups organic pineapple, finely chopped
- 1 small organic red onion, diced
- 1 organic red bell pepper, chopped
- 1 organic jalapeño, diced
- 1/4 cup organic fresh cilantro, chopped
- 1 tbsp organic lime juice
- 1 tbsp organic sea salt
- 2 cups filtered water (to create the brine)

Instructions:

1. Prepare the Pineapple Salsa Base:
   Combine pineapple, red onion, bell pepper, jalapeño, cilantro, and lime juice in a clean jar.
2. Create the Brine:
   Dissolve the sea salt in filtered water and pour over the salsa mixture, ensuring everything is fully submerged.
3. Ferment the Salsa:
   Cover the jar with a breathable cloth and let it ferment at room temperature for 2-3 days. Taste daily to monitor the fermentation process.
4. Serve:
   Once fermented, refrigerate and use within 1-2 weeks. The sweetness of the pineapple pairs wonderfully with the tanginess of fermentation, making this salsa perfect for pairing with grilled fish, meats, or roasted vegetables.
   Tip: Fermented pineapple adds a tropical depth, balancing sweetness with acidity. Use this salsa as a unique topping for tacos or as a vibrant dip.

Nutritional Information (per serving):

- Calories: 15
- Protein: 0g
- Fat: 0g
- Carbohydrates: 4g
- Fiber: 1g

BASE RECIPES

CLEAN-EATING CHICKEN BONE BROTH

Serves: 4 quarts
Prep Time: 20 minutes
Cook Time: 12-24 hours

Ingredients:
- 3-4 lbs organic chicken bones (from pasture-raised chickens)
- 2 organic celery stalks, roughly chopped
- 1 organic onion, quartered
- 1 organic garlic head, halved crosswise
- 1 tbsp organic apple cider vinegar
- 1 tsp sea salt
- 1/2 tsp organic black peppercorns
- 2 organic bay leaves
- 2 tbsp organic coconut oil
- Filtered water

Instructions:
1. Place chicken bones in a large stockpot and cover with cold filtered water. Add apple cider vinegar and let sit for 30 minutes to help extract nutrients from the bones.
2. Add celery, onion, garlic, salt, peppercorns, and bay leaves to the pot.
3. Bring the mixture to a boil over high heat, then reduce heat to low and simmer, partially covered, for 12-24 hours. Skim off any foam or impurities that rise to the surface.
4. Remove from heat and let cool slightly. Strain the broth through a fine-mesh sieve, discarding the solids.
5. Let the broth cool completely, then stir in coconut oil until melted. Transfer to airtight containers. Store in the refrigerator for up to 5 days or freeze for up to 6 months.

Tips:
- Roast the bones before simmering for a richer, more complex flavor.
- Add a handful of fresh herbs like parsley or thyme in the last 30 minutes of cooking for added depth and antioxidants.
- Sip on its own for a nourishing, gut-healing drink or use as a base for keto-friendly soups and stews.
- Chicken bones are rich in collagen, which supports healthy skin, hair, nails, and joints, while coconut oil provides satiating, energizing medium-chain triglycerides (MCTs).

Nutritional Information (per cup):
- Calories: 50
- Protein: 5g
- Fat: 3g
- Carbohydrates: 1g
- Fiber: 0g

GUT-HEALING BEEF BONE BROTH

Serves: 4 quarts
Prep Time: 20 minutes
Cook Time: 24-48 hours

Ingredients:
- 3-4 lbs organic grass-fed beef bones (knuckle, short rib, and marrow bones)
- 2 organic carrots, roughly chopped
- 2 organic celery stalks, roughly chopped
- 1 organic onion, quartered
- 1 organic garlic head, halved crosswise
- 1 tbsp organic apple cider vinegar
- 1 tsp sea salt
- 1/2 tsp organic black peppercorns
- 2 organic bay leaves
- 2 tbsp organic grass-fed ghee
- Filtered water

Instructions:
1. Preheat the oven to 400°F. Place beef bones on a baking sheet and roast for 30-40 minutes until browned.
2. Transfer roasted bones to a large stockpot and cover with cold filtered water. Add apple cider vinegar and let sit for 30 minutes to help extract nutrients from the bones.
3. Add carrots, celery, onion, garlic, salt, peppercorns, and bay leaves to the pot.
4. Bring the mixture to a boil over high heat, then reduce heat to low and simmer, partially covered, for 24-48 hours. Skim off any foam or impurities that rise to the surface.
5. Remove from heat and let cool slightly. Strain the broth through a fine-mesh sieve, discarding the solids.
6. Let the broth cool completely, then stir in ghee until melted. Transfer to airtight containers. Store in the refrigerator for up to 5 days or freeze for up to 6 months.

Tips:
- For a more gelatinous broth, add organic chicken feet or pig's feet to the pot for extra collagen.
- Add a splash of red wine for depth and complexity.
- Sip on its own for a nourishing, gut-healing drink or use as a base for low-carb soups and stews.
- Beef bones are rich in minerals like calcium, magnesium, and phosphorus, which support bone health, while ghee provides anti-inflammatory conjugated linoleic acid (CLA) and butyrate for gut health.

Nutritional Information (per cup):
- Calories: 70
- Protein: 6g
- Fat: 5g
- Carbohydrates: 1g
- Fiber: 0g

PROBIOTIC VEGETABLE BROTH

Serves: 2 quarts
Prep Time: 20 minutes
Cook Time: 1-2 hours

Ingredients:
- 1 lb organic low-carb vegetable scraps (broccoli stalks, kale stems, zucchini ends, etc.)
- 1 organic onion, quartered
- 2 organic celery stalks, roughly chopped
- 1 organic leek, roughly chopped (white and green parts)
- 4 organic garlic cloves, smashed
- 1 organic bay leaf
- 1/2 tsp organic black peppercorns
- 1/2 cup organic fermented vegetable brine (from sauerkraut or kimchi)
- 1 tsp sea salt
- 1 tbsp organic coconut oil
- Filtered water

Instructions:
1. In a large stockpot, combine vegetable scraps, onion, celery, leek, garlic, bay leaf, peppercorns, and fermented vegetable brine.
2. Cover with cold filtered water and add salt. Bring the mixture to a boil over high heat, then reduce heat to low and simmer, partially covered, for 1-2 hours.

3. Remove from heat and let cool slightly. Strain the broth through a fine-mesh sieve, pressing on the solids to extract as much liquid as possible. Discard the solids.
4. Let the broth cool completely, then stir in coconut oil until melted. Transfer to airtight containers. Store in the refrigerator for up to 5 days or freeze for up to 6 months.

Tips:

- Use low-carb, nutrient-dense vegetable scraps for a blood sugar-friendly broth.
- Roast the vegetables before simmering for a richer, more complex flavor.
- Use as a base for low-carb soups, stews, or sauces, or cook non-starchy vegetables in it for added flavor and nutrition.
- Fermented vegetable brine adds beneficial probiotics and umami depth to the broth for improved gut health and digestion.

Nutritional Information (per serving):

- Calories: 50
- Protein: g
- Fat: 2 g
- Carbohydrates: 6 g
- Fiber: g

IMMUNE-BOOSTING MUSHROOM BROTH

Serves: 2 quarts
Prep Time: 20 minutes
Cook Time: 1-2 hours

Ingredients:

- 1 lb organic mixed medicinal mushrooms (shiitake, maitake, reishi, chaga, etc.), roughly chopped
- 1 organic onion, quartered
- 2 organic celery stalks, roughly chopped
- 4 organic garlic cloves, smashed
- 1 organic bay leaf

- 1/2 tsp organic black peppercorns
- 1 tbsp organic coconut aminos
- 1 tsp sea salt
- 1 tbsp organic coconut oil
- Filtered water

Instructions:

1. In a large stockpot, combine mushrooms, onion, celery, garlic, bay leaf, peppercorns, and coconut aminos.
2. Cover with cold filtered water and add salt. Bring the mixture to a boil over high heat, then reduce heat to low and simmer, partially covered, for 1-2 hours.
3. Remove from heat and let cool slightly. Strain the broth through a fine-mesh sieve, pressing on the solids to extract as much liquid as possible. Discard the solids.
4. Let the broth cool completely, then stir in coconut oil until melted. Transfer to airtight containers. Store in the refrigerator for up to 5 days or freeze for up to 6 months.

Tips:

- Use a variety of medicinal mushrooms for a complex, immune-boosting flavor profile.
- Simmer the broth longer for a more concentrated, intense flavor.
- Use as a base for low-carb soups, stews, or sauces, or sip on its own for a nourishing, immune-supportive drink.
- Medicinal mushrooms provide beta-glucans, antioxidants, and adaptogenic compounds for enhanced immune function and overall health.

Nutritional Information (per serving):

- Calories: 60
- Protein: 3 g
- Fat: 3 g
- Carbohydrates: 7 g
- Fiber: 1 g

SNACKS AND APPETIZERS

CHEESY BROCCOLI "POPCORN" BITES

Prep Time: 15 minutes
Cook Time: 15 minutes
Serves: 4

Ingredients:

- 4 cups organic broccoli florets, cut into small pieces
- 1 cup organic grass-fed cheddar cheese, grated
- 2 organic pasture-raised eggs, beaten
- 1/4 cup organic coconut flour
- 1 tsp organic garlic powder
- 1/2 tsp sea salt
- 1/4 tsp organic black pepper
- 2 tbsp organic ghee, melted

Instructions:

1. Preheat oven to 375°F (190°C).
2. Steam broccoli florets until tender, then chop into small pieces.
3. In a large bowl, mix chopped broccoli, cheese, eggs, coconut flour, garlic powder, salt, and pepper.
4. Form mixture into small, bite-sized balls.
5. Place balls on a parchment-lined baking sheet and brush with melted ghee.
6. Bake for 15 minutes, or until golden brown and crispy.

Tip: For extra flavor, add a pinch of smoked paprika to the mixture.

Nutritional Information (per serving):

- Calories: 250
- Protein: 15g
- Fat: 18g
- Carbohydrates: 10g

- Fiber: 4g

AVOCADO AND BACON DEVILED EGGS

Prep Time: 15 minutes
Cook Time: 10 minutes
Serves: 4

Ingredients:

- 6 organic, pasture-raised eggs
- 1 large organic avocado
- 4 slices organic, pasture-raised bacon, cooked and crumbled
- 1 tbsp organic Dijon mustard
- 1 tbsp organic apple cider vinegar
- Sea salt and black pepper to taste
- 1/4 cup organic fresh chives, chopped

Instructions:

1. Place eggs in a pot and cover with water. Bring to a boil, then reduce heat and simmer for 10 minutes. Cool in ice water and peel.
2. Slice eggs in half and remove yolks.
3. In a bowl, mash avocado and yolks together. Stir in bacon, Dijon mustard, apple cider vinegar, salt, and pepper.
4. Spoon the mixture back into egg whites.
5. Garnish with fresh chives and serve.

Tip: For perfectly smooth filling, use a food processor to blend the avocado and yolk mixture.

Nutritional Information (per serving):

- Calories: 250
- Protein: 12g
- Fat: 20g

- Carbohydrates: 6g
- Fiber: 3g

SARDINE AND AVOCADO STUFFED ENDIVES

Prep Time: 15 minutes
Cook Time: 0 minutes
Serves: 4

Ingredients:
- 2 cans (4 oz each) wild-caught sardines in olive oil, drained and flaked
- 2 large organic avocados, mashed
- 1 organic lemon, juiced
- 1/4 cup organic red onion, finely chopped
- 1/4 cup organic fresh parsley, chopped
- 1 tsp organic Dijon mustard
- Sea salt and black pepper to taste
- 12 organic endive leaves

Instructions:
1. In a bowl, mix together flaked sardines, mashed avocados, lemon juice, red onion, parsley, Dijon mustard, salt, and pepper.
2. Spoon the mixture into the endive leaves.
3. Arrange on a platter and serve immediately.

Tip: For added texture and flavor, sprinkle some toasted pine nuts or sunflower seeds on top.

Nutritional Information (per serving):
- Calories: 250
- Protein: 18g
- Fat: 20g
- Carbohydrates: 8g
- Fiber: 6g

AVOCADO AND ANCHOVY STUFFED EGGS WITH SMOKED PAPRIKA

Prep Time: 15 minutes
Cook Time: 10 minutes
Serves: 4

Ingredients:
- 6 organic, pasture-raised eggs
- 1 large organic avocado, mashed
- 6 wild-caught anchovy fillets, minced
- 1 tbsp organic lemon juice
- 1 tbsp organic mayonnaise (preferably homemade with avocado oil, see recipe)
- 1/4 tsp smoked paprika
- Sea salt and black pepper to taste

Instructions:
1. Place eggs in a saucepan and cover with cold water. Bring to a boil, then reduce heat and simmer for 10 minutes.
2. Drain hot water and immediately place eggs in a bowl of ice water to cool.
3. Peel eggs and cut in half lengthwise. Carefully remove yolks and place in a bowl.
4. Mash yolks with avocado, minced anchovies, lemon juice, mayonnaise, smoked paprika, salt, and pepper.
5. Spoon or pipe the yolk mixture back into the egg whites.
6. Sprinkle with additional smoked paprika and serve.

Tip: For smoother deviled eggs, push the yolk mixture through a fine-mesh sieve before filling the egg whites.

Nutritional Information (per serving):
- Calories: 220
- Protein: 12g
- Fat: 18g
- Carbohydrates: 3g
- Fiber: 2g

COCONUT-CRUSTED SCOTCH EGGS WITH TURMERIC AIOLI

Prep Time: 25 minutes
Cook Time: 20 minutes
Serves: 4

Ingredients:
- 6 organic, pasture-raised eggs
- 1 lb organic, grass-fed ground pork
- 1/4 cup organic fresh parsley, finely chopped
- 1 tsp organic garlic powder
- 1 tsp organic onion powder
- 1/2 cup organic coconut flour
- 1/2 cup organic shredded coconut
- 2 tbsp organic coconut oil, melted

For the Aioli:
- 1/2 cup organic mayonnaise (preferably homemade with avocado oil, see recipe)
- 1 tsp organic ground turmeric
- 1 organic garlic clove, minced
- 1 tsp organic lemon juice
- Sea salt and black pepper to taste

Instructions:
1. Soft boil 4 eggs for 6 minutes. Cool in ice water, then peel carefully.
2. Mix ground pork with parsley, garlic powder, and onion powder.
3. Wrap each egg in the pork mixture, ensuring even coverage.
4. Beat remaining 2 eggs in a bowl. In another bowl, mix coconut flour and shredded coconut.
5. Dip each wrapped egg in beaten egg, then roll in coconut mixture.
6. Preheat oven to 375°F (190°C). Place eggs on a baking sheet and brush with melted coconut oil.
7. Bake for 20 minutes, turning halfway through, until golden brown.
8. For the aioli, mix all ingredients until smooth.
9. Serve Scotch eggs with turmeric aioli.

Tip: For perfect soft-boiled eggs, start with room temperature eggs and immediately transfer them to ice water after boiling.

Nutritional Information (per serving):
- Calories: 520
- Protein: 28g
- Fat: 42g
- Carbohydrates: 10g
- Fiber: 4g

WALNUT AND GOAT CHEESE STUFFED DATES WITH PROSCIUTTO

Prep Time: 15 minutes
Cook Time: 5 minutes
Serves: 4 (12 stuffed dates)

Ingredients:
- 12 organic Medjool dates, pitted
- 1/4 cup organic goat cheese, softened
- 2 tbsp organic walnuts, finely chopped
- 6 slices organic prosciutto, cut in half lengthwise

Instructions:
1. Preheat oven to 400°F (200°C).
2. In a small bowl, mix together goat cheese and chopped walnuts.
3. Stuff each date with a heaping teaspoon of the goat cheese-walnut mixture.
4. Wrap each stuffed date with a half-slice of prosciutto, securing it with a toothpick.
5. Arrange the stuffed dates on a baking sheet and bake for 5 minutes, or until the prosciutto is crispy.
6. Serve the warm, stuffed dates immediately.

Tip: For a more pronounced walnut flavor, toast the chopped walnuts in a dry skillet for 2-3 minutes before mixing with the goat cheese.

Nutritional Information (per serving):
- Calories: 120 (per 3 stuffed dates)
- Protein: 6g
- Fat: 8g
- Carbohydrates: 10g
- Fiber: 2g

KOHLRABI CHIPS WITH AVOCADO DIP

Prep Time: 10 minutes
Cook Time: 30 minutes
Serves: 4

Ingredients:
- 2 large organic kohlrabi, peeled and thinly sliced
- 2 tbsp organic avocado oil
- Sea salt and black pepper to taste

For the Avocado Dip:
- 2 large organic avocados, mashed
- 2 tbsp organic lime juice
- 1 organic garlic clove, minced
- 1/4 cup organic fresh cilantro, chopped
- Sea salt and black pepper to taste

Instructions:
1. Preheat oven to 375°F (190°C).
2. Toss kohlrabi slices with avocado oil, salt, and pepper.
3. Arrange the slices in a single layer on a baking sheet lined with parchment paper.
4. Bake for 25-30 minutes, flipping halfway through, until crisp and golden.
5. For the dip, mix mashed avocados, lime juice, minced garlic, cilantro, salt, and pepper in a bowl.
6. Serve the kohlrabi chips with the avocado dip on the side.

Tip: For even cooking, make sure the kohlrabi slices are uniform in thickness.

Nutritional Information (per serving):
- Calories: 240
- Protein: 3g
- Fat: 20g
- Carbohydrates: 16g
- Fiber: 8g

CAULIFLOWER PIZZA BITES

Prep Time: 20 minutes
Cook Time: 15 minutes
Serves: 4

Ingredients:
- 1 large head organic cauliflower, riced
- 1 organic egg, beaten
- 1/2 cup organic full-fat grass-fed mozzarella cheese, shredded
- 1/4 cup organic full-fat grass-fed Parmesan cheese, grated
- 1 tsp organic Italian seasoning (preferably homemade, see recipe)
- 1/2 cup organic marinara sauce (preferably homemade, see recipe)
- 1/4 cup organic grass-fed mini pepperoni slices or diced organic turkey sausage (optional)
- 2 tbsp organic extra-virgin olive oil
- Sea salt and black pepper to taste

Instructions:
1. Preheat oven to 425°F (220°C) and grease a mini muffin tin with avocado oil.
2. In a large bowl, mix together riced cauliflower, beaten egg, mozzarella cheese, Parmesan cheese, Italian seasoning, salt, and pepper.
3. Press the mixture firmly into the mini muffin tin to form bite-sized pizza crusts.

4. Bake for 10 minutes until set and lightly browned.
5. Remove from oven and top each bite with a small amount of marinara sauce, mini pepperoni slices or diced turkey sausage (if using), and additional mozzarella cheese.
6. Return to oven and bake for another 5 minutes until cheese is melted and bubbly.
7. Let cool slightly before serving.

Tip: For a crispier crust, broil the pizza bites for the last 1-2 minutes of baking.

Nutritional Information (per serving):
- Calories: 250
- Protein: 16g
- Fat: 18g
- Carbohydrates: 10g
- Fiber: 3g

DUKKAH-CRUSTED AVOCADO WITH SMOKED SALMON AND FERMENTED RADISH

Prep Time: 10 minutes
Cook Time: 0 minutes
Serves: 2

Ingredients:
- 1 large organic avocado, halved and pitted
- 2 tbsp organic dukkah
- 4 oz organic smoked salmon, thinly sliced
- 1/4 cup organic fermented radish, chopped
- 1 tbsp organic lemon juice

Instructions:
1. Brush cut side of avocado halves with lemon juice.
2. Press dukkah onto the avocado halves, coating them evenly.
3. Arrange smoked salmon slices on top of the avocado and sprinkle with fermented radish.
4. Serve immediately.

Tip: For a visually appealing presentation, use a variety of colorful fermented radishes.

Nutritional Information (per serving):
- Calories: 320
- Protein: 14g
- Fat: 26g
- Carbohydrates: 8g
- Fiber: 4g

CRISPY TOFU WITH AVOCADO HERB DRESSING

Prep Time: 10 minutes
Cook Time: 25 minutes
Serves: 4

Ingredients:
- 14 oz extra-firm tofu, drained and pressed
- 2 tbsp arrowroot powder (or tapioca starch)
- 2 tbsp avocado oil
- 1 tsp smoked paprika
- 1/2 tsp ground cumin
- Sea salt and black pepper to taste

For the Avocado Herb Dressing:
- 1 ripe avocado
- 1/4 cup fresh cilantro, chopped
- 1/4 cup fresh parsley, chopped
- 1 tbsp lemon juice
- 1 clove garlic, minced
- 2-3 tbsp water to thin
- Sea salt to taste

Instructions:
1. Prepare the Tofu: Preheat the oven to 400°F (200°C). Slice the pressed tofu into cubes. Toss the tofu cubes with arrowroot powder, smoked paprika, cumin, salt, and pepper.

2. Bake the Tofu: Spread the tofu cubes on a baking sheet lined with parchment paper. Drizzle with avocado oil and bake for 20-25 minutes, flipping halfway, until golden and crispy.
3. Make the Avocado Herb Dressing: In a blender or food processor, combine avocado, cilantro, parsley, lemon juice, garlic, salt, and water. Blend until smooth and creamy, adjusting the water for your desired consistency.
4. Serve: Serve the crispy tofu with a generous drizzle of the avocado herb dressing and a side of sauerkraut for probiotics.

Tip: Pressing the tofu removes excess moisture, helping it achieve maximum crispiness when baked. The arrowroot powder creates a light, crispy coating on the tofu.

Nutritional Information (per serving):
- Calories: 220
- Protein: 10 g
- Fat: 16 g
- Carbohydrates: 12 g
- Fiber: 5 g

ENERGY BALLS AND BARS

These are great natural and easy-to-make energy bar, that can help you avoid getting them packaged if you make them part of your weekly meal prep. These can help you give a jolt of energy without wreaking havoc on your blood sugar. Consume sparingly as they are very high in calories.

HEMP SEED ENERGY BALLS WITH COCONUT AND ALMOND BUTTER

Prep Time: 15 minutes
Cook Time: 0 minutes (plus 30 minutes chilling)
Serves: 4 (makes 12 balls)

Ingredients:
- 1 cup organic almond butter
- 1/2 cup organic hemp seeds
- 1/2 cup organic shredded coconut
- 1/4 cup organic coconut flour
- 1/4 cup organic coconut oil, melted
- 1 tbsp organic vanilla extract
- 1 tsp organic cinnamon
- Pinch of sea salt

Instructions:
1. In a large bowl, mix almond butter, hemp seeds, shredded coconut, coconut flour, melted coconut oil, vanilla extract, cinnamon, and salt until well combined.
2. Roll the mixture into 1-inch balls and place on a parchment-lined baking sheet.
3. Chill in the refrigerator for at least 30 minutes until firm.
4. Store in an airtight container in the refrigerator.

Tip: For added texture, roll the energy balls in extra shredded coconut before chilling.

Nutritional Information (per serving):
- Calories: 220 (per ball)
- Protein: 6g
- Fat: 18g
- Carbohydrates: 8g
- Fiber: 4g

AVOCADO TRUFFLES WITH PISTACHIOS

Prep Time: 20 minutes
Cook Time: 10 minutes (plus 30 minutes chilling)
Serves: 12 truffles

Ingredients:
- 2 ripe organic avocados
- 1/4 cup organic unsweetened cocoa powder
- 1/4 cup organic coconut flour
- 2 tbsp organic coconut oil, melted
- 1/4 cup organic coconut yogurt
- 1 tsp organic vanilla extract
- 1/2 cup organic pistachios, finely chopped

Instructions:
1. In a medium mixing bowl, mash the avocados until smooth with no lumps.
2. Add the cocoa powder, coconut flour, melted coconut oil, coconut yogurt, and vanilla extract. Mix until well combined.
3. Using a small cookie scoop or your hands, scoop about 1 tablespoon of the mixture and roll into a ball. Repeat with the remaining mixture to form about 12 truffles.
4. Roll each truffle in the finely chopped pistachios until fully coated and place the coated truffles on a parchment-lined baking sheet.
5. Refrigerate the truffles for at least 30 minutes to firm up before serving.
6. Serve the avocado truffles chilled as a delightful and nutritious snack or dessert.

Tip: For an extra layer of flavor, lightly toast the chopped pistachios in a dry skillet over medium heat for 3-4 minutes, stirring frequently, until golden and fragrant. Let cool before coating the truffles.

Nutritional Information (per truffle):
- Calories: 90
- Protein: 2g
- Fat: 8g
- Carbohydrates: 5g
- Fiber: 3g

MATCHA PISTACHIO ENERGY BARS

Prep Time: 10 minutes
Cook Time: 1 hour
Serves: 8 bars

Ingredients:
- 1 cup organic pistachios, chopped
- 1/4 cup coconut oil, melted
- 1 tbsp organic matcha powder
- 1 tbsp chia seeds

Instructions:
1. Mix the **Ingredients:** Combine chopped pistachios, melted coconut oil, matcha powder, and chia seeds in a bowl.
2. Form Bars: Press the mixture into a lined baking pan and refrigerate for 1 hour.
3. Serve: Once firm, cut into bars.

Tip: Sprinkle sea salt on top before chilling for a savory-sweet balance.

Nutritional Information (per bar):
- Calories: 140
- Protein: 3g
- Healthy Fats: 11g
- Fiber: 3g

COCONUT RASPBERRY LAYER BARS

Prep Time: 15 minutes
Cook Time: 2 hours
Serves: 9 bars

Ingredients:
- 1 cup organic shredded coconut
- 1/4 cup coconut oil, melted
- 1/2 cup organic raspberries
- 1 tbsp chia seeds

Instructions:

1. Make the Base Layer: In a bowl, combine shredded coconut and melted coconut oil. Press into a lined baking pan.
2. Make the Raspberry Chia Layer: Mash the raspberries with chia seeds and spread evenly over the coconut layer.
3. Chill: Refrigerate for 2 hours until set, then cut into bars.

Tip: Lightly toast the coconut for a nuttier flavor before mixing it with the coconut oil.

Nutritional Information (per bar):
- Calories: 110 kcal
- Protein: 2g
- Fat: 9g
- Carbohydrates: 5g
- Fiber: 4g

HAZELNUT CHOCOLATE BLISS BALLS

Prep Time: 10 minutes
Cook Time: 30 minutes
Serves: 10

Ingredients:
- 1/2 cup organic hazelnuts, finely chopped
- 1/4 cup organic cacao powder
- 1/4 cup coconut oil, melted
- 2 tbsp organic chia seeds
- 1 tsp organic vanilla extract

Instructions:
1. Mix Ingredients: In a bowl, mix chopped hazelnuts, cacao powder, melted coconut oil, chia seeds, and vanilla.
2. Form Balls: Roll the mixture into small balls.
3. Chill: Refrigerate for 30 minutes.

Tip: Lightly toast the hazelnuts before using to enhance their flavor.

Nutritional Information (per bliss ball):
- Calories: 110
- Protein: 2g
- Fat: 11g
- Carbohydrates: 5g
- Fiber: 2g

PISTACHIO-COCONUT ENERGY BITES

Prep Time: 10 minutes
Cook Time: 30 minutes
Serves: 10

Ingredients:
- 1/2 cup organic pistachios, chopped
- 1/4 cup organic coconut flakes
- 1 tbsp chia seeds
- 1/4 cup organic almond butter

Instructions:
1. Mix the Ingredients: In a bowl, combine chopped pistachios, coconut flakes, chia seeds, and almond butter.
2. Form Balls: Roll the mixture into small balls.
3. Chill: Refrigerate for 30 minutes until firm.

Tip: Lightly toast the pistachios and coconut flakes for a nuttier, richer flavor.

Nutritional Information (per bite):
- Calories: 90

- Protein: 3g
- Fat: 8g
- Carbohydrates: 4g
- Fiber: 2g

GINGER TURMERIC BLISS BALLS

Prep Time: 15 minutes
Cook Time: 1 hour
Serves: 12

Ingredients:
- 1 cup organic almond flour
- 1/4 cup organic coconut oil, melted
- 1 tbsp organic ground ginger
- 1 tsp organic turmeric
- 1/4 cup shredded coconut

Instructions:
1. Mix Ingredients: In a bowl, combine almond flour, coconut oil, ginger, turmeric, and shredded coconut.
2. Form Balls: Roll the mixture into small balls and place on a lined tray.
3. Chill: Refrigerate for 1 hour until firm.

Tip: Ginger and turmeric provide anti-inflammatory benefits and add a warming spice profile to these bliss balls.

Nutritional Information (per bliss ball):
- Calories: 80
- Protein: 2 g
- Fat: 7 g
- Carbohydrates: 3 g
- Fiber: 1 g

CARROT CAKE ENERGY BALLS

Prep Time: 15 minutes
Cook Time: 1 hour
Serves: 12

Ingredients:
- 1 cup organic shredded carrots
- 1/2 cup organic almond flour
- 1/4 cup organic coconut flour
- 1 tsp organic cinnamon
- 1/4 cup organic coconut oil, melted
- 1/4 cup organic walnuts, chopped

Instructions:
1. Combine Ingredients: In a bowl, mix shredded carrots, almond flour, coconut flour, cinnamon, coconut oil, and walnuts.
2. Shape into Balls: Form into balls and place on a lined tray.
3. Chill: Refrigerate for 1 hour.

Tip: For more sweetness, mix in 2 tablespoons of chopped dates.

Nutritional Information (per energy ball):
- Calories: 70
- Protein: 2 g
- Fat: 6 g
- Carbohydrates: g
- Fiber: 2

NO-GRAIN BREADS

ALMOND FLOUR BREAD

Prep Time: 10 minutes
Cook Time: 40-45 minutes
Serves: 1 loaf (10 slices)

Ingredients:
- 2 cups organic almond flour
- 4 organic, pasture-raised eggs
- 1/4 cup organic ghee or avocado oil
- 1 tsp organic apple cider vinegar (unpasteurized)
- 1 tsp organic baking soda (grain-free)
- 1/4 tsp sea salt

Instructions:
1. Preheat Oven:
   Preheat your oven to 350°F (175°C). Line a 9x5-inch loaf pan with parchment paper.
2. Mix the Wet **Ingredients:**
   In a bowl, whisk together the eggs, ghee (or avocado oil), and apple cider vinegar.
3. Combine the Dry **Ingredients:**
   In another bowl, combine the almond flour, baking soda, and sea salt.
4. Mix the Batter:
   Slowly add the dry ingredients to the wet mixture and stir until fully combined.
5. Bake the Bread:
   Pour the batter into the prepared loaf pan and smooth the top with a spatula. Bake for 40-45 minutes or until a toothpick inserted into the center comes out clean.
   Tip: For a more even texture, tap the loaf pan gently on the counter before baking to remove any air bubbles.
6. Cool and Serve:
   Allow the bread to cool completely before slicing. This bread can be stored in an airtight container in the refrigerator for up to 5 days or frozen for longer storage.
   Tip: To toast the bread slices without drying them out, use a skillet with a little ghee or avocado oil for added crispness and flavor.

Nutritional Information (per serving):
- Calories: 180
- Protein: 6 g
- Fat: 16 g
- Carbohydrates: 4 g
- Fiber: 2 g

COCONUT FLOUR BREAD

Prep Time: 10 minutes
Cook Time: 30-35 minutes
Serves: 1 loaf (10 slices)

Ingredients:
- 1/2 cup organic coconut flour
- 6 organic, pasture-raised eggs
- 1/4 cup organic coconut oil, melted
- 1 tsp organic apple cider vinegar (unpasteurized)
- 1/2 tsp organic baking soda
- 1/4 tsp sea salt

Instructions:
1. Preheat Oven:
   Preheat your oven to 350°F (175°C). Line a small loaf pan (8x4 inches) with parchment paper.
2. Mix Wet Ingredients
   In a bowl, whisk together eggs, melted coconut oil, and apple cider vinegar until fully combined.
3. Combine Dry Ingredients
   In another bowl, mix the coconut flour, baking soda, and sea salt.
4. Blend the Mixture:
   Gradually add the dry ingredients to the wet mixture, stirring well to incorporate. Coconut flour absorbs a lot of moisture, so the batter will thicken quickly. Let it sit for a minute or two to fully hydrate.
5. Bake the Bread:
   Pour the batter into the prepared loaf pan and smooth the top. Bake for 30-35 minutes, or until the top is golden and a toothpick inserted into the center comes out clean.
6. Cool and Slice:
   Let the bread cool completely before slicing to prevent crumbling. Store in the refrigerator for up to 5 days or freeze for longer use.
   Tip: Coconut flour is delicate, so avoid overmixing to keep the bread tender. Coconut flour bread pairs beautifully with nut butters and fresh fruit for a wholesome snack.

Nutritional Information (per slice):
- Calories: 120
- Protein: 5 g
- Fat: 9 g
- Carbohydrates: 4 g
- Fiber: 2 g

FLAXSEED BREAD

Prep Time: 10 minutes
Cook Time: 45-50 minutes
Serves: 1 loaf (10 slices)

Ingredients:
- 1 1/2 cups organic flaxseed meal (ground flaxseeds)
- 5 organic, pasture-raised eggs
- 1/4 cup organic avocado oil
- 1 tsp organic apple cider vinegar
- 1 tsp organic baking soda
- 1/2 tsp sea salt
- 1 tbsp organic dried herbs (optional, for flavor)

Instructions:
1. Preheat Oven: Preheat your oven to 350°F (175°C). Grease a 9x5-inch loaf pan or line with parchment paper.
2. Mix the Wet Ingredients: In a bowl, whisk together eggs, avocado oil, and apple cider vinegar.
3. Combine the Dry Ingredients: In another bowl, mix the flaxseed meal, baking soda, sea salt, and optional dried herbs.
4. Prepare the Batter: Gradually stir the dry ingredients into the wet mixture. The batter will thicken as the flax absorbs the liquid.
5. Bake the Bread: Pour the batter into the prepared loaf pan and bake for 45-50 minutes, or until the top is firm and a toothpick inserted comes out clean.:
6. Cool and Slice: Let the bread cool completely before slicing. This bread keeps well in the fridge for up to a week or in the freezer for 2 months.
   Tip: Flaxseed meal adds moisture to the bread, making it dense and filling. Use herbs to infuse different flavors into the loaf. This bread is packed with fiber and omega-3s, making it an excellent base for sandwiches or a hearty breakfast toast.

Nutritional Information (per slice):
- Calories: 150
- Protein: 6 g
- Fat: 11 g
- Carbohydrates: 5 g
- Fiber: 4 g

CASSAVA FLOUR FLATBREAD

Prep Time: 10 minutes
Cook Time: 10 minutes
Serves: 4 flatbreads

Ingredients:
- 1 cup organic cassava flour
- 1/2 cup filtered water
- 1 tbsp organic olive oil or avocado oil
- 1/4 tsp sea salt
- 1/4 tsp organic garlic powder (optional)

Instructions:
1. **Mix the Dough:** In a bowl, combine cassava flour, water, olive oil, sea salt, and garlic powder (if using). Mix until a dough forms.
2. **Shape the Flatbreads:** Divide the dough into 4 equal portions. Roll each portion into a ball and then flatten it into a thin circle using your hands or a rolling pin.
3. **Cook the Flatbreads:** Heat a dry skillet over medium heat. Cook each flatbread for 2-3 minutes on each side until golden and slightly puffed.
4. **Serve or Store:** Serve immediately with your favorite fillings or store in an airtight container for up to 3 days. Reheat on a skillet for a quick meal.
   Tip: Cassava flour has a neutral flavor, making these flatbreads versatile for both sweet and savory toppings. These flatbreads are excellent for making grain-free wraps or tacos.

Nutritional Information (per flatbread):
- Calories: 140
- Protein: 1 g
- Fat: 4 g
- Carbohydrates: 27 g
- Fiber: 1 g

ZUCCHINI AND ALMOND FLOUR BREAD

Prep Time: 15 minutes
Cook Time: 45-50 minutes
Serves: 1 loaf (10 slices)

Ingredients:
- 2 cups organic almond flour
- 1 cup organic zucchini, grated and squeezed dry
- 3 organic, pasture-raised eggs
- 1/4 cup organic avocado oil
- 1 tsp organic baking soda
- 1/2 tsp sea salt
- 1 tsp organic dried oregano (optional)

Instructions:
1. Preheat Oven: Preheat your oven to 350°F (175°C). Grease a loaf pan with avocado oil or line with parchment paper.
2. Prepare the Zucchini: Grate the zucchini and squeeze out any excess moisture using a clean towel or cheesecloth. This helps prevent soggy bread.
3. Mix Wet and Dry Ingredients: In a large bowl, mix the almond flour, baking soda, sea salt, and oregano (if using). In a separate bowl, whisk together the eggs, avocado oil, and zucchini.
4. Combine the Mixture: Gradually stir the dry ingredients into the wet mixture until fully combined.
5. Bake the Bread: Pour the batter into the prepared loaf pan and bake for 45-50 minutes, or until the top is golden and a toothpick inserted into the center comes out clean.:
6. Cool and Slice: Let the bread cool before slicing. Store in the refrigerator for up to 5 days or freeze for longer storage.
   Tip: Squeezing excess water from the zucchini is essential for the bread to have the right texture. Adding herbs like oregano gives a savory touch to the loaf. This zucchini bread is moist and pairs well with savory spreads like guacamole or hummus.

Nutritional Information (per slice):
- Calories: 160
- Protein: 5 g
- Fat: 14 g
- Carbohydrates: 4 g
- Fiber: 2 g

SEEDED BREAD (FLAX, SUNFLOWER, AND PUMPKIN SEEDS)

Prep Time: 15 minutes
Cook Time: 50-60 minutes
Serves: 1 loaf (10 slices)

Ingredients:
- 1 cup organic flaxseed meal (ground flaxseeds)
- 1/4 cup organic sunflower seeds
- 1/4 cup organic pumpkin seeds
- 1/4 cup organic chia seeds
- 1/2 cup organic almond flour
- 4 organic, pasture-raised eggs
- 1/4 cup organic avocado oil
- 1 tsp organic baking soda
- 1 tsp organic apple cider vinegar
- 1/2 tsp sea salt
- 1/4 tsp organic dried thyme (optional)

Instructions:
1. Preheat Oven: Preheat your oven to 350°F (175°C). Grease a 9x5-inch loaf pan or line it with parchment paper.
2. Mix Wet Ingredients: In a bowl, whisk together the eggs, avocado oil, and apple cider vinegar.
3. Mix Dry Ingredients: In a separate bowl, combine flaxseed meal, sunflower seeds, pumpkin seeds, chia seeds, almond flour, baking soda, sea salt, and thyme.
4. Combine and Mix: Gradually add the dry ingredients to the wet mixture, stirring until well combined.
5. Bake the Bread: Pour the batter into the prepared loaf pan and bake for 50-60 minutes, or until the top is firm and a toothpick inserted into the center comes out clean.
6. Cool and Slice: Let the bread cool completely before slicing. This bread can be stored in the fridge for up to a week or frozen for longer storage.
   Tip: If the seeds on top start to brown too quickly, loosely cover the loaf with foil during the last 10 minutes of baking. Toast the slices in a skillet with ghee for extra crunch and flavor.

Nutritional Information (per slice):
- Calories: 190
- Protein: 7 g
- Fat: 16 g
- Carbohydrates: 6 g
- Fiber: 5 g

SWEET POTATO FLATBREAD

Prep Time: 10 minutes
Cook Time: 10 minutes
Serves: 4 flatbreads

Ingredients:
- 1 cup organic sweet potato, mashed (about 1 medium sweet potato)
- 1/4 cup organic cassava flour
- 1/4 cup organic coconut flour
- 1 tbsp organic olive oil or ghee
- 1/2 tsp sea salt

Instructions:
1. **Prepare the Sweet Potato:** Peel and boil or steam the sweet potato until tender. Mash it well and let it cool slightly.
2. **Mix the Dough:** In a bowl, combine the mashed sweet potato, cassava flour, coconut flour, olive oil (or ghee), and sea salt. Stir until a dough forms. If the dough is too sticky, add more coconut flour, 1 tbsp at a time, until it's pliable.

3. **Shape and Cook the Flatbreads:** Divide the dough into 4 equal portions. Roll each portion into a ball and flatten into a round, about 1/4 inch thick.
4. **Cook the Flatbreads:** Heat a skillet over medium heat and cook each flatbread for 2-3 minutes on each side, or until golden brown.
   Tip: If you want softer flatbreads, reduce the cooking time slightly to maintain a chewy texture.

Nutritional Information (per flatbread):
- Calories: 120
- Protein: 2 g
- Fat: 4 g
- Carbohydrates: 19 g
- Fiber: 3 g

HAZELNUT AND ALMOND FLOUR BREAD

Prep Time: 15 minutes
Cook Time: 45 minutes
Serves: 1 loaf (10 slices)

Ingredients:
- 1 cup organic almond flour
- 1/2 cup organic hazelnut flour (or finely ground hazelnuts)
- 4 organic, pasture-raised eggs
- 1/4 cup organic avocado oil or melted coconut oil
- 1/2 tsp organic baking soda
- 1 tsp organic apple cider vinegar
- 1/4 tsp sea salt
- 1/4 cup organic hazelnuts, roughly chopped (optional, for texture)

Instructions:
1. **Preheat Oven:** Preheat your oven to 350°F (175°C). Grease a 9x5-inch loaf pan or line it with parchment paper.
2. **Mix Wet Ingredients:** In a bowl, whisk together the eggs, avocado oil, and apple cider vinegar.
3. **Combine Dry Ingredients:** In another bowl, mix the almond flour, hazelnut flour, baking soda, and sea salt.
4. **Prepare the Batter:** Gradually add the dry ingredients to the wet mixture, stirring to combine. Fold in the chopped hazelnuts for extra texture.
5. **Bake the Bread:** Pour the batter into the prepared loaf pan and bake for 40-45 minutes, or until golden brown and a toothpick inserted into the center comes out clean.
6. **Cool and Slice:** Allow the bread to cool completely before slicing. Store in the fridge for up to 5 days or freeze for longer storage.

Tip: Let the loaf cool in the pan for at least 10 minutes before transferring it to a wire rack. This helps the bread firm up.

Nutritional Information (per slice):
- Calories: 180
- Protein: 6 g
- Fat: 16 g
- Carbohydrates: 5 g
- Fiber: 3 g

ALMOND FLOUR DINNER ROLLS

Prep Time: 15 minutes
Cook Time: 25-30 minutes
Serves: 6 rolls

Ingredients:
- 2 cups organic almond flour
- 2 organic pasture-raised eggs
- 2 tbsp organic ghee or avocado oil
- 1 tsp organic apple cider vinegar (unpasteurized)
- 1/2 tsp organic baking soda
- 1/2 tsp sea salt
- 1 tbsp organic fresh rosemary, chopped (optional)

Instructions:
1. **Preheat Oven:** Preheat your oven to 350°F (175°C). Line a baking sheet with parchment paper.
2. **Mix Wet Ingredients:** In a bowl, whisk together the eggs, ghee (or avocado oil), and apple cider vinegar.
3. **Combine Dry Ingredients:** In another bowl, combine almond flour, baking soda, sea salt, and rosemary (if using).
4. **Form the Dough:** Gradually stir the dry ingredients into the wet mixture until a dough forms. The dough should be soft and slightly sticky.
5. **Shape the Rolls:** Divide the dough into 6 equal portions. Roll each portion into a ball and place them on the prepared baking sheet.
6. **Bake the Rolls:** Bake for 25-30 minutes, or until the rolls are golden brown and a toothpick inserted into the center comes out clean.
7. **Cool and Serve:** Let the rolls cool slightly before serving. They can be stored in an airtight container at room temperature for 2 days or in the fridge for up to 5 days.
   Tip: For an extra-crispy crust, brush the tops with melted ghee before baking. These rolls pair beautifully with herb butter or avocado slices for a nutritious snack or side.

Nutritional Information (per serving):
- Calories: 220
- Protein: 8g
- Fat: 19g
- Carhydrates: 7g
- Fiber: 4g

COCONUT FLOUR GARLIC-HERB ROLLS

Prep Time: 10 minutes
Cook Time: 25-30 minutes
Serves: 6 rolls

Ingredients:
- 1/2 cup organic coconut flour
- 4 organic, pasture-raised eggs
- 2 tbsp organic ghee, melted
- 1 tsp organic garlic powder
- 1/2 tsp organic dried oregano
- 1/2 tsp organic baking soda
- 1/4 tsp sea salt
- 1/4 cup filtered water (or more as needed)

Instructions:
1. **Preheat Oven:** Preheat your oven to 350°F (175°C). Line a baking sheet with parchment paper.
2. **Mix Wet Ingredients:** In a bowl, whisk together the eggs, melted ghee, and water.
3. **Combine Dry Ingredients:** In another bowl, mix the coconut flour, garlic powder, oregano, baking soda, and sea salt.
4. **Make the Dough:** Gradually add the dry ingredients to the wet mixture, stirring to combine. Let the dough sit for a minute to allow the coconut flour to absorb the moisture. If the dough seems too dry, add an extra tablespoon of water.
5. **Shape the Rolls:** Divide the dough into 6 equal portions. Roll each into a ball and place them on the baking sheet.
6. **Bake the Rolls:** Bake for 25-30 minutes, or until the rolls are lightly golden and set. Brushing the tops with extra ghee or olive oil right before baking gives the rolls a beautiful golden finish and enhances the flavor.
7. **Serve:** Let the rolls cool slightly before serving. These rolls are best enjoyed fresh but can be stored in an airtight container in the fridge for up to 5 days.
   Tip: Coconut flour is very absorbent, so be mindful of the dough's consistency. It should be soft but not too sticky. Add more water if needed.

Nutritional Information (per serving):
- Calories: 130, Protein: 5g, Fat: 9g, Carbohydrates: 6g, Fiber: 3g

CAULIFLOWER TORTILLA WRAPS

Prep Time: 15 minutes
Cook Time: 20 minutes
Serves: 4 wraps

Ingredients:

- 1 medium **organic cauliflower** head, riced (about 3 cups)
- 2 **organic, pasture-raised eggs**
- 1/4 cup **organic almond flour**
- 1 tbsp **organic olive oil**
- 1/2 tsp **sea salt**
- 1/4 tsp **organic cumin powder** (optional, for flavor)

Instructions:

1. **Prepare the Cauliflower:** Preheat the oven to 375°F (190°C). Line a baking sheet with parchment paper. Pulse the cauliflower in a food processor until it resembles rice. Transfer the cauliflower to a microwave-safe bowl and microwave for 5 minutes. Let it cool slightly, then squeeze out as much moisture as possible using a clean kitchen towel.
   The key to a pliable wrap is removing all excess moisture from the cauliflower. This step is crucial for achieving the right texture.
2. **Mix the Batter:** In a bowl, mix the dried cauliflower, eggs, almond flour, olive oil, salt, and cumin (if using) until it forms a dough-like consistency.
3. **Shape and Bake the Wraps:** Divide the mixture into 4 equal parts. Press each part into a thin circle (about 6 inches in diameter) on the prepared baking sheet. Bake for 15-20 minutes, flipping halfway through, until the wraps are golden and firm but still flexible.
4. **Serve:** Use these wraps for tacos, burritos, or sandwiches. They can be stored in an airtight container in the fridge for up to 4 days or frozen for up to a month.
   Tip: To get crisp edges or reheat the wraps, gently warm them in a dry skillet or toaster oven for a few minutes before serving.

Nutritional Information (per serving):

- Calories: 90, Protein: 5g, Fat: 6g, Carbohydrates: 6g, Fiber: 2g

SWEET POTATO AND CASSAVA FLOUR WRAPS

Prep Time: 10 minutes
Cook Time: 10 minutes
Serves: 4 wraps

Ingredients:

- 1 cup organic sweet potato, mashed (about 1 medium sweet potato)
- 1/2 cup organic cassava flour
- 1 tbsp organic avocado oil (for cooking)
- 1/4 tsp sea salt
- 1/4 tsp organic cinnamon (optional, for sweetness)

Instructions:

1. **Prepare the Sweet Potato:** Peel and boil the sweet potato until tender. Drain and mash it until smooth. Allow it to cool slightly before mixing with the other ingredients.
2. **Mix the Dough:** In a bowl, combine the mashed sweet potato, cassava flour, sea salt, and cinnamon (if using). Mix until a dough forms. If the dough is too sticky, add a little more cassava flour until it's pliable.
3. **Shape and Cook the Wraps:** Divide the dough into 4 equal portions. Roll each into a ball, then flatten between two pieces of parchment paper into a circle about 6 inches in diameter. Heat a skillet over medium heat and cook each wrap for about 2 minutes on each side, until lightly browned and flexible.
4. **Serve:** These wraps are excellent for pairing with both sweet and savory fillings. Store them in the fridge for up to 4 days or freeze for longer-term storage.
   Tip: Cassava flour makes these wraps soft and chewy, while sweet potato adds a touch of natural sweetness and moisture, keeping the wraps pliable. Reheat the wraps by lightly toasting them in a dry skillet to enhance their chewiness and flavor.

Nutritional Information (per serving):

- Calories: 160, Protein 2g, Fat: 4g, Carbohydrates: 31g, Fiber: 3g

SIDES

ROASTED BROCCOLI WITH ANCHOVY-GARLIC DRESSING

Prep Time: 15 minutes
Cook Time: 20 minutes
Serves: 4

Ingredients:

- 4 cups organic broccoli florets
- 6 fillets wild-caught anchovies, finely chopped
- 2 organic garlic cloves, minced
- 1/4 cup organic extra-virgin olive oil
- 2 tbsp organic lemon juice
- 1/4 cup organic pine nuts, toasted
- Sea salt and black pepper to taste

Instructions:

1. Preheat oven to 400°F (200°C).
2. Toss broccoli florets with 2 tbsp olive oil, salt, and pepper. Spread on a baking sheet and roast for 15-20 minutes until tender and slightly charred.
3. In a small saucepan, heat remaining olive oil over medium heat. Add anchovies and garlic, cooking until fragrant and anchovies dissolve.
4. Remove from heat and stir in lemon juice.
5. Drizzle anchovy-garlic dressing over the roasted broccoli and sprinkle with toasted pine nuts before serving.

Tip: Avoid burning the garlic in the dressing by cooking it gently over medium heat.

Nutritional Information (per serving):

- Calories: 220

- Protein: 5g
- Fat: 20g
- Carbohydrates: 8g
- Fiber: 4g

ROASTED GARLIC CAULIFLOWER WITH LEMON TAHINI DRIZZLE

Prep Time: 10 minutes
Cook Time: 25 minutes
Serves: 4

Ingredients:

- 1 large organic cauliflower, cut into florets
- 2 tbsp organic extra-virgin olive oil
- 1 tbsp organic garlic, minced
- 1 tbsp organic tahini
- 1 tbsp organic lemon juice
- 1/4 cup water

Instructions:

1. **Preheat the Oven:** Preheat to 400°F (200°C).
2. **Roast the Cauliflower:** Toss cauliflower florets with oil, garlic, salt, and pepper. Spread on a sheet pan and roast for 25 minutes, stirring halfway.
3. **Make the Tahini Drizzle:** In a small bowl, whisk together tahini, lemon juice, water, and salt until smooth.
4. **Serve:** Drizzle the roasted cauliflower with the tahini sauce before serving.

Tip: Roasting cauliflower at a high temperature caramelizes the edges for an extra nutty flavor.

Pair with grilled grass-fed lamb or wild-caught salmon.
Nutritional Information (per serving):

- Calories 130
- Protein: 4g
- Fat: 9g
- Carbohydrates: 11g
- Fiber: 4g

CRISPY ROASTED BRUSSELS SPROUTS WITH BACON AND BALSAMIC GLAZE

Prep Time: 15 minutes
Cook Time: 25 minutes
Serves: 4

Ingredients:

- 1 lb organic Brussels sprouts, trimmed and halved
- 4 slices organic, pasture-raised bacon, chopped
- 2 tbsp organic avocado oil
- 1 tbsp organic balsamic vinegar
- 1 tbsp organic coconut aminos
- 1 tsp organic Dijon mustard
- Sea salt and black pepper to taste

Instructions:

1. Preheat oven to 400°F (200°C).
2. In a large bowl, toss Brussels sprouts with avocado oil, salt, and pepper.
3. Spread in a single layer on a baking sheet.
4. Roast for 15 minutes.
5. While the Brussels sprouts are roasting, cook bacon in a skillet over medium heat until crisp. Remove bacon and set aside, reserving the fat.
6. In a small bowl, whisk together balsamic vinegar, coconut aminos, and Dijon mustard.
7. Remove Brussels sprouts from the oven and add the bacon and balsamic glaze to the baking sheet.
8. Toss to coat and roast for an additional 10 minutes, or until the Brussels sprouts are tender and slightly charred.

Tip: Make sure the Brussels sprouts are spread in a single layer on the baking sheet to ensure even browning.
Nutritional Information (per serving):

- Calories: 180
- Protein: 8g
- Fat: 14g
- Carbohydrates: 9g
- Fiber: 5g

SHAVED BRUSSELS SPROUTS SALAD WITH TOASTED ALMONDS AND LEMON VINAIGRETTE

Prep Time: 15 minutes
Cook Time: 0 minutes
Serves: 4

Ingredients:

- 1 lb organic Brussels sprouts, trimmed and thinly shaved
- 1/2 cup organic slivered almonds, toasted
- 1/4 cup organic dried cranberries (unsweetened)
- 1/4 cup organic crumbled goat cheese
- 2 tbsp organic extra-virgin olive oil
- 1 tbsp organic lemon juice
- 1 tsp organic Dijon mustard
- Sea salt and black pepper to taste

Instructions:

1. In a large bowl, combine shaved Brussels sprouts, toasted almonds, dried cranberries, and goat cheese.
2. In a small bowl, whisk together olive oil, lemon juice, Dijon mustard, salt, and pepper.
3. Pour the dressing over the salad and toss to coat.
4. Serve immediately or chill for later.

Tip: Toasting the almonds enhances their flavor and adds a satisfying crunch to the salad.
Nutritional Information (per serving):

- Calories: 230
- Protein: 8g
- Fat: 18g
- Carbohydrates: 12g
- Fiber: 6g

BRUSSELS SPROUTS WITH SESAME SEEDS

Prep Time: 15 minutes
Cook Time: 20 minutes
Serves: 4

Ingredients:

- 1 lb organic Brussels sprouts, trimmed and halved
- 2 tbsp organic coconut oil
- 2 tbsp organic coconut aminos
- 1 tbsp toasted sesame oil
- 1 tbsp sesame seeds, toasted
- 1 tsp grated fresh ginger
- 1 garlic clove, minced
- Pinch of red pepper flakes

Instructions:

1. Preheat oven to 400°F (200°C).
2. In a large bowl, toss Brussels sprouts with coconut oil, coconut aminos, sesame oil, ginger, garlic, and red pepper flakes.
3. Spread in a single layer on a baking sheet.
4. Roast for 15-20 minutes, or until tender and slightly charred.
5. Sprinkle with toasted sesame seeds before serving.

Tip: Don't be afraid to get a bit of char on the Brussels sprouts; it adds a delicious smoky flavor.
Nutritional Information (per serving):

- Calories: 190
- Protein: 6g
- Fat: 16g
- Carbohydrates: 9g
- Fiber: 5g

CARROT AND COCONUT "RICE" PILAF

Prep Time: 15 minutes
Cook Time: 15 minutes
Serves: 4

Ingredients:

- 4 cups organic carrots, riced in a food processor
- 1 cup organic unsweetened shredded coconut
- ½ cup organic cashews, chopped
- ¼ cup organic raisins
- 2 tbsp organic coconut oil
- 1 tsp organic ground cinnamon
- ½ tsp organic ground cardamom
- Sea salt to taste
- ¼ cup organic fresh mint, chopped

Instructions:

1. In a large skillet, heat coconut oil over medium heat.
2. Add riced carrots and sauté for 5-7 minutes until tender.
3. Stir in shredded coconut, cashews, raisins, cinnamon, cardamom, and salt.
4. Cook for another 5 minutes, stirring frequently.
5. Remove from heat and stir in fresh mint.
6. Serve warm as a side dish or light meal.

Tip: For added protein, serve this pilaf alongside grilled chicken or fish.
Nutritional Information (per serving):

- Calories: 320
- Protein: 6g
- Fat: 24g

- Carbohydrates: 26g
- Fiber: 8g

CRISPY BAKED OKRA WITH LEMON-GARLIC DIP

Prep Time: 15 minutes
Cook Time: 20 minutes
Serves: 4

Ingredients:
- 1 lb organic okra, trimmed
- 2 tbsp organic avocado oil
- 1 tsp organic garlic powder
- 1/2 tsp organic onion powder
- Sea salt and black pepper to taste

For the Lemon-Garlic Dip:
- 1/2 cup organic coconut yogurt
- 1 organic lemon, juiced
- 1 organic garlic clove, minced
- Sea salt and black pepper to taste

Instructions:
1. Preheat oven to 400°F (200°C).
2. Toss okra with avocado oil, garlic powder, onion powder, salt, and pepper.
3. Spread okra in a single layer on a baking sheet.
4. Bake for 15-20 minutes, turning halfway through, until crispy and slightly browned.
5. While okra is baking, whisk together coconut yogurt, lemon juice, garlic, salt, and pepper in a small bowl to make the dip.
6. Serve the crispy baked okra with the lemon-garlic dip.

Tip: For extra crispy okra, toss with a little bit of almond flour before baking.

Nutritional Information (per serving):
- Calories: 180
- Protein: 4g
- Fat: 14g
- Carbohydrates: 12g
- Fiber: 5g

SHIRAZI SALAD

Prep Time: 15 minutes
Cook Time: 0 minutes
Serves: 4

Ingredients:
- 2 large organic tomatoes, diced
- 2 organic Persian cucumbers, diced
- 1 small organic red onion, finely diced
- 1/4 cup organic fresh mint leaves, chopped
- 1/4 cup organic fresh parsley, chopped
- 2 tbsp organic extra-virgin olive oil
- 2 tbsp organic fresh lemon juice
- 1 tsp organic sumac (optional)
- Sea salt and freshly ground black pepper to taste

Instructions:
1. In a large bowl, combine the diced tomatoes, cucumbers, and red onion. Add the chopped mint and parsley to the bowl.
2. In a small bowl, whisk together the olive oil and lemon juice. Season with sea salt and freshly ground black pepper to taste.
3. Pour the dressing over the vegetables and herbs and gently toss to combine, ensuring all ingredients are evenly coated.
4. Sprinkle sumac over the salad, if using.
5. Let the salad sit for about 5 minutes to allow flavors to meld then serve immediately as a refreshing side dish or light meal.

Tip: For the best flavor and texture, prepare this salad just before serving. If you need to make it in advance, keep the dressing separate and combine it with the vegetables just before serving to prevent the salad from becoming soggy.

Nutritional Information (per serving):
- Calories: 90
- Protein: 2g
- Fat: 7g
- Carbohydrates: 8g
- Fiber: 2g

GRAIN-FREE TABBOULEH

Prep Time: 20 minutes
Cook Time: 0 minutes
Serves: 4

Ingredients:
- 1 head organic cauliflower, riced
- 1 cup organic cherry tomatoes, halved
- 1 cup organic cucumber, diced
- 1/2 cup organic fresh parsley, finely chopped
- 1/4 cup organic fresh mint, finely chopped
- 1/4 cup organic red onion, finely chopped
- 2 tbsp organic lemon juice
- 2 tbsp organic extra-virgin olive oil
- 1 tsp organic ground cumin
- 1/2 tsp sea salt
- 1/4 tsp freshly ground black pepper

Instructions:
1. In a food processor, pulse the cauliflower florets until they resemble the texture of bulgur wheat. Transfer to a large bowl.
2. To the riced cauliflower, add the halved cherry tomatoes, diced cucumber, chopped parsley, mint, and red onion. Toss to combine.
3. In a small bowl, whisk together the lemon juice, olive oil, cumin, salt, and pepper.
4. Pour the dressing over the cauliflower and vegetable mixture, and toss gently to coat everything evenly.
5. Cover the tabbouleh and refrigerate for at least 30 minutes to allow the flavors to meld.

Tip: For a more uniform texture, grate the cucumber on a box grater instead of dicing it.

Nutritional Information (per serving):
- Calories: 150
- Protein: 4g
- Fat: 12g
- Carbohydrates: 10g
- Fiber: 4g

ROASTED SPAGHETTI SQUASH WITH PESTO AND PINE NUTS

Prep Time: 10 minutes
Cook Time: 40 minutes
Serves: 4

Ingredients:
- 1 large **organic spaghetti squash**, halved and seeded
- 2 tbsp **organic olive oil**
- 1/4 cup **organic pesto** (no added sugars)
- 2 tbsp **organic pine nuts**, toasted

Instructions:
1. **Preheat the Oven:** Preheat to 400°F (200°C).
2. **Roast the Squash:** Rub the cut side of the squash with olive oil and roast cut-side down for 40 minutes, or until tender.
3. **Toss with Pesto:** Scrape out the squash strands with a fork and toss with pesto. Top with toasted pine nuts.

Tip: Toasting pine nuts adds a nutty, crunchy element that complements the fresh pesto. Serve alongside grilled chicken or baked fish.

Nutritional Information (per serving):
- Calories: 210
- Protein: 3g

- Fat: 18g
- Carbohydrates: 11g
- Fiber: 3g

GRILLED PORTOBELLO MUSHROOMS WITH GARLIC AND PARSLEY

Prep Time: 5 minutes
Cook Time: 10 minutes
Serves: 4

Ingredients:
- 4 large organic Portobello mushrooms
- 2 tbsp organic olive oil
- 2 cloves organic garlic, minced
- 1 tbsp organic fresh parsley, chopped

Instructions:
1. Preheat the Grill: Preheat to medium heat.
2. Grill the Mushrooms: Brush mushrooms with olive oil, season with salt and pepper, and grill for 5 minutes per side.
3. Finish with Garlic and Parsley: Top the grilled mushrooms with minced garlic and fresh parsley before serving.

Tip: Grilling mushrooms brings out their meaty texture and rich, umami flavor. Ideal with grilled steak or chicken thighs.

Nutritional Information (per serving):
- Calories: 90
- Protein: 3g
- Fat: 8g
- Carbohydrates: 5g
- Fiber: 2g

ROASTED CHERRY TOMATOES WITH BASIL AND BALSAMIC VINEGAR

Prep Time: 5 minutes
Cook Time: 15 minutes
Serves: 4

Ingredients:
- 2 cups organic cherry tomatoes
- 2 tbsp organic olive oil
- 1 tbsp organic balsamic vinegar
- 1 tbsp organic fresh basil, chopped

Instructions:
1. Preheat the Oven: Preheat to 400°F (200°C).
2. Roast the Tomatoes: Toss the tomatoes with olive oil, salt, and pepper. Roast for 15 minutes until blistered.
3. Finish with Balsamic and Basil: Drizzle with balsamic vinegar and garnish with fresh basil.

Tip: Roasting cherry tomatoes brings out their natural sweetness, and balsamic adds a tangy depth.

Nutritional Information (per serving):
- Calories: 80
- Protein: 1g
- Fat: 7g
- Carbohydrates: 5g
- Fiber: 2g

SAUTÉED SWISS CHARD WITH GARLIC AND LEMON ZEST

Prep Time: 5 minutes
Cook Time: 10 minutes
Serves: 4

Ingredients:
- 1 bunch organic Swiss chard, stems removed and chopped
- 2 tbsp organic olive oil
- 2 cloves organic garlic, minced
- 1 tbsp organic lemon zest

Instructions:
1. Sauté the Garlic: Heat olive oil in a skillet over medium heat. Sauté garlic until fragrant, about 1 minute.

2. Cook the Chard: Add Swiss chard and cook, stirring frequently, until wilted, about 5 minutes.
3. Finish with Lemon Zest: Stir in lemon zest and season with salt and pepper before serving.

Tip: Lemon zest brightens the earthy flavor of the Swiss chard. Perfect with grilled fish or roast lamb.

Nutritional Information (per serving):
- Calories: 70
- Protein: 2g
- Fat: 7g
- Carbohydrates: 4g
- Fiber: 2g

ROASTED RED CABBAGE WEDGES WITH BALSAMIC GLAZE

Prep Time: 5 minutes
Cook Time: 20 minutes
Serves: 4

Ingredients:
- 1 small organic red cabbage, cut into wedges
- 2 tbsp organic olive oil
- 1 tbsp organic balsamic vinegar
- 1 tbsp organic fresh parsley, chopped

Instructions:
1. Preheat the Oven: Preheat to 425°F (220°C).
2. Roast the Cabbage: Drizzle cabbage wedges with olive oil, season with salt and pepper, and roast for 20 minutes until tender and slightly caramelized.
3. Drizzle with Balsamic: Finish with a drizzle of balsamic vinegar and sprinkle with parsley.

Tip: Roasting red cabbage intensifies its sweetness, and the balsamic glaze adds a tangy finish. Pair with grilled sausages or roasted chicken.

Nutritional Information (per serving):
- Calories: 90
- Protein: 1g
- Fat: 7g
- Carbohydrates: 7g
- Fiber: 2

ROASTED BUTTERNUT SQUASH WITH CINNAMON AND WALNUTS

Prep Time: 10 minutes
Cook Time: 30 minutes
Serves: 4

Ingredients:
- 1 medium organic butternut squash, peeled, seeded, and cubed
- 2 tbsp organic coconut oil, melted
- 1 tsp organic cinnamon
- 1/4 cup organic walnuts, chopped and toasted

Instructions:
1. Preheat the Oven: Preheat to 400°F (200°C).
2. Roast the Squash: Toss the butternut squash cubes with melted coconut oil, cinnamon, salt, and pepper. Roast for 30 minutes, stirring halfway through.
3. Top with Walnuts: Garnish with toasted walnuts before serving.

Tip: Cinnamon and coconut oil bring out the natural sweetness of the butternut squash, while walnuts add a crunchy texture.

Nutritional Information (per serving):
- Calories: 180
- Protein: 2g
- Fat 11g
- Carbohydrates: 20g
- Fiber: 4g

CELERIAC PURÉE WITH GARLIC AND OLIVE OIL

Prep Time: 10 minutes
Cook Time: 20 minutes
Serves: 4

Ingredients:
- 1 large organic celeriac (celery root), peeled and cubed
- 2 cloves organic garlic, minced
- 2 tbsp organic olive oil
- 1 tbsp organic lemon juice

Instructions:
1. Boil the Celeriac: Boil celeriac cubes in salted water for 15-20 minutes until tender.
2. Mash the Celeriac: Drain and mash the celeriac with garlic, olive oil, and lemon juice. Season with salt and pepper.

Tip: Celeriac has a subtle, nutty flavor, and mashing it with garlic creates a creamy, rich side dish.

Nutritional Information (per serving):
- Calories: 110
- Protein: 1g
- Fat: 7g
- Carbohydrates: 10g
- Fiber: 3g

LEMON AND HERB ROASTED CARROTS WITH PISTACHIOS

Prep Time: 5 minutes
Cook Time: 25 minutes
Serves: 4

Ingredients:
- 6 large organic carrots, peeled and halved
- 2 tbsp organic olive oil
- 1 tbsp organic lemon juice
- 1 tbsp organic fresh parsley, chopped
- 1/4 cup organic pistachios, chopped

Instructions:
1. Preheat the Oven: Preheat to 400°F (200°C).
2. Roast the Carrots: Toss carrots with olive oil, salt, and pepper. Roast for 25 minutes, until tender and caramelized.
3. Serve with Lemon and Pistachios: Drizzle the roasted carrots with lemon juice, garnish with parsley, and sprinkle with pistachios.

Tip: The roasted carrots' natural sweetness is enhanced by the lemon, and the pistachios add a satisfying crunch.

Nutritional Information (per serving):
- Calories: 150
- Protein: 2g
- Fat: 11g
- Carbohydrates: 12g
- Fiber: 4g

MASHED PARSNIPS WITH GARLIC AND CHIVES

Prep Time: 10 minutes
Cook Time: 15 minutes
Serves: 4

Ingredients:
- 4 large organic parsnips, peeled and chopped
- 2 cloves organic garlic, minced
- 2 tbsp organic ghee
- 1 tbsp organic fresh chives, chopped

Instructions:
1. Cook the Parsnips: Boil parsnips in salted water for 10-12 minutes until tender. Drain well.
2. Mash the Parsnips: In a bowl, mash parsnips with ghee and garlic. Season with salt and pepper.
3. Serve with Chives: Garnish with fresh chives before serving.

Tip: Ghee adds richness, while garlic provides depth to the natural sweetness of parsnips.

Nutritional Information (per serving):
- Calories: 140
- Protein: 2g
- Fat: 6g
- Carbohydrates: 21g
- Fiber: 5g

COCONUT-ROASTED DELICATA SQUASH WITH PEPITAS

Prep Time: 10 minutes
Cook Time: 25 minutes
Serves: 4

Ingredients:
- 2 organic delicata squash, sliced into rings
- 2 tbsp organic coconut oil, melted
- 1 tbsp organic pepitas (pumpkin seeds)

Instructions:
1. Preheat the Oven: Preheat to 400°F (200°C).
2. Roast the Squash: Toss delicata squash rings with coconut oil, salt, and pepper. Spread on a sheet pan and roast for 25 minutes, flipping halfway.
3. Garnish with Pepitas: Sprinkle roasted squash with pepitas before serving.

Tip: The naturally sweet squash pairs beautifully with the nutty crunch of pepitas. Pair with grilled pork chops or baked chicken thighs.

Nutritional Information (per serving):
- Calories: 160
- Protein: 2g
- Fat: 12g
- Carbohydrates: 14g
- Fiber: 3g

DIPS, SAUCES, AND DRESSINGS

Dips, sauces, and dressings are among the most common sources of processed and ultra-processed foods we consume without even thinking about it. You can carefully select organic, gluten-free, no added sugar or preservatives alternatives from a well stock grocery store and you can even find some easy substitution at Walmart and Costco. Still, I believe homemade is always better, you'll be able to source the whole food ingredients and create something that can nourish you for weeks and months. The flavor are so much stronger and complex when we make something from scratch!

CHIMICHURRI SAUCE

Prep Time: 10 minutes
Serves: 1 cup

Ingredients:

- 1 cup organic cilantro leaves
- 1 cup organic parsley leaves
- 1/2 cup organic avocado oil
- 1/4 cup organic red wine vinegar
- 2 organic garlic cloves, minced
- 1 organic shallot, minced
- 1 tsp sea salt
- 1/2 tsp organic red pepper flakes
- 1/4 tsp organic black pepper

Instructions:

1. In a food processor or blender, combine cilantro, parsley, avocado oil, vinegar, garlic, shallot, salt, red pepper flakes, and black pepper.
2. Pulse until the herbs are finely chopped and the ingredients are well combined, scraping down the sides as needed.
3. Taste and adjust seasoning as needed. Use immediately or store in the refrigerator for up to 1 week.

Tips:

- For a chunkier texture, finely chop the ingredients by hand instead of using a food processor.
- Add a splash of organic lime juice for extra tang.
- Serve as a condiment for grilled grass-fed steak or drizzle over roasted vegetables.
- Cilantro and parsley provide antioxidants and fresh, herbaceous flavor.

Nutritional Information (per serving):

- Calories: 140
- Protein: 1g
- Fat: 15g
- Carbohydrates: 2g
- Fiber: 1g

LEMON CAPER SAUCE

Prep Time: 10 minutes
Cook Time: 5 minutes
Serves: 1 cup

Ingredients:

- 1/2 cup organic chicken or vegetable broth
- 1/4 cup organic lemon juice
- 2 tbsp organic ghee or grass-fed butter
- 2 tbsp organic capers, drained and rinsed
- 1 tbsp organic Dijon mustard
- 1 organic garlic clove, minced
- 1/2 tsp sea salt
- 1/4 tsp organic black pepper

Instructions:

1. In a small saucepan, whisk together broth, lemon juice, ghee, capers, mustard, garlic, salt, and pepper.
2. Bring the mixture to a simmer over medium heat, stirring occasionally.

3. Reduce the heat to low and simmer for 3-5 minutes until slightly thickened and the flavors have melded.
4. Remove from heat and let cool slightly. If the sauce is too thick, gradually whisk in additional broth 1 teaspoon at a time until desired consistency is reached.
5. Taste and adjust seasoning as needed. Use immediately or store in the refrigerator for up to 5 days.

Tips:

- For a smoother sauce, strain through a fine-mesh sieve before serving.
- Add a pinch of organic red pepper flakes for a spicy kick.
- Serve over pan-seared wild-caught fish or roasted organic chicken.
- Lemon juice provides vitamin C and bright acidity while capers add briny, salty flavor.

Nutritional Information (per serving):

- Calories: 60
- Protein: 1g
- Fat: 5g
- Carbohydrates: 3g
- Fiber: 0g

NOMATO KETCHUP

Prep Time: 15 minutes
Cook Time: 30 minutes
Serves: 2 cups

Ingredients:

- 2 cups organic pumpkin puree
- 1/2 cup organic apple cider vinegar
- 1/4 cup organic beet juice
- 2 tbsp organic coconut aminos
- 1 tbsp organic garlic powder
- 1 tbsp organic onion powder
- 1 tsp sea salt
- 1/2 tsp organic ground cloves
- 1/4 tsp organic ground cinnamon

Instructions:

1. In a medium saucepan, whisk together pumpkin puree, vinegar, beet juice, coconut aminos, garlic powder, onion powder, salt, cloves, and cinnamon.
2. Bring the mixture to a simmer over medium heat, stirring occasionally.
3. Reduce the heat to low and simmer, uncovered, for 25-30 minutes until thickened, whisking occasionally to prevent scorching.
4. Remove from heat and let cool completely. Transfer to an airtight container and refrigerate for up to 2 weeks.

Tips:

- For a smoother consistency, blend the cooled ketchup in a high-speed blender or food processor.
- Adjust the sweetness by adding a few drops of liquid stevia or monk fruit extract.
- Delicious as a dipping sauce for jicama fries or grain-free chicken nuggets.
- Pumpkin provides vitamin A and fiber while beet juice adds natural sweetness and vibrant color.

Nutritional Information (per serving):

- Calories: 25
- Protein: 0g
- Fat: 0g
- Carbohydrates: 6g
- Fiber: 1g

GARLIC AVOCADO AIOLI

Prep Time: 10 minutes
Total Time: 10 minutes
Serves: 1 cup

Ingredients:

- 1 organic avocado, pitted and peeled
- 1/4 cup organic avocado oil
- 2 tbsp organic lemon juice
- 2 organic garlic cloves, minced
- 1/2 tsp sea salt
- 1/4 tsp organic black pepper

Instructions:

1. In a food processor or blender, combine avocado, avocado oil, lemon juice, garlic, salt, and pepper.
2. Process until smooth and creamy, scraping down the sides as needed.
3. If the aioli is too thick, gradually blend in filtered water 1 teaspoon at a time until desired consistency is reached.
4. Taste and adjust seasoning as needed. Use immediately or store in the refrigerator for up to 3 days.

Tips:

- For a milder garlic flavor, roast the cloves before blending.
- Add a pinch of organic cayenne pepper for a spicy kick.
- Serve as a dip for raw vegetables or dollop on top of grilled wild-caught salmon.
- Avocado provides heart-healthy monounsaturated fats and fiber.

Nutritional Information (per serving):

- Calories: 100
- Protein: 1g
- Fat: 10g
- Carbohydrates: 3g
- Fiber: 2g

FERMENTED CHILI OIL

Prep Time: 10 minutes
Fermentation Time: 1 week
Serves: 1 cup

Ingredients:

- 1 cup organic avocado oil
- 1/4 cup organic red pepper flakes
- 2 tbsp organic fermented vegetables (like sauerkraut or kimchi)
- 1 organic garlic clove, minced
- 1 tsp sea salt

Instructions:

1. In a small saucepan, heat avocado oil over medium-low heat until warm but not simmering.
2. Remove from heat and stir in red pepper flakes, fermented vegetables, garlic, and salt.
3. Transfer the mixture to a sterilized glass jar and let cool to room temperature.
4. Cover the jar with a tight-fitting lid and store at room temperature away from direct sunlight for 1 week to allow the flavors to develop.
5. Strain the oil through a fine-mesh sieve into a clean jar, pressing on the solids to extract as much oil as possible. Discard the solids.
6. Store the fermented chili oil in the refrigerator for up to 6 months.

Tips:

- Use as a finishing oil for stir-fries, soups, or grain-free noodle dishes.
- Adjust the heat level by increasing or decreasing the amount of red pepper flakes.
- Fermented vegetables provide beneficial probiotics and complex flavor.
- Chili oil may solidify when refrigerated; let stand at room temperature for a few minutes before using.

Nutritional Information (per serving):

- Calories: 120
- Protein: 0g
- Fat: 14g
- Carbohydrates: 0g
- Fiber: 0g

COCONUT PEANUT SAUCE

Prep Time: 10 minutes
Cook Time: 5 minutes
Serves: 1 1/2 cups

Ingredients:

- 1 cup organic coconut milk
- 1/2 cup organic unsweetened peanut butter
- 2 tbsp organic lime juice
- 1 tbsp organic coconut aminos
- 1 tsp organic fish sauce
- 1 tsp organic grated ginger
- 1 organic garlic clove, grated
- 1/4 tsp organic red pepper flakes

Instructions:

1. In a medium saucepan, whisk together coconut milk, peanut butter, lime juice, coconut aminos, fish sauce, ginger, garlic, and red pepper flakes.
2. Heat the mixture over medium heat, whisking constantly, until smooth and slightly thickened, about 5 minutes.
3. Remove from heat and let cool slightly. If the sauce is too thick, gradually whisk in filtered water 1 tablespoon at a time until desired consistency is reached.
4. Taste and adjust seasoning as needed. Use immediately or store in the refrigerator for up to 1 week.

Tips:

- For a smoother sauce, blend the cooled mixture in a high-speed blender until creamy.
- Add a splash of organic rice vinegar for extra tang.
- Toss with spiralized vegetables or use as a dipping sauce for grilled organic chicken skewers.
- Coconut milk and peanut butter provide healthy fats and creamy texture.

Nutritional Information (per serving):

- Calories: 130
- Protein: 3g
- Fat: 12g
- Carbohydrates: 5g
- Fiber: 1g

CILANTRO "RANCH" DRESSING

Prep Time: 10 minutes
Serves: 1 1/2 cups

Ingredients:

- 1 cup organic coconut yogurt
- 1/2 cup organic cilantro leaves
- 1/4 cup organic avocado oil mayonnaise
- 2 tbsp organic lime juice
- 1 tbsp organic apple cider vinegar
- 1 tsp organic onion powder
- 1/2 tsp organic garlic powder
- 1/2 tsp sea salt
- 1/4 tsp organic black pepper

Instructions:

1. In a food processor or blender, combine coconut yogurt, cilantro, mayonnaise, lime juice, vinegar, onion powder, garlic powder, salt, and pepper.
2. Process until smooth and creamy, scraping down the sides as needed.
3. If the dressing is too thick, gradually blend in filtered water 1 tablespoon at a time until desired consistency is reached.

4. Taste and adjust seasoning as needed. Use immediately or store in the refrigerator for up to 3 days.

Tips: Dip organic crudités or drizzle over fish tacos or a Mexican-inspired salad.

Nutritional Information (per serving):
- Calories: 60
- Protein: 1g
- Fat: 6g
- Carbohydrates: 2g
- Fiber: 0g

MUHAMMARA WITH FERMENTED ROASTED PEPPERS

Prep Time: 15 minutes
Cook Time: 10 minutes
Serves: 4

Ingredients:
- 2 large organic red bell peppers, roasted and skin removed
- 1/2 cup fermented roasted red peppers (for probiotics)
- 1/4 cup organic walnuts, toasted
- 2 tbsp organic extra virgin olive oil
- 1 tbsp organic pomegranate molasses (no sugar added or homemade)
- 1 clove organic garlic, minced
- 1 tsp organic cumin

Instructions:
1. **Prepare the Muhammara:**
   In a food processor, combine the roasted red peppers, fermented red peppers, walnuts, olive oil, pomegranate molasses, garlic, and cumin. Blend until smooth but slightly chunky. Season with salt and pepper.
2. **Serve:**
   Transfer the muhammara to a serving dish, drizzle with a little extra olive oil, and serve with sliced vegetables or grain-free crackers.
   Tip: Toast the walnuts lightly for 2-3 minutes to bring out their natural oils and enhance their nutty flavor.

Nutritional Information (per serving):
- Calories: 150
- Protein: 2g
- Fat: 12g
- Carbohydrates: 9g
- Fiber: 3g

BABA GHANOUSH WITH FERMENTED VEGETABLES

Prep Time: 15 minutes
Cook Time: 40 minutes
Serves: 4

Ingredients:
- 2 large organic eggplants
- 1/4 cup organic tahini
- 2 organic garlic cloves, minced
- 1 organic lemon, juiced
- 2 tbsp organic extra-virgin olive oil
- Sea salt and black pepper to taste
- 1/4 cup organic fermented vegetables (such as sauerkraut or kimchi), finely chopped
- 1/4 cup organic fresh parsley, chopped
- Organic vegetable crudités for serving

Instructions:
1. Preheat the oven to 400°F (200°C).
2. Prick the eggplants several times with a fork and place them on a baking sheet. Roast for 35-40 minutes, until the skin is charred and the flesh is tender.
3. Let the eggplants cool slightly, then scoop out the flesh and place it in a food processor.
4. Add tahini, garlic, lemon juice, olive oil, salt, and pepper. Blend until smooth and creamy.
5. Transfer to a serving bowl and stir in the chopped fermented vegetables.

6. Garnish with fresh parsley and a drizzle of olive oil.
7. Serve with vegetable crudités.

Tip: For extra smoky flavor, grill the eggplants over an open flame before roasting them.

Nutritional Information (per serving):
- Calories: 160
- Protein: 3g
- Fat: 12g
- Carbohydrates: 11g
- Fiber: 5g

ROASTED CAULIFLOWER HUMMUS

Prep Time: 10 minutes
Cook Time: 40 minutes
Serves: 4

Ingredients:
- 1 large organic cauliflower, chopped
- 1 can (15 oz) organic chickpeas, drained and rinsed
- 1 tbsp organic tahini (optional)
- 1 tbsp organic extra-virgin olive oil
- Sea salt and black pepper to taste

Instructions:
1. Preheat oven to 400°F (200°C).
2. In a large bowl, mix chopped cauliflower, drained chickpeas, water, and salt to taste. Let sit for 10 minutes to allow flavors to meld.
3. Drain the cauliflower and chickpeas mixture thoroughly.
4. Return the cauliflower to a baking dish, spread evenly, and drizzle with olive oil.
5. Roast for 30-40 minutes until tender and lightly golden.
6. Serve hot with a sprinkle of salt and pepper, and a drizzle of tahini (if using).

Tip: For a smoother, creamier texture, blend half of the chickpeas before mixing with the cauliflower with an ice cube. For extra flavor, roast the garlic cloves along with the cauliflower. This will mellow the garlic's sharpness and add a caramelized sweetness to the hummus.

Nutritional Information (per serving):
- Calories: 220
- Protein: 8g
- Fat: 14g
- Carbohydrates: 14g
- Fiber: 5g

BEET HUMMUS WITH SAUERKRAUT AND HERBS

Prep Time: 15 minutes
Cook Time: None
Serves: 4

Ingredients:
- 1 cup organic cooked beets, chopped
- 1/2 cup organic tahini
- 2 tbsp organic lemon juice
- 1/2 cup organic sauerkraut (for probiotics)
- 1 clove organic garlic, minced
- 2 tbsp organic fresh dill, chopped
- 2 tbsp organic extra virgin olive oil

Instructions:
1. In a blender, combine the beets, tahini, lemon juice, garlic, and olive oil. Blend until smooth. Season with salt to taste.
2. Stir in the sauerkraut and fresh dill.
3. Serve the beet hummus in a bowl, drizzled with a bit more olive oil. Garnish with extra dill and serve with vegetable sticks.
   Tip: The sweetness of the beets pairs well with the tangy sauerkraut, creating a unique and vibrant hummus variation.

Nutritional Information (per serving):
- Calories: 170
- Protein: 4g

- Fat: 12g
- Carbohydrates: 13g
- Fiber: 3g

FERMENTED BEET AND HEMP SEED HUMMUS

Prep Time: 15 minutes
Cook Time: None (plus optional fermentation time for beets)
Serves: 4

Ingredients:
- 1 cup organic fermented beets (or roast and ferment your own beets)
- 1/4 cup organic hemp seeds
- 1/4 cup organic tahini
- 2 tbsp organic lemon juice
- 1 tbsp organic apple cider vinegar (unpasteurized)
- 1 clove organic garlic, minced
- 1 tbsp organic extra virgin olive oil
- 1/4 tsp sea salt
- 1 tbsp organic fresh dill, chopped (for garnish)

Instructions:
1. **Blend the Base:**
   In a blender or food processor, combine fermented beets, hemp seeds, tahini, lemon juice, apple cider vinegar, garlic, olive oil, and sea salt. Blend until smooth.
2. **Adjust the Texture:**
   Add water if needed to adjust the consistency of the hummus. This hummus should be creamy but slightly thicker.
3. **Serve and Garnish:**
   Spoon the hummus into a bowl and garnish with fresh dill for added flavor and brightness.
   Tip: This hummus pairs well with fermented vegetables like kimchi or sauerkraut, boosting both flavor and probiotic benefits.

Nutritional Information (per serving):
- Calories: 180
- Protein: 6g
- Fat: 13g
- Carbohydrates: 11g
- Fiber: 4g

SMOKY MACKEREL AND ROASTED RED PEPPER DIP

Prep Time: 15 minutes
Cook Time: 10 minutes (for roasting peppers)
Serves: 4

Ingredients:
- 2 fresh mackerel fillets, cooked and flaked
- 1 large organic red bell pepper, roasted and peeled
- 1/4 cup organic olive oil
- 1 tbsp organic apple cider vinegar (unpasteurized)
- 1/2 tsp organic smoked paprika
- 1 clove organic garlic, minced
- Sea salt & pepper to taste

Instructions:
1. Roast the Red Pepper: Roast the red bell pepper under a broiler or over a gas flame until charred. Peel and remove seeds, then roughly chop.
2. Prepare the Dip: In a blender or food processor, combine the roasted red pepper, olive oil, apple cider vinegar, smoked paprika, and garlic. Blend until smooth.
3. Add the Mackerel: Fold in the flaked mackerel and season with salt and pepper.
4. Serve with raw veggies, lettuce cups, or grain-free crackers for a smoky, flavorful dip.

Nutritional Information (per serving):
- Calories: 220
- Protein: 14g
- Fat: 18g

- Carbohydrates:3g
- Fiber: 1g

YOGURT-HERB DRESSING WITH FERMENTED SAUERKRAUT

Prep Time: 5 minutes
Cook Time: None
Serves: 4

Ingredients:
- 1/2 cup organic coconut yogurt (unsweetened, probiotic-rich)
- 2 tbsp organic extra virgin olive oil
- 2 tbsp organic lemon juice
- 1 tbsp organic fresh parsley, chopped
- 1 tbsp organic fresh dill, chopped
- 2 tbsp organic fermented sauerkraut, finely chopped
- 1 clove organic garlic, minced
- 1/4 tsp sea salt
- 1/4 tsp ground black pepper
- 1 tbsp filtered water (optional, for consistency)

Instructions:
1. Mix the Dressing Base:
   In a medium bowl, whisk together the coconut yogurt, olive oil, lemon juice, garlic, sea salt, and black pepper.
2. Add Herbs and Sauerkraut:
   Stir in the chopped parsley, dill, and sauerkraut. The sauerkraut adds a probiotic boost and a tangy, slightly salty flavor to the dressing.
3. Adjust Consistency:
   If the dressing is too thick, thin it out with a tablespoon of water. Taste and adjust seasoning as needed.
4. Serve or Store:
   Serve over fresh salads, grilled fish, or as a dip for roasted vegetables. Store in the refrigerator for up to 3 days.
   Tip: Chop the sauerkraut finely so that it incorporates evenly into the dressing without overwhelming the texture.

Nutritional Information (per serving):
- Calories: 70
- Protein: 1g
- Fat: 7g
- Carbohydrates: 2g
- Fiber: 0g

AVOCADO-GREEN GODDESS DRESSING

Prep Time: 5 minutes
Cook Time: None
Serves: 4

Ingredients:
- 1 large organic avocado, ripe
- 1/4 cup organic fresh parsley, chopped
- 1/4 cup organic fresh cilantro or basil, chopped
- 1/4 cup organic coconut yogurt (unsweetened, probiotic-rich)
- 2 tbsp organic extra virgin olive oil
- 1 tbsp organic apple cider vinegar (unpasteurized)
- 2 tbsp organic lemon juice (freshly squeezed)
- 1 clove organic garlic, minced
- 1/4 tsp sea salt
- 1-2 tbsp filtered water (to adjust consistency)

Instructions:
1. Blend the **Ingredients**: In a blender or food processor, combine the avocado, parsley, cilantro (or basil), coconut yogurt, olive oil, apple cider vinegar, lemon juice, garlic, and sea salt. Blend until smooth and creamy.
2. Adjust Consistency: If the dressing is too thick, add water 1 tablespoon at a time until you reach your desired consistency.
3. Serve or Store: Serve immediately over salads, grilled fish, or as a dip for raw vegetables. This dressing can be stored

in an airtight container in the refrigerator for up to 3 days.

Tip: Fresh herbs like parsley and cilantro bring vibrant, earthy flavors that balance the richness of the avocado and yogurt. Blending these herbs at the last minute ensures they keep their fresh, bright green color. For a pop of extra flavor, you can add a teaspoon of Dijon mustard, which adds a slight tang and depth to the dressing.

Nutritional Information (per serving):

- Calories: 140
- Protein: 2g
- Fat: 14g
- Carbohydrates: 5g
- Fiber: 3g

FERMENTED GINGER-TURMERIC DRESSING

Prep Time: 10 minutes
Fermentation Time: 2-3 days
Serves: 6 (dressing portions)

Ingredients:

- 1 tbsp organic fresh ginger, minced
- 1 tsp organic turmeric powder
- 2 tbsp organic lemon juice
- 1 tbsp organic apple cider vinegar (unpasteurized)
- 1 tbsp organic kimchi brine (or sauerkraut brine, probiotic-rich)
- 1/4 cup organic extra virgin olive oil
- Sea salt & pepper to taste

Instructions:

1. **Ferment the Base:** Combine ginger, turmeric, lemon juice, apple cider vinegar, and kimchi brine in a jar. Cover with a breathable cloth and let ferment at room temperature for 2-3 days.
2. **Blend the Dressing:** Once fermented, whisk in the olive oil and season with salt and pepper.
3. **Serve:** Refrigerate and use within 1 week. This anti-inflammatory dressing pairs well with green salads, roasted vegetables, or grilled fish.

Tip: Fermenting ginger and turmeric not only enhances their flavors but also boosts their bioavailability, making this dressing both flavorful and nutritious.

Nutritional Information (per serving):

- Calories: 70
- Protein: 0g
- Fat: 7g
- Carbohydrates: 1g
- Fiber: 0g

SWEETS AND DESSERTS

Sweets without sugar seems counterintuitive, but that is just because we are addicted to the overly sweet taste of industrially processed desserts and ingredients. Just a few days into a no-sugar diet will restore your palate to your natural state and allow you to appreciate the natural sweetness of fruits paired with the complexity of nuts, seeds, and other natural ingredients.

CAKES AND PIES

NO BAKE BLUEBERRY CASHEW CHEESECAKE

Prep Time: 20 minutes
Cook Time: 3 hours
Serves: 8

Ingredients:

- 1 cup organic cashews, soaked overnight
- 1/4 cup organic coconut cream
- 1/4 cup organic blueberries
- 1 tsp organic vanilla extract
- 1/2 cup almond flour (for crust)
- 1/4 cup coconut oil, melted (for crust)

Instructions:

1. Make the Crust: Mix almond flour and coconut oil, then press into a tart or springform pan.
2. Make the Filling: Blend soaked cashews, coconut cream, blueberries, and vanilla until smooth. Pour over the crust.
3. Chill: Refrigerate for at least 3 hours until set.

Tip: Garnish with fresh blueberries or a drizzle of melted dark chocolate for added flair.

Nutritional Information (per serving):

- Calories: 250
- Protein: 5g
- Fat: 22g
- Carbohydrates: 12g
- Fiber: 2g

ALMOND BUTTER CHOCOLATE TART

Prep Time: 15 minutes
Cook Time: 2 hours
Serves: 8

Ingredients:
- 1 cup almond flour (for crust)
- 1/4 cup coconut oil, melted (for crust)
- 1/2 cup almond butter
- 1/4 cup organic cacao powder
- 1/4 cup organic coconut cream

Instructions:
1. Make the Crust: Mix almond flour and coconut oil. Press into a tart pan.
2. Make the Filling: Blend almond butter, cacao powder, and coconut cream until smooth. Pour over the crust.
3. Chill: Refrigerate for 2 hours.

Tip: Garnish with shaved dark chocolate or crushed nuts for a rich presentation.

Nutritional Information (per serving):
- Calories: 210
- Protein: 6g
- Fat: 18g
- Carbohydrates: 8g
- Fiber:4g

PUMPKIN COCONUT CREAM PIE

Prep Time: 15 minutes
Cook Time: 2 hours
Serves: 8

Ingredients:
- 1 cup organic pumpkin puree
- 1 cup organic coconut cream
- 1 tsp organic pumpkin spice
- 1/2 cup almond flour (for crust)
- 1/4 cup coconut oil (for crust)

Instructions:
1. Make the Crust: Mix almond flour and melted coconut oil. Press into the bottom of a pie pan.
2. Make the Filling: Blend pumpkin puree, coconut cream, and pumpkin spice until smooth. Pour over the crust.
3. Chill: Refrigerate for at least 2 hours before serving.

Tip: Add chopped nuts on top for added texture and crunch.

Nutritional Information (per slice):
- Calories: 220
- Protein: 3g
- Fat: 19g
- Carbohydrates: 10g
- Fiber: 3g

LEMON BLUEBERRY MUFFINS

Prep Time: 10 minutes
Cook Time: 25 minutes
Serves: 8 muffins

Ingredients:
- 1 cup almond flour
- 1/4 cup coconut flour
- 1/4 cup coconut oil, melted
- 1/2 cup organic blueberries
- Zest and juice of 1 organic lemon

Instructions:
1. Mix the Ingredients: In a bowl, combine almond flour, coconut flour, melted coconut oil, blueberries, lemon zest, and juice.
2. Bake: Spoon the batter into a lined muffin tin and bake at 350°F for 20-25 minutes.

Tip: Add a pinch of Himalayan salt to enhance the lemon flavor.

Nutritional Information (per muffin):
- Calories: 130
- Protein: 4g
- Fat: 9g
- Carbohydrates: 10g
- Fiber: 3g

CHOCOLATE CHIP BANANA BREAD

Prep Time: 10 minutes
Cook Time: 40 minutes
Serves: 10 slices

Ingredients:
- 2 ripe organic bananas, mashed
- 1/2 cup almond flour
- 1/4 cup coconut flour
- 2 tbsp coconut oil, melted
- 1/4 cup organic dark chocolate chips

Instructions:
1. Mix the Ingredients: In a bowl, combine mashed bananas, almond flour, coconut flour, coconut oil, and chocolate chips.
2. Bake: Pour the batter into a greased loaf pan and bake at 350°F for 35-40 minutes, until a toothpick comes out clean.

Tip: For a nutty twist, sprinkle chopped walnuts over the batter before baking.

Nutritional Information (per slice):
- Calories: 130
- Protein: 3g
- Fat: 8g
- Carbohydrates: 12g
- Fiber: 3g

COOKIES, BROWNIES, AND CRUMBLES

ALMOND FLOUR SHORTBREAD COOKIES

Prep Time: 10 minutes
Cook Time: 12 minutes
Serves: 12 cookies

Ingredients:
- 1 cup almond flour
- 1/4 cup coconut oil, melted
- 1 tsp organic vanilla extract
- Pinch of Himalayan salt

Instructions:
1. Make the Dough: In a bowl, combine almond flour, melted coconut oil, vanilla, and salt.
2. Shape the Cookies: Form small cookies and place them on a lined baking sheet.
3. Bake: Bake at 350°F for 10-12 minutes until golden.

Tip: For a flavor twist, add a dash of cinnamon or lemon zest to the dough.

Nutritional Information (per cookie):
- Calories: 100
- Protein: 2g
- Fat: 9g
- Carbohydrates: 3g
- Fiber: 1g

CINNAMON CASHEW COOKIES

Prep Time: 10 minutes
Cook Time: 15 minutes
Serves: 12 cookies

Ingredients:
- 1 cup organic cashew butter
- 1/4 cup coconut flour
- 1/4 cup coconut oil, melted
- 1 tsp organic cinnamon
- 1/2 tsp organic vanilla extract

Instructions:
1. Mix the Ingredients: In a bowl, combine cashew butter, coconut flour, coconut oil, cinnamon, and vanilla until a dough forms.
2. Form Cookies: Scoop spoonfuls of dough onto a lined baking sheet and flatten.
3. Bake: Bake at 350°F for 12-15 minutes, until lightly golden.

Tip: Sprinkle additional cinnamon on top before baking for an extra spicy kick.

Nutritional Information (per cookie):
- Calories: 140
- Protein: 4g
- Fat: 11g
- Carbohydrates: 6g
- Fiber: 2g

CHOCOLATE ZUCCHINI BROWNIES

Prep Time: 10 minutes
Cook Time: 30 minutes
Serves: 9

Ingredients:
- 1 medium organic zucchini, grated
- 1/2 cup almond flour
- 1/4 cup organic cacao powder
- 1/4 cup coconut oil, melted
- 1 tsp organic vanilla extract

Instructions:
1. Mix the Ingredients: In a bowl, mix grated zucchini, almond flour, cacao powder, melted coconut oil, and vanilla extract.
2. Bake: Pour the mixture into a greased baking pan and bake at 350°F for 25-30 minutes, until set.

Tip: Squeeze out excess moisture from the zucchini before mixing for a denser texture.

Nutritional Information (per brownie):
- Calories: 130
- Protein: 4g
- Fat: 9g
- Carbohydrates: 10g
- Fiber: 3g

CHOCOLATE AVOCADO BROWNIES

Prep Time: 10 minutes
Cook Time: 25 minutes
Serves: 9 brownies

Ingredients:
- 2 ripe organic avocados
- 1/2 cup organic cacao powder
- 1/4 cup coconut flour
- 1/4 cup coconut oil, melted
- 1/2 tsp organic vanilla extract

Instructions:
1. Blend the Ingredients: In a blender, combine avocados, cacao powder, coconut flour, coconut oil, and vanilla. Blend until smooth.
2. Bake: Pour the mixture into a greased pan and bake at 350°F for 20-25 minutes, until set.

Tip: Add a pinch of Himalayan salt to enhance the chocolate flavor and balance the sweetness.

Nutritional Information (per brownie):
- Calories: 150
- Protein: 3g
- Fat: 11g
- Carbohydrates: 10g
- Fiber: 4g

CINNAMON APPLE CRUMBLE

Prep Time: 10 minutes
Cook Time: 25 minutes
Serves: 6

Ingredients:
- 4 organic apples, peeled and sliced
- 1/2 tsp cinnamon
- 1/2 cup almond flour
- 1/4 cup organic walnuts, chopped
- 2 tbsp coconut oil, melted

Instructions:
1. Prepare the Apples: Toss apple slices with cinnamon and arrange in a baking dish.
2. Make the Crumble Topping: Mix almond flour, walnuts, and melted coconut oil. Spread over the apples.
3. Bake: Bake at 350°F for 20-25 minutes until the topping is golden brown.

Tip: Add a dash of nutmeg or ground ginger to the topping for extra warmth and spice.

Nutritional Information (per serving):
- Calories: 140
- Protein: 3g
- Fat: 8g
- Carbohydrates: 17g
- Fiber: 4g

PUDDINGS AND MOUSSES

COCONUT CHIA PUDDING WITH MANGO

Prep Time: 5 minutes
Cook Time: 2 hours
Serves: 2

Ingredients:

- 1 cup organic coconut milk
- 2 tbsp chia seeds
- 1/2 cup organic mango, diced

Instructions:

1. Mix the **Ingredients:** Combine coconut milk and chia seeds in a bowl, and stir to mix well.
2. Chill: Refrigerate for 2 hours, stirring occasionally for smooth consistency.
3. Top with Mango: Add fresh diced mango on top before serving.

Tip: For a tropical flavor boost, add a squeeze of fresh lime juice and some shredded coconut.

Nutritional Information (per serving):

- Calories: 160
- Protein: 3g
- Fat: 10g
- Carbohydrates:15g
- Fiber: 6g

TURMERIC GOLDEN CHIA PUDDING WITH MACADAMIA-CASHEW CREAM

Prep Time: 10 minutes (plus overnight soaking)
Cook Time: None
Serves: 4

Ingredients:

- For the Chia Pudding:
  - 1/4 cup **organic chia seeds**
  - 1 1/2 cups **organic cashew milk** (unsweetened, or homemade)
  - 1/2 tsp **organic ground turmeric**
  - 1/4 tsp **organic cinnamon**
  - 1/4 tsp **organic ginger powder**
  - 1/2 tsp **organic vanilla extract**
  - Pinch of sea salt
- For the Macadamia-Cashew Cream:
  - 1/4 cup **organic raw macadamia nuts**, soaked overnight
  - 1/4 cup **organic raw cashews**, soaked overnight
  - 1 tbsp **organic lemon juice**
  - 1/2 tsp **organic vanilla extract**
  - 1 tbsp **organic water** (as needed)

Instructions:

1. **Prepare the Turmeric Chia Pudding:**
   In a bowl, whisk together chia seeds, cashew milk, turmeric, cinnamon, ginger, vanilla, and sea salt. Stir well and refrigerate overnight.
   Tip: Turmeric adds anti-inflammatory benefits while cinnamon and ginger enhance its warming, earthy flavor, making this a comforting, nutrient-dense treat.
2. **Make the Macadamia-Cashew Cream:**
   Drain and rinse the soaked macadamia nuts and cashews. In a blender, combine the nuts with lemon juice, vanilla extract, and a tablespoon of water. Blend until smooth and creamy, adding more water if needed for a silky texture.
   Tip: Soaking the nuts overnight softens them, resulting in a luxuriously smooth cream that perfectly complements the rich turmeric pudding.
3. **Assemble and Serve:**
   Layer the turmeric chia pudding with a generous spoonful of macadamia-cashew cream. Garnish with a sprinkle of

cinnamon and a few chopped macadamia nuts for extra texture.

Nutritional Information (per serving):

- Calories: 260
- Protein: 8g
- Fat: 20g
- Carbohydrates: 16g
- Fiber: 7g

CHOCOLATE CHIA-BASIL SEED PUDDING WITH HAZELNUT BUTTER AND BERRIES

Prep Time: 10 minutes (plus 30 minutes soaking)
Cook Time: None
Serves: 4

Ingredients:

- 2 tbsp organic chia seeds
- 2 tbsp organic basil seeds
- 1 1/2 cups organic almond milk (unsweetened)
- 2 tbsp organic raw cacao powder
- 1 tsp organic vanilla extract
- 2 tbsp organic hazelnut butter
- 1 cup organic mixed berries (blueberries, raspberries, strawberries)
- 1 tbsp organic cacao nibs (for topping)

Instructions:

1. In a medium bowl, whisk together chia seeds, basil seeds, almond milk, cacao powder, and vanilla extract until well combined. Allow the mixture to sit for 30 minutes, stirring occasionally to avoid clumping.
2. Once the seeds have absorbed the liquid and formed a pudding-like consistency, stir in the hazelnut butter until fully incorporated for an added layer of richness.
3. Divide the pudding into bowls and top with mixed berries and cacao nibs for a crunchy finish.
   Tip: If you want a creamier pudding, blend the mixture with an immersion blender before adding the hazelnut butter.

Nutritional Information (per serving):

- Calories: 350
- Protein: 8g
- Fat: 26g
- Carbohydrates: 23g
- Fiber: 12g

SPICED CHIA SEED PUDDING WITH APPLE AND WALNUTS

Prep Time: 10 minutes (plus overnight soaking)
Cook Time: None
Serves: 4

Ingredients:

- 1/4 cup organic chia seeds
- 1 1/2 cups organic cashew milk (unsweetened)
- 1/2 tsp organic ground cinnamon
- 1/4 tsp organic ground nutmeg
- 1 medium organic apple, diced
- 2 tbsp organic walnuts, chopped
- 1 tbsp organic coconut flakes (for topping)

Instructions:

1. In a medium-sized bowl, whisk chia seeds, cashew milk, cinnamon, and nutmeg. Stir well to combine and refrigerate overnight.
2. In the morning, stir the chia pudding well and spoon it into serving bowls. Top with diced apple and chopped walnuts.

3. Sprinkle with coconut flakes and an extra dash of cinnamon if desired.
   Tip: For extra warmth and depth of flavor, lightly sauté the diced apple in ghee for 2-3 minutes before adding it to the pudding. This caramelizes the natural sugars in the apple and brings out its sweetness. For a creamier consistency, use full-fat coconut milk or a mix of cashew and almond milk.

Nutritional Information (per serving):
- Calories: 260
- Protein: 7g
- Fat: 16g
- Carbohydrates: 24g
- Fiber: 8g

TROPICAL CHIA-BASIL SEED PUDDING WITH PINEAPPLE AND MINT

Prep Time: 10 minutes (plus 30 minutes soaking)
Cook Time: None
Serves: 4

Ingredients:
- 1 tbsp organic chia seeds
- 1 tbsp organic basil seeds
- 1 1/2 cups organic coconut water (no added sugar)
- 1 tsp organic lime zest
- 1 cup organic fresh pineapple, diced
- 1 tbsp organic fresh mint, chopped
- 2 tbsp organic macadamia nuts, chopped (for topping)

Instructions:
1. Mix the **Seed Base:** In a medium bowl, whisk together chia seeds, basil seeds, coconut water, and lime zest. Let the mixture sit for 30 minutes to thicken, stirring occasionally.
2. Assemble the Pudding: Once the pudding has set, divide it into bowls. Top with diced pineapple, fresh mint, and chopped macadamia nuts.
3. Serve and Garnish: For a refreshing twist, garnish with extra lime zest or a few mint leaves.
   Tip: Coconut water provides natural sweetness and electrolytes, making this pudding hydrating and refreshing.

Nutritional Information (per serving):
- Calories: 240
- Protein: 5g
- Fat: 14g
- Carbohydrates: 25g
- Fiber: 6g

CHOCOLATE AVOCADO PUDDING

Prep Time: 5 minutes
Cook Time: 30 minutes
Serves: 4

Ingredients:
- 2 ripe organic avocados
- 1/4 cup organic raw cacao powder
- 1/4 cup organic coconut milk
- 1 tsp organic vanilla extract
- Pinch of Himalayan salt

Instructions:
1. Blend the **Ingredients:** In a blender, combine avocados, cacao powder, coconut milk, vanilla, and salt. Blend until smooth.
2. Chill: Refrigerate for 30 minutes before serving.

Tip: For added sweetness, drizzle with coconut nectar or mix in a handful of dark chocolate chips.

Nutritional Information (per serving):
- Calories: 160 kcal
- Protein: 3g

- Healthy Fats: 12g
- Fiber: 7g

ALMOND BUTTER CHOCOLATE MOUSSE

Prep Time: 5 minutes
Cook Time: 30 minutes
Serves: 4

Ingredients:
- 1/2 cup almond butter
- 1/4 cup organic cacao powder
- 1/4 cup coconut milk
- 1 tsp organic vanilla extract

Instructions:
1. Blend the **Ingredients:** In a blender, combine almond butter, cacao powder, coconut milk, and vanilla until smooth.
2. Chill: Refrigerate for 30 minutes before serving.

Tip: Garnish with crushed nuts or a sprinkle of cacao nibs for extra crunch.

Nutritional Information (per serving):
- Calories: 160
- Protein: 3g
- Fat: 12g
- Carbohydrates: 14g
- Fiber: 7g

VANILLA ALMOND PANNA COTTA

Prep Time: 10 minutes
Cook Time: 2 hours
Serves: 4

Ingredients:
- 1 cup organic coconut milk
- 1 tsp organic vanilla extract
- 1/4 cup almond butter
- 2 tbsp chia seeds

Instructions:
1. Mix the **Ingredients:** In a bowl, whisk together coconut milk, vanilla extract, almond butter, and chia seeds.
2. Chill: Refrigerate for 2 hours, stirring occasionally for even chia seed absorption.

Tip: Serve with fresh berries or a drizzle of almond butter for extra flavor and texture.

Nutritional Information (per serving):
- Calories: 180
- Protein: 4g
- Fat: 14g
- Carbohydrates: 10g
- Fiber: 5g

CASHEW VANILLA ICE CREAM

Prep Time: 10 minutes
Freeze Time: 4 hours
Serves: 4

Ingredients:
- 1 cup organic cashews, soaked overnight
- 1/2 cup organic coconut milk
- 1 tsp organic vanilla extract
- Pinch of Himalayan salt

Instructions:
1. Blend the **Ingredients:** In a blender, combine soaked cashews, coconut milk, vanilla, and salt. Blend until creamy.
2. Freeze: Pour into a container and freeze for 4 hours, stirring halfway through for even texture.

Tip: Stirring while freezing helps to prevent ice crystals and keeps the ice cream creamy.

Nutritional Information (per serving):
- Calories: 180
- Protein: 4g

- Fat: 14g
- Carbohydrates: 10g
- Fiber: 2g

MATCHA COCONUT PUDDING

Prep Time: 5 minutes
Cook Time: 30 minutes
Serves: 2

Ingredients:
- 1 cup organic coconut milk
- 1 tsp organic matcha powder
- 2 tbsp chia seeds
- 1/2 tsp organic vanilla extract

Instructions:
1. **Mix the Ingredients:** In a bowl, whisk together coconut milk, matcha powder, chia seeds, and vanilla.
2. Chill: Refrigerate for 30 minutes, stirring occasionally to ensure even chia seed absorption.

Tip: Stir halfway through chilling to prevent clumping of chia seeds for a smooth consistency.

Nutritional Information (per serving):
- Calories: 180
- Protein: 4g
- Fat: 14g
- Carbohydrates: 9g
- Fiber: 5g

FRUIT DESSERTS

CARAMELIZED PEARS WITH COCONUT CREAM

Prep Time: 5 minutes
Cook Time: 10 minutes
Serves: 4

Ingredients:
- 2 medium organic pears, sliced
- 1 tbsp coconut oil
- 1 tsp cinnamon
- 1 cup organic coconut cream

Instructions:
1. Cook the Pears: Heat coconut oil in a pan over medium heat. Add pear slices and cinnamon, and cook until caramelized, about 5 minutes per side.
2. Serve with Coconut Cream: Top the warm pears with chilled coconut cream.

Tip: A sprinkle of crushed nuts like walnuts or pecans adds a delightful crunch to this dessert.

Nutritional Information (per serving):
- Calories: 180
- Protein: 1g
- Fat: 14g
- Carbohydrates: 16g
- Fiber: 4g

CHOCOLATE DIPPED STRAWBERRIES

Prep Time: 10 minutes
Cook Time: 10 minutes
Serves: 10

Ingredients:
- 1/2 cup organic dark chocolate, melted
- 10 organic strawberries

Instructions:
1. Dip the Strawberries: Dip each strawberry into the melted dark chocolate and place them on a parchment-lined tray.
2. Chill: Refrigerate for 10 minutes to set the chocolate.

Tip: For added texture and flavor, sprinkle with crushed nuts or shredded coconut before the chocolate sets.

Nutritional Information (per strawberry):
- Calories: 45
- Protein: 0g
- Fat: 3g
- Carbohydrates: 5g
- Fiber: 1g

RASPBERRY COCONUT CREAM PARFAIT

Prep Time: 5 minutes
Serves: 2

Ingredients:
- 1 cup organic coconut yogurt
- 1/2 cup organic raspberries
- 2 tbsp shredded coconut
- 1 tsp organic vanilla extract

Instructions:
1. **Layer the Ingredients:** In small jars or bowls, layer coconut yogurt, raspberries, and shredded coconut.
2. **Serve:** Top with more raspberries and a sprinkle of coconut.

Tip: For added texture, toast the shredded coconut before layering it in the parfait.

Nutritional Information (per serving):
- Calories: 130
- Protein: 2g
- Fat: 8g
- Carbohydrates: 14g
- Fiber: 3g

BLUEBERRY COCONUT ICE CREAM

Prep Time: 10 minutes
Freeze Time: 4 hours
Serves: 4

Ingredients:
- 1 cup organic coconut milk
- 1/2 cup organic blueberries
- 1/4 cup coconut cream
- 1 tsp organic vanilla extract

Instructions:
1. Blend the **Ingredients:** In a blender, combine coconut milk, blueberries, coconut cream, and vanilla. Blend until smooth.
2. Freeze: Pour into a container and freeze for 4 hours, stirring halfway through.

Tip: Add more blueberries for a bolder flavor and beautiful purple hue.

Nutritional Information (per serving):
- Calories: 140
- Protein: 2g
- Fat: 12g
- Carbohydrates: 8g
- Fiber: 2g

FUNCTIONAL

Dr. Casey Means recommends cutting out alcohol completely and giving it up is much easier if you have a healthy alternative. These mocktails are loaded with antioxidants and anti-inflammatory ingredients for a fun and healthy evening drink, and you can start drinking in the morning too!

FERMENTED DRINKS

Probiotics are an essential part of the Good Energy Diet. Make sure to find good reliable brands for our favorite fermented drink, but you can also make your own.

COCONUT KEFIR

Prep Time: 5 minutes
Fermentation Time: 24-48 hours
Serves: 4

Ingredients:
- 4 cups organic coconut water
- 1/4 cup water kefir grains (available online or at health stores)

Instructions:
1. Ferment the Kefir: Place the water kefir grains in a large jar. Pour in the coconut water and cover with a breathable cloth secured with a rubber band.
2. Fermentation: Allow the mixture to ferment at room temperature for 24-48 hours. Taste after 24 hours and continue fermenting until you reach your desired flavor (more time creates a stronger tang).
3. Strain and Serve: Strain the kefir grains and store the coconut kefir in the fridge for up to 1 week. The grains can be reused for future batches.

Tip: Ferment in a warm spot (about 75°F) for the best results. The tangy, slightly fizzy coconut kefir can be consumed alone or added to smoothies for a probiotic boost.

Nutritional Information (per 1 cup serving):
- Calories: 40
- Protein: 0g
- Fat: 0g
- Carbohydrates: 10g
- Fiber: 0g

GINGER TURMERIC KOMBUCHA

Prep Time: 10 minutes
Fermentation Time: 7-10 days (for primary fermentation) + 2-3 days (for secondary fermentation)
Serves: 8

Ingredients:
- 8 cups organic black or green tea (brewed and cooled)
- 1 cup organic sugar (the sugar is consumed during fermentation)
- 1 SCOBY (symbiotic culture of bacteria and yeast)
- 1-inch piece organic fresh ginger, thinly sliced
- 1 tsp organic ground turmeric or 1-inch piece fresh
- 1/4 cup organic lemon juice

Instructions:
1. Primary Fermentation: In a large glass jar, combine the brewed tea, sugar, and SCOBY. Cover with a breathable cloth and let it ferment for 7-10 days at room temperature.
2. Secondary Fermentation: Once the tea is tangy and slightly fizzy, remove the SCOBY and set aside for future use. Pour the fermented tea into clean bottles, add ginger, turmeric, and lemon juice. Seal tightly and ferment for another 2-3 days at room temperature for carbonation.

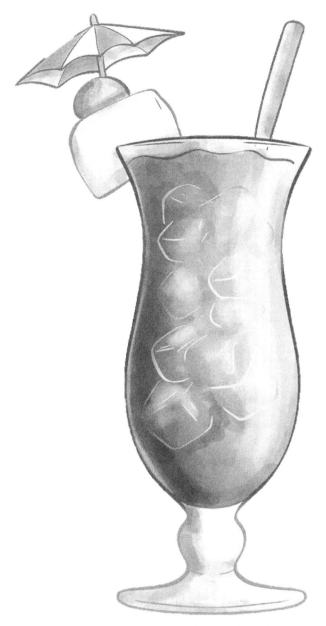

3. Serve: Once fizzy, refrigerate the kombucha and enjoy chilled.

Tip: Adjust the secondary fermentation time to achieve your desired carbonation. Fresh ginger adds spice, while turmeric provides anti-inflammatory properties.

Nutritional Information (per 1 cup serving):
- Calories: 30
- Protein: 0g
- Fat: 0g
- Carbohydrates: 7g
- Fiber: 0g

DAIRY-FREE PROBIOTIC COCONUT LASSI

Prep Time: 5 minutes
Serves: 2

Ingredients:
- 1 cup organic coconut yogurt (for probiotics)
- 1/2 cup organic coconut water
- 1/2 tsp organic ground cardamom
- 1 tbsp organic lemon juice
- Ice cubes (optional)

Instructions:
1. Blend the **Ingredients:** In a blender, combine the coconut yogurt, coconut water, cardamom, lemon juice, and ice cubes (if using). Blend until smooth.
2. Serve: Pour into glasses and enjoy immediately.

Tip: This dairy-free lassi is light and refreshing. You can adjust the thickness by adding more or less coconut water.

Nutritional Information (per serving):
- Calories: 120
- Protein: 2g
- Fat: 8g
- Carbohydrates: 10g
- Fiber: 2g

WATER KEFIR LEMONADE

Prep Time: 5 minutes
Fermentation Time: 24-48 hours
Serves: 4

Ingredients:
- 4 cups filtered water
- 1/4 cup organic sugar (consumed during fermentation)
- 1/4 cup water kefir grains
- 1/4 cup organic lemon juice
- 1 tbsp organic lemon zest

Instructions:
1. Ferment the Water Kefir: In a large jar, combine water and sugar, stirring until the sugar dissolves. Add the water kefir grains and let it ferment for 24-48 hours.
2. Strain and Flavor: Strain the kefir grains and set them aside for future use. Stir in the lemon juice and lemon zest. Let it ferment for another 12-24 hours for extra fizz, or refrigerate and serve chilled.

Tip: Water kefir is a great base for probiotic-rich lemonade, and you can experiment with different fruit juices and herbs.

Nutritional Information (per 1 cup serving):
- Calories: 40
- Protein: 0g
- Fat: 0g
- Carbohydrates: 10g
- Fiber: 0g

DAIRY-FREE CASHEW YOGURT DRINK

Prep Time: 10 minutes
Fermentation Time: 24-48 hours
Serves: 2

Ingredients:
- 1 cup organic raw cashews, soaked for 4 hours
- 1/2 cup filtered water
- 1 tbsp organic lemon juice
- 2 tbsp organic coconut yogurt (as a starter culture)

Instructions:
1. **Blend the Cashews:** Drain the soaked cashews and blend with water and lemon juice until smooth.
2. **Ferment:** Stir in the coconut yogurt and transfer the mixture to a sterilized jar. Cover loosely and let it ferment at room temperature for 24-48 hours.
3. **Serve:** Once fermented, refrigerate and serve chilled.

Tip: This cashew yogurt drink is creamy and tangy. Add a touch of cinnamon or vanilla for extra flavor.

Nutritional Information (per serving):
- Calories: 150
- Protein: 4g
- Fat: 12g
- Carbohydrates: 8g
- Fiber: 2g

BEET KVASS

Prep Time: 10 minutes
Fermentation Time: 7-10 days
Serves: 4

Ingredients:
- 2 large organic beets, peeled and chopped
- 1 tbsp Himalayan salt
- 4 cups filtered water
- 1 tsp organic caraway seeds (optional, for added flavor)

Instructions:
1. Prepare the Beets: Place the chopped beets into a sterilized jar.
2. Make the Brine: Dissolve the salt in the filtered water and pour the brine over the beets. Add the caraway seeds if using. Ensure the beets are fully submerged, using a fermentation weight if necessary.
3. Ferment: Cover the jar with a breathable cloth or loosely fit lid. Let the kvass ferment at room temperature for 7-10 days. Taste periodically, and once the kvass has a tangy flavor, strain and store the liquid in the fridge.
4. Serve: Once strained, beet kvass can be enjoyed on its own or mixed with sparkling water for a refreshing drink.

Tip: The longer the fermentation, the more tangy and earthy the beet kvass will become. You can also reuse the beets for a second batch by refilling the jar with water and salt.

Nutritional Information (per 1 cup serving):
- Calories: 20
- Protein: 1g
- Fat: 0g
- Carbohydrates: 5g
- Fiber: 0g

FERMENTED CABBAGE JUICE (CABBAGE KVASS)

Prep Time: 15 minutes
Fermentation Time: 5-7 days
Serves: 4

Ingredients:
- 1 medium organic green cabbage, chopped
- 1 tbsp Himalayan salt
- 4 cups filtered water
- 2 cloves organic garlic, crushed (optional, for extra flavor)

Instructions:
1. Prepare the Cabbage: Place the chopped cabbage into a large glass jar. Press it down firmly to release some natural juice.
2. Make the Brine: Dissolve the salt in the filtered water and pour it over the cabbage. Add crushed garlic if you prefer a more complex flavor.
3. Ferment: Seal the jar loosely and leave it at room temperature for 5-7 days. Check daily, and taste until it reaches your preferred level of sourness.
4. Strain and Serve: Strain the liquid into a bottle and refrigerate. Enjoy the cabbage juice cold, or mix it with other vegetable juices for a nutrient-packed drink.

Tip: The liquid from fermented cabbage (kvass) is an excellent digestive tonic. You can adjust the flavor by mixing in some fermented carrot or beet juice.

Nutritional Information (per 1 cup serving):
- Calories: 15
- Protein: 1g
- Fat: 0g
- Carbohydrates: 3g
- Fiber: 0g

FERMENTED CUCUMBER AND DILL DRINK

Prep Time: 10 minutes
Fermentation Time: 5-7 days
Serves: 4

Ingredients:

- 2 medium organic cucumbers, chopped
- 1 tbsp Himalayan salt
- 4 cups filtered water
- 1 tbsp organic fresh dill, chopped
- 2 cloves organic garlic, crushed

Instructions:

1. Prepare the Cucumbers: Place the chopped cucumbers in a sterilized jar with the garlic and dill.
2. Make the Brine: Dissolve the salt in the filtered water and pour it over the cucumbers. Ensure the cucumbers are fully submerged.
3. Ferment: Cover loosely and let the mixture ferment at room temperature for 5-7 days. Taste the drink after a few days, and once it reaches your desired sourness, strain the liquid.
4. Store: Refrigerate the strained cucumber drink and serve cold. Optionally, garnish with fresh dill for extra flavor.

Tip: Fermented cucumber drinks have a light, refreshing taste. You can add lemon zest or ginger during fermentation for an extra burst of flavor.

Nutritional Information (per 1 cup serving):

- Calories: 10
- Protein: 0g
- Fat 0g
- Carbohydrates: 2g
- Fiber: 0g

CARROT AND GINGER KVASS

Prep Time: 15 minutes
Fermentation Time: 5-7 days
Serves: 4

Ingredients:

- 4 large organic carrots, peeled and chopped
- 1-inch piece organic fresh ginger, sliced
- 1 tbsp Himalayan salt
- 4 cups filtered water

Instructions:

1. Prepare the Carrots: Place the chopped carrots and sliced ginger into a sterilized jar.
2. Make the Brine: Dissolve the salt in the filtered water and pour the brine over the carrots and ginger. Ensure the vegetables are fully submerged.
3. Ferment: Cover loosely and let the mixture ferment for 5-7 days at room temperature. Taste daily, and once the drink is tangy and lightly fermented, strain the liquid.
4. Store: Transfer the strained liquid to a bottle and refrigerate. Drink chilled, and optionally, garnish with a slice of fresh ginger.

Tip: This carrot-ginger kvass is naturally sweet with a subtle spice. You can also reuse the carrots and ginger for a second round of fermentation.

Nutritional Information (per 1 cup serving):

- Calories: 30
- Protein: 1g
- Fat: 0g
- Carbohydrates: 7g
- Fiber: 1g

FERMENTED CELERY AND APPLE DRINK

Prep Time: 15 minutes
Fermentation Time: 5-7 days
Serves: 4

Ingredients:

- 4 stalks organic celery, chopped
- 1 medium organic apple, cored and chopped
- 1 tbsp Himalayan salt
- 4 cups filtered water
- 1 tbsp organic fresh lemon juice (optional)

Instructions:

1. Prepare the Vegetables: Place the chopped celery and apple in a sterilized jar.
2. Make the Brine: Dissolve the salt in the filtered water and pour the brine over the celery and apple. Add lemon juice for extra tang if desired.
3. Ferment: Seal the jar loosely and ferment at room temperature for 5-7 days. Once the drink has a mild, tangy flavor, strain the liquid.
4. Store: Refrigerate the strained drink and serve cold.

Tip: This fermented drink has a fresh, slightly sweet flavor from the apple, balanced by the celery's earthiness. It's perfect for sipping as a digestive tonic.

Nutritional Information (per 1 cup serving):

- Calories 20
- Protein: 0g
- Fat: 0g
- Carbohydrates: 5g
- Fiber: 0

ANTIOXIDANTS MOCKTAILS

PURPLE RAIN

Prep Time: 5 minutes
Cook Time: 0 minutes
Serves: 2

Ingredients:

- 1/2 cup organic blueberries
- 1 tbsp organic basil leaves, chopped
- 1 tbsp organic lemon juice
- 1 tsp organic apple cider vinegar (with "mother")
- 2 cups filtered water
- Ice cubes

Instructions:

1. Muddle the Blueberries and Basil: In a glass, gently muddle the blueberries and basil leaves to release their juices.
2. Mix the **Ingredients:** Add the lemon juice, apple cider vinegar, and water. Stir well.
3. Serve: Pour over ice and enjoy the beautiful, deep purple drink.

Tip: Blueberries are packed with antioxidants that give this drink its bold color, while basil adds a fresh and herbaceous note.

Nutritional Information (per serving):

- Calories: 30
- Protein: 0g
- Fat: 0g
- Carbohydrates: 7g
- Fiber: 1g

SPICED CITRUS PUNCH

Prep Time: 5 minutes
Cook Time: 0 minutes
Serves: 2

Ingredients:

- 1/4 cup organic orange juice
- 1/4 cup organic apple juice

- 1 tbsp organic lemon juice
- 1/4 tsp organic ground cinnamon
- 1/4 tsp organic ground ginger
- 1/8 tsp organic ground nutmeg
- 1 cup sparkling water
- Ice cubes
- Orange slices and star anise for garnish

Instructions:
1. Mix the Juices and Spices: In a glass, combine orange juice, apple juice, lemon juice, cinnamon, ginger, and nutmeg. Stir well.
2. Add Sparkling Water: Pour in sparkling water and stir gently.
3. Serve: Pour over ice and garnish with orange slices and star anise for a festive touch.

Tip: The combination of citrus and spices boosts metabolism, supports digestion, and provides immune-boosting vitamin C.

Nutritional Information (per serving):
- Calories: 45
- Protein: 0g
- Fat: 0g
- Carbohydrates: 11g
- Fiber: 0g

MOCK NEGRONI TWIST

Inspired by the Negroni, this mocktail uses berries and kombucha to create a rich, tangy flavor profile.

Prep Time: 5 minutes
Cook Time: 0 minutes
Serves: 2

Ingredients:
- 1/2 cup organic mixed berries (blueberries, raspberries, blackberries)
- 1 tbsp organic lime juice
- 1/4 cup organic pomegranate juice
- 1/2 cup kombucha (probiotic-rich)
- Ice cubes
- Orange peel for garnish

Instructions:
1. Muddle the Berries: Gently muddle the mixed berries in a glass until they release their juices.
2. Add Kombucha and Juice: Pour in lime juice, pomegranate juice, and kombucha. Stir gently.
3. Serve: Pour over ice, garnish with an orange peel, and enjoy.

Tip: The berries and pomegranate juice are loaded with antioxidants, while kombucha adds gut-friendly probiotics and a fizzy kick that resembles the bitter notes of a Negroni.

Nutritional Information (per serving):
- Calories: 60
- Protein: 1g
- Fat: 0g
- Carbohydrates: 15g
- Fiber: 2g

CITRUS SPARKLER

Prep Time: 5 minutes
Cook Time: 0 minutes
Serves: 2

This refreshing mocktail mimics the look and feel of an Aperol Spritz, with a burst of citrus and a light fizz.

Ingredients:
- 1/2 cup organic grapefruit juice
- 1/4 cup organic orange juice
- 1 tsp organic lemon juice
- 1/2 tsp organic apple cider vinegar (for a bitter edge)
- 1 cup sparkling water

- Ice cubes
- Orange slices and rosemary sprigs for garnish

Instructions:
1. Mix the Juices: In a glass, mix grapefruit juice, orange juice, lemon juice, and apple cider vinegar.
2. Add Sparkling Water: Top with sparkling water and stir gently.
3. Serve: Pour over ice and garnish with orange slices and rosemary sprigs.

Tip: The combination of citrus juices boosts metabolism and detoxifies the body, while apple cider vinegar gives it a slight bitterness, mimicking the Aperol taste.

Nutritional Information (per serving):
- Calories: 40
- Protein: 1g
- Fat: 0g
- Carbohydrates: 10g
- Fiber: 0g

BERRY BELLINI BLISS

Prep Time: 5 minutes
Cook Time: 0 minutes
Serves: 2

Ingredients:
- 1/2 cup organic mixed berries (strawberries, blueberries, raspberries)
- 1 tsp organic lemon juice
- 1/4 cup organic kombucha (probiotic-rich)
- 1 cup sparkling water
- Ice cubes
- Mint leaves for garnish

Instructions:
1. Muddle the Berries: In a glass, gently muddle the mixed berries with the lemon juice until they release their juices.
2. Add the Kombucha: Pour in the kombucha and sparkling water, and stir gently.
3. Serve: Pour over ice and garnish with mint leaves.

Tip: Kombucha adds probiotics to support gut health, while berries provide antioxidants and a natural sweetness without the need for added sugars.

Nutritional Information (per serving):
- Calories: 25
- Protein: 0g
- Fat: 0g
- Carbohydrates: 6g
- Fiber: 1g

RED COOLER

Prep Time: 5 minutes
Cook Time: 0 minutes
Serves: 2

Ingredients:
- 1 tbsp dried hibiscus flowers
- 1 tbsp dried rose hips
- 2 cups filtered water
- 1 tbsp organic lime juice
- Ice cubes
- Edible flowers for garnish (optional)

Instructions:
1. Steep the Hibiscus and Rose Hips: In a teapot, steep the hibiscus flowers and rose hips in hot water for 5 minutes. Strain and let cool.
2. Add Lime Juice: Stir in the lime juice once the tea has cooled.
3. Serve: Pour over ice and garnish with edible flowers for a beautiful presentation.

Tip: Hibiscus is naturally tart and gives this mocktail a deep red color, while rose hips add a subtle floral flavor and are rich in vitamin C.

Nutritional Information (per serving):

- Calories: 10
- Protein: 0g
- Fat: 0g
- Carbohydrates: 2g
- Fiber: 0g

PURPLE SWEET POTATO AND LAVENDER FIZZ

Prep Time: 10 minutes
Cook Time: 10 minutes
Serves: 2

Ingredients:

- 1 medium organic purple sweet potato, peeled and chopped
- 1 tsp organic dried lavender flowers
- 1 cup filtered water
- 1 tbsp organic lemon juice
- Sparkling water
- Ice cubes

Instructions:

1. **Cook the Sweet Potato:** Steam or boil the sweet potato for 10 minutes until tender. Let it cool.
2. **Blend the Ingredients:** In a blender, blend the cooked sweet potato with water, lemon juice, and lavender flowers.
3. **Strain and Serve:** Strain the liquid into a glass, pour over ice, and top with sparkling water for a fizzy finish.

Tip: Purple sweet potatoes are high in anthocyanins, which give them their vibrant color and antioxidant power. The lavender adds a floral note that pairs beautifully with the sweetness of the potato.

Nutritional Information (per serving):

- Calories: 60
- Protein: 1g
- Fat: 0g
- Carbohydrates:
- Fiber: 2g

TURMERIC MANGO LASSI

Prep Time: 5 minutes
Cook Time: 0 minutes
Serves: 2

Ingredients:

- 1/2 cup organic mango, peeled and chopped
- 1 cup organic coconut yogurt (probiotic-rich)
- 1/2 tsp organic ground turmeric

- 1/4 tsp black pepper (to activate turmeric)
- 1 tbsp organic lime juice
- Ice cubes

Instructions:

1. **Blend the Ingredients:** In a blender, combine mango, coconut yogurt, turmeric, black pepper, and lime juice. Blend until smooth.
2. **Serve:** Pour over ice and enjoy the rich golden color and bold flavors.

Tip: The black pepper enhances the bioavailability of curcumin in turmeric, boosting its anti-inflammatory properties. Turmeric and mango create a beautiful contrast of sweet and savory.

Nutritional Information (per serving):

- Calories 120
- Protein: 3g
- Fat: 6g
- Carbohydrates: 15g
- Fiber: 2g

ELECTRIC BLUE LEMONADE

Prep Time: 5 minutes
Cook Time: 0 minutes
Serves: 2

Ingredients:

- 1/4 tsp blue spirulina powder (natural algae, antioxidant-rich)
- 2 tbsp organic lemon juice
- 2 cups filtered water
- Ice cubes
- Lemon slices for garnish

Instructions:

1. **Mix the Ingredients:** In a glass, dissolve the spirulina powder in lemon juice and water.
2. **Stir and Serve:** Pour over ice and garnish with lemon slices for a pop of color.

Tip: Blue spirulina not only gives this lemonade an electric blue hue but also provides a strong dose of antioxidants. You can make this drink fizzy by using sparkling water instead of still.

Nutritional Information (per serving):

- Calories: 20
- Protein: 0g
- Fat: 0g
- Carbohydrates: 5g
- Fiber: 0g

DIGESTIVE MOCKTAILS

SPICED APPLE FIZZ

Prep Time: 5 minutes
Cook Time: 0 minutes
Serves: 2

Ingredients:

- 1/2 cup organic apple juice (fresh, unsweetened)
- 1 tbsp organic lemon juice
- 1 tsp organic cinnamon
- 1/4 tsp organic ground ginger
- 1 cup sparkling water
- Ice cubes
- Cinnamon sticks and apple slices for garnish

Instructions:

1. **Mix the Ingredients:** In a glass, combine apple juice, lemon juice, cinnamon, and ground ginger.
2. Add Sparkling Water: Pour in sparkling water and stir gently.
3. Serve: Pour over ice, garnish with cinnamon sticks and apple slices.

Tip: Cinnamon helps regulate blood sugar, while ginger and apple give this mocktail a warming yet refreshing twist, perfect for digestion.

Nutritional Information (per serving):

- Calories: 30
- Protein: 0g
- Fat: 0g
- Carbohydrates: 8g
- Fiber: 0g

COCONUT COOLER

Prep Time: 5 minutes
Cook Time: 0 minutes
Serves: 2

Ingredients:

- 1/2 cup organic pineapple, chopped
- 1/4 cup organic coconut cream
- 1/2 cup organic coconut water
- 1 tsp organic lime juice

- Ice cubes
- Pineapple slices for garnish

Instructions:
1. Blend the **Ingredients:** In a blender, combine pineapple, coconut cream, coconut water, and lime juice. Blend until smooth.
2. Serve: Pour over ice and garnish with pineapple slices.

Tip: Pineapple contains bromelain, an enzyme that aids digestion and supports metabolism, while coconut provides electrolytes and healthy fats.

Nutritional Information (per serving):
- Calories: 100
- Protein: 1g
- Fat: 6g
- Carbohydrates: 11g
- Fiber: 1g

GOLDEN GINGER MULE

Prep Time: 5 minutes
Cook Time: 0 minutes
Serves: 2

Ingredients:
- 1 tsp organic fresh ginger, grated
- 1/2 tsp organic ground turmeric
- 1 tbsp organic apple cider vinegar
- 1/2 cup organic coconut water
- 1 cup sparkling water
- Ice cubes
- Lime slices and mint sprigs for garnish

Instructions:
1. Muddle the Ginger: Muddle the fresh ginger and turmeric in a glass to release the flavors.
2. Add Liquids: Pour in apple cider vinegar, coconut water, and sparkling water. Stir well.
3. Serve: Pour over ice and garnish with lime slices and mint sprigs.

Tip: The turmeric and ginger are anti-inflammatory powerhouses, while the apple cider vinegar supports metabolism and digestion.

Nutritional Information (per serving):
- Calories: 15
- Protein: 0g
- Fat: 0g
- Carbohydrates: 4g
- Fiber: 0g

CUCUMBER-COOL MULE

Prep Time: 5 minutes
Cook Time: 0 minutes
Serves: 2

Ingredients:
- 1/2 cup organic cucumber, sliced
- 1 tsp organic fresh ginger, grated
- 1 tbsp organic lime juice
- 1 cup sparkling water
- Ice cubes
- Cucumber slices and lime wedges for garnish

Instructions:
1. Muddle the Cucumber: In a glass, gently muddle the cucumber slices and grated ginger until they release their juices.
2. Add the Liquid: Pour in the lime juice and sparkling water, and stir well.

3. Serve: Pour over ice and garnish with cucumber slices and lime wedges.

Tip: Ginger enhances digestion and stimulates metabolism, while cucumber keeps you hydrated and adds a crisp flavor.

Nutritional Information (per serving):
- Calories: 10
- Protein: 0g
- Fat: 0g
- Carbohydrates: 2g
- Fiber: 0g

PINK COOLER

Prep Time: 5 minutes
Cook Time: 0 minutes
Serves: 2

Ingredients:
- 1/2 medium organic beet, peeled and grated
- 1 cup organic coconut kefir (probiotic-rich)
- 1/2 cup organic coconut water
- 1 tbsp organic lemon juice
- Ice cubes
- Fresh mint for garnish

Instructions:
1. Grate the Beet: Grate the beet finely. You can blend it for a smoother texture or leave it as is for texture.
2. Mix the **Ingredients:** In a glass jar, mix coconut kefir, coconut water, lemon juice, and grated beet. Stir well.
3. Serve: Pour over ice, garnish with fresh mint, and enjoy.

Tip: The natural sugars in beets add sweetness and balance the tanginess of the kefir. For a more intense pink color, allow the beets to steep longer before serving.

Nutritional Information (per serving):
- Calories: 80
- Protein: 2g
- Fat: 5g
- Carbohydrates: 7g
- Fiber: 2g

KALE AND APPLE DETOX MOCKTAIL

Prep Time: 5 minutes
Cook Time: 0 minutes
Serves: 2

Ingredients:
- 1 cup organic kale leaves, chopped
- 1/2 organic green apple, chopped
- 1/2 cup organic coconut water
- 1 tbsp organic lemon juice
- Ice cubes

Instructions:
1. Blend the **Ingredients:** In a blender, combine kale, apple, coconut water, and lemon juice. Blend until smooth.
2. Strain and Serve: If you prefer a smoother texture, strain the mocktail through a fine mesh sieve. Pour over ice and serve immediately.

Tip: Kale is rich in fiber and chlorophyll, which supports detoxification, while apples provide pectin, a fiber that promotes fullness and digestive health.

Nutritional Information (per serving):
- Calories: 35
- Protein: 1g
- Fat: 0g
- Carbohydrates: 8g
- Fiber: 2g

ENERGY BOOSTING MOCKTAILS

MATCHA AND COCONUT CREAM FIZZ

Prep Time: 5 minutes
Cook Time: 0 minutes
Serves: 2

Ingredients:
- 1 tsp organic matcha powder (rich in antioxidants)
- 1/4 cup organic coconut cream
- 1 cup sparkling water
- 1 tbsp organic lime juice
- Ice cubes

Instructions:
1. Mix the Matcha: In a glass, whisk the matcha powder with lime juice until smooth.
2. Add Coconut Cream: Pour the coconut cream into the matcha mixture and stir gently.
3. Serve: Top with sparkling water and ice cubes for a refreshing, creamy drink.

Tip: Matcha powder is a potent source of antioxidants (particularly EGCG), which can help boost metabolism. The coconut cream adds richness and healthy fats that provide satiety.

Nutritional Information (per serving):
- Calories: 70
- Protein: 1g
- Fat: 6g
- Carbohydrates: 3g
- Fiber: 0g

COCONUT COOLER

Prep Time: 5 minutes
Cook Time: 0 minutes
Serves: 2

Ingredients:
- 1/2 cup organic pineapple, chopped
- 1/4 cup organic coconut cream
- 1/2 cup organic coconut water
- 1 tsp organic lime juice
- Ice cubes
- Pineapple slices for garnish

Instructions:
1. Blend the **Ingredients:** In a blender, combine pineapple, coconut cream, coconut water, and lime juice. Blend until smooth.
2. Serve: Pour over ice and garnish with pineapple slices.

Tip: Pineapple contains bromelain, an enzyme that aids digestion and supports metabolism, while coconut provides electrolytes and healthy fats.

Nutritional Information (per serving):
- Calories: 100
- Protein: 1g
- Fat: 6g
- Carbohydrates: 11g
- Fiber: 1g

AVOCADO COCONUT LASSI

Prep Time: 5 minutes
Cook Time: 0 minutes
Serves: 2

Ingredients:
- 1/2 medium organic avocado
- 1 cup organic coconut yogurt (probiotic-rich)
- 1/2 cup organic coconut water
- 1 tbsp organic lime juice
- 1 tbsp organic fresh mint, chopped
- Ice cubes

Instructions:
1. Blend the **Ingredients:** In a blender, combine avocado, coconut yogurt, coconut water, lime juice, and mint. Blend until smooth.
2. Serve: Pour over ice and enjoy immediately.

Tip: Avocado and coconut yogurt provide healthy fats, which help maintain satiety and stable energy levels. The lime juice enhances the flavor by adding a tangy brightness, while the probiotics aid digestion.

Nutritional Information (per serving):
- Calories: 150
- Protein: 3g
- Fat: 12g
- Carbohydrates: 10g
- Fiber: 4g

CUCUMBER AND MINT KOMBUCHA COOLER

Prep Time: 5 minutes
Cook Time: 0 minutes
Serves: 2

Ingredients:
- 1 cup organic plain kombucha (probiotic-rich)
- 1 cup filtered water
- 1 medium organic cucumber, sliced
- 1 tbsp organic fresh mint, chopped
- 1 tbsp organic lemon juice
- Ice cubes

Instructions:
1. Prepare the **Ingredients:** Slice the cucumber and chop the mint.
2. Mix: In a pitcher, combine kombucha, water, cucumber slices, mint, and lemon juice. Stir gently.
3. Serve: Pour into glasses over ice and garnish with extra mint or cucumber slices.

Tip: Kombucha adds a fizzy, probiotic punch to this mocktail, which can improve digestion and aid in metabolic efficiency. For an extra chill, freeze the cucumber slices beforehand.

Nutritional Information (per serving):
- Calories: 20
- Protein: 0g
- Fat: 0g
- Carbohydrates: 5g
- Fiber: 0g

BERRY BEET TONIC

Prep Time: 5 minutes
Cook Time: 0 minutes
Serves: 2

Ingredients:
- 1 small organic beet, peeled and chopped
- 1/2 cup organic mixed berries (blueberries, strawberries, raspberries)
- 1 tbsp organic lime juice
- 1/2 tsp organic fresh ginger, grated
- 1 cup sparkling water
- Ice cubes
- Lime wedges and basil leaves for garnish

Instructions:
1. Juice the Beet: Using a blender or juicer, blend the beet until smooth. Strain if needed.
2. Muddle the Berries: In a glass, muddle the mixed berries and ginger.
3. Mix the **Ingredients:** Pour in beet juice, lime juice, and sparkling water. Stir well.

4. Serve: Pour over ice, garnish with lime wedges and basil leaves.

Tip: Beets are a great source of natural nitrates, which help improve circulation and boost energy. Combined with berries, this mocktail is both delicious and detoxifying.

Nutritional Information (per serving):
- Calories: 45
- Protein: 1g
- Fat: 0g
- Carbohydrates: 11g
- Fiber: 2g

THE FAUX-GARITA

Prep Time: 5 minutes
Cook Time: 0 minutes
Serves: 2

Ingredients:
- 1 tbsp organic lime juice
- 1/2 tsp organic lemon juice
- 1/2 tsp organic orange zest (or juice)
- 1 tsp organic apple cider vinegar (for a tequila-like kick)
- 1/4 tsp organic cayenne pepper (optional, for a spicy kick)
- 1 cup sparkling water
- Ice cubes
- Lime wedges and sea salt for rimming the glass

Instructions:
1. Rim the Glass: Rub a lime wedge around the rim of your glass and dip it into sea salt for that classic margarita look.
2. Mix the **Ingredients:** In a shaker or glass, combine lime juice, lemon juice, orange zest, apple cider vinegar, and cayenne. Stir or shake well.
3. Serve: Pour over ice, top with sparkling water, and garnish with lime wedges.

Tip: The cayenne pepper and apple cider vinegar help boost metabolism, while the citrus provides a refreshing tartness.

Nutritional Information (per serving):
- Calories: 10
- Protein: 0
- Fat: 0g
- Carbohydrates: 2g
- Fiber: 0g

MOJITO REBOOT

Prep Time: 5 minutes
Cook Time: 0 minutes
Serves: 2

Ingredients:
- 1/4 cup organic fresh mint leaves
- 1 tbsp organic lime juice
- 1 tsp organic apple cider vinegar (with "mother")
- 1/2 cup organic coconut water
- 1 tbsp organic raw honey (optional)
- 1 cup sparkling water
- Ice cubes
- Mint sprigs and lime wedges for garnish

Instructions:
1. Muddle the Mint: In a glass, gently muddle the fresh mint with lime juice and honey (if using) to release the mint's flavor.
2. Add the Liquid: Pour in the coconut water, apple cider vinegar, and sparkling water. Stir well.
3. Serve: Pour over ice and garnish with extra mint sprigs and lime wedges.

Tip: Apple cider vinegar adds a metabolic boost, while the coconut water provides electrolytes for hydration.

Nutritional Information (per serving):
- Calories: 25
- Protein: 0g
- Fat: 0g
- Carbohydrates: 6g
- Fiber: 0g

BONUSES FOOD LIST +120-DAY MEAL PLAN BONUS

Now it's time to take your journey even further! For easy access to the exact food items recommended by Dr. Casey Means, download the most extensive **GOOD ENERGY FOOD LIST** on the market! This comprehensive resource, along with a **PRINTABLE MEAL PLAN** designed to guide you through your first 90 days, will ensure that you seamlessly implement all of Dr. Casey's recommendations. Just scan the **QR code** to download these amazing bonuses, including a **shopping list** that makes every grocery trip stress-free and meal prep effortless.

SCAN THE QR CODE TO GET YOUR 2 BONUSES

GOOD ENERGY FOOD LIST +120-DAY MEAL PLAN BONUS

INDEX

CONCLUSION

As you've journeyed through this cookbook, you've taken a powerful step toward reclaiming your health and embracing a lifestyle rooted in whole, nourishing foods. The recipes and advice within these pages are not just about following a diet—they represent a commitment to your long-term well-being, vitality, and energy.

By now, you've seen how simple, delicious, and satisfying it can be to prioritize whole, unprocessed foods. You've learned that by fueling your body with nutrient-dense ingredients, you're not only enhancing your daily energy and mood, but you're also preventing and reversing the chronic diseases that plague so many. Every recipe, from the high-protein breakfasts to the fiber-rich dinners, has been designed with your metabolic health in mind, ensuring that each meal works with your body, not against it.

What's most important to remember is that this cookbook is just the beginning. The choices you make in your kitchen ripple out into every aspect of your life—your energy levels, your mental clarity, your ability to thrive. By incorporating these meals into your daily routine, you're actively lowering your risk of chronic disease, stabilizing blood sugar, reducing inflammation, and fostering a vibrant, healthy life.

The power to change your health lies in your hands. Through thoughtful meal prep and mindful choices, you've proven that eating for health doesn't have to be difficult, bland, or time-consuming. With this knowledge, you can confidently step away from the processed and ultra-processed foods that dominate our shelves, and instead, embrace the rich flavors and life-giving nutrients that come from real, whole food.

If you found this cookbook helpful,
please consider leaving a review.

Your feedback helps others discover the life-changing power
of real, whole food and supports our mission to
bring health and vitality to more people.

Here's to your continued journey of
health, happiness, and energy!

Thank you.

Made in United States
Orlando, FL
21 June 2025